The Catholic Companion to Jesus

The Catholic Companion to Jesus

Mary Kathleen Glavich, SND

THE CATHOLIC COMPANION TO JESUS
by Mary Kathleen Glavich, SND

Edited by Gregory F. Augustine Pierce
Cover design by Tom A. Wright
Cover art by M.P. Wiggens, www.thespiritsource.com
Text Design and Typesetting by Patricia A. Lynch

Published by ACTA Publications, 5559 W. Howard Street, Skokie, IL 60077-2621, (800) 397-2282, www.actapublications.com

Library of Congress Catalog number: 2009944226
ISBN-13: 978-0-87946-422-6
Printed in the United States of America by Evangel Press

Year 16 14 13 12 11 10
Printing 8 7 6 5 4 3 2 First

CONTENTS

To Jesus Christ,
my Lord and God,
to whom I owe
my life and joy.

The Lord is the goal of human history,
the focal point of the longings of history and of civilization,
the center of the human race,
the joy of every heart,
and the answer to all its yearnings.

Gaudium et Spes
Second Vatican Council

Introduction

Jesus is probably the most famous person in the world. Although he lived 2,000 years ago, today he is still very much alive for billions of people. They strive to follow his teachings and meet regularly to celebrate his life and works. Children are taught to ask themselves, "What would Jesus do?" And in the last century more Christians have laid down their lives for him than in all other centuries combined. About one-third of the world (more than two billion people) are Christians (although over the centuries they broke into several different rites and denominations). Another one-fifth of the world's population, Muslims, regard Jesus as a great prophet. Albert Einstein admitted, "I am a Jew, but I am enthralled by the luminous figure of the Nazarene." And Mahatma Gandhi stated, "I tell the Hindus that their lives will be imperfect if they do not also study reverently the teaching of Jesus."

At first glance, Jesus seems an unlikely candidate for the "most famous person in history" award. He was born a first-century Jew in Palestine, a small country at the eastern end of the Mediterranean Sea occupied at the time by Rome; and he spent almost all of his relatively short life in obscurity, the so-called "hidden" years. In the end, Jesus was executed in the prime of his life, one of thousands at that time who were crucified by the Romans in order to squelch rebellion and dissent. He left behind no writings. There are no paintings or statues of him created by his contemporaries. Why then are there millions of books about him? Why does artwork from every age and country depict him? Why has his movement outlasted the very Roman Empire that executed him and persecuted his followers? Why is his name used even today (sometimes by the same people) both to curse and to pray?

One reason for Jesus' widespread influence is his unique, powerful, but short ministry. He taught and healed for at most three years, possibly only one year, around the year 30 A.D. This was a mere flash in time compared to the Buddha, for example, who taught for forty-five years, or Mohammed, who taught about twenty years, or Moses, who lived to be over a hundred. Moreover, the ministry of Jesus was carried out in a world that didn't enjoy the instant communication of today's mass media. Yet the striking words and awesome deeds of Jesus altered the course of the history of humankind.

One of the main reasons for the enduring attraction of Jesus is the strong belief on the part of his followers that he is alive today. His disciples claimed to be eyewitnesses to the fact that Jesus had come back from the dead. The resurrection of Jesus gave credibility for them to everything he taught, including his good news that the kingdom of God has already begun and that death is not the end of the road for us. This risen Jesus promised to be with his followers always, and he kept his promise. Through the Spirit of Jesus alive in them, the first Christians formed a Church, which down through twenty centuries has continuously proclaimed that Jesus is with us, acting with the same power and loving compassion as when he walked the rocky roads of Palestine. What's more astounding is that the early Christians came to believe that Jesus is more than human, in fact that he is divine: God in the form of a human being.

Who Is Jesus?

Jesus is a man of mystery. In his time people surmised that he might be John the Baptist, or Elijah, or Jeremiah, or another of the Hebrew prophets. To some he was a troublemaker, even an ally of Satan. Jesus once asked his disciples, "Who do you say that I am?" It was Simon Peter, who ultimately became the leader of the disciples and the head of the Church, who answered: "You are the Son of the living God." Jesus said, "Blessed are you, Simon bar Jonah, for flesh and blood has not revealed this to you, but my Father in heaven" (see Matthew 16:15–17).

The Church has taken Peter's answer and interpreted it differently over the years, influenced by different cultures and world events. Sometimes she views Jesus more "divinely" (this is known as "high" Christology or Christology from above), and sometimes she emphasizes his humanity (this is known as "low" Christology or Christology from below). Like a shape shifter, Jesus has been perceived at times not only as the long-promised Jewish Messiah who redeemed the world but also as a hippie, a king, a sage, a revolutionary, a feminist, and even the last pharaoh!

Our understanding of Jesus' identity changes, depending on our individual life experience. The more we know about him and, more importantly, the more we know him personally, the more accurate will be our answer to the question: "Who do you say I am?" And this answer is crucial. For as Scripture says, '"God gave us eternal life, and this life is in his Son. Whoever has the Son has life; whoever does not have the Son of God does not have life" (1 John 5:11–12).

The Catholic Companion to Jesus is intended to be a catalyst for anyone who wishes to know Jesus better. We come to know people by learning about their family, their country, their job, what they say and do, and what others think about them. Likewise, this is how we get to know Jesus. In these pages you will find information about the historical person Jesus of Nazareth based on Scripture and scholarly research and reflection. You will also learn, or be reminded of, what the Catholic Church believes about him. (While this book is written by a Catholic and intended for Catholics, it should also be of interest to those who want to know more about how Catholics understand their Lord and Savior.)

The best and most effective way to know someone, however, is by personal interaction. For this reason, in addition to presenting the facts about Jesus of Nazareth, this book offers ideas for developing a deeper relationship with the one the prophet Isaiah foretold would be called "Emmanuel," which means "God with us." One suggestion is to read the stories of Jesus' life in your Bible. They are presented here in abbreviated and combined forms, but along with Scripture references that direct you to the sources. May every reader share the desires of the thirteenth-century bishop St. Richard of Chichester, whose prayer was popularized by the musical *Godspell*:

Thanks be to thee, my Lord Jesus Christ,
for all the benefits thou hast given me,

for all the pains and insults you have borne for me.
O most merciful redeemer, friend and brother,
may I know thee more clearly,
love thee more dearly,
and follow thee more nearly,
day by day.

Mary Kathleen Glavich, SND
South Euclid, Ohio
January 2010

1 Jesus: The Christ

The birth of Jesus signaled the beginning of a new era for humankind. In fact, the new calendar decreed by Pope Gregory XIII in 1582 marked years starting from what was assumed the year of Christ's birth. (We know now that the monk who calculated this date in the sixth century was off by a few years.) Gradually years came to be denoted as B.C. (Before Christ) or A.D. (Anno Domini, the year of the Lord). This was fitting in the West at the time, when almost everyone was Christian and saw Jesus' birth as the most important turning point of history. Today, of course, we are more aware and respectful of other religious traditions, and so the initials B.C.E. (Before the Common Era) and C.E. (Common Era) are increasingly used to indicate dates. But it is interesting that year one of the Common Era is the same year that the Gregorian calendar assigned to the birth of Jesus. (Since this book is aimed at Christians, we will use the more familiar B.C. and A.D. to designate dates.)

Jesus as Messiah

For us Christians, all of Jewish history, as recorded in what we call the Old Testament, was a preparation for the coming of Jesus. The Jews were (and still remain) for us God's chosen people, who received God's promise of salvation and blessing to the entire world, a promise revealed to Abraham, the founder of the Hebrew race. Eventually, the Jews came to believe that a great leader would arise among them and lead them to final victory. Israelite prophets gave insight into this prom-

The chi-rho symbol for Jesus is the merging of the first letters in the Greek for Christ, which are chi (X) and rho (P), to form:

ised one, and Israelite heroes foreshadowed him. The Israelites yearned for him, especially after they were conquered and exiled and conquered again by one nation after another. Most of them felt that this God-sent person would be the descendant of their greatest king, David, and re-establish Israel as the independent country it had been during David's reign. During the time of Jesus, the Jews were being oppressed by Rome and longed especially for just such a liberator.

Israelite leaders—their priests, kings, and prophets—were anointed with oil in rituals that consecrated them for their special tasks. It follows then that the person they were awaiting was thought of as "the anointed one" or Messiah, which in Greek is *Christos*. This title quickly evolved into a kind of surname for Jesus, who today is known as Jesus Christ, which actually means "Jesus, the Anointed One."

Around the time of Jesus, there were others, such as Judas the Galilean (circa 6 B.C.) and Bar Kochba (Son of the Star, circa 132 A.D.), who were thought by their followers to be the Jewish Messiah as they led rebellions against their oppressors. But all of these "messiahs" were eventually vanquished. When Jesus, the true Messiah, did appear on the scene, he wasn't recognized by the majority of the Jewish people (although all of his original disciples were Jews).

For one thing, Jesus didn't fit the image of the Jewish Messiah. His battles were with a far mightier foe than Rome: They were with evil itself. His kingdom was not "of" this world, but is a spiritual kingdom of peace, love, and justice that Jesus proclaimed had already begun and was "within" us. His followers conquer not by the sword but by love.

Another difference between Jesus and the expected Messiah was that his rule encompasses not only Israel but is meant for "all nations" and the heavens as well. What's more, Jesus didn't comply with all the Jewish rules and traditions. For example, he healed on the Sabbath, a day when work wasn't to be done; he associated with outcasts; and he spoke to women in public, which was taboo. Jesus' disregard for certain practices sparked the Jewish leaders' antagonism and contempt. To add coals to the fire, his popularity garnered him their jealousy. And the mobs he drew gave rise to a concern on their part that Rome would clamp down with even fiercer oppression.

So Jesus is the Messiah, at least as far as Christians are concerned, although he is certainly not the one that most Jews were expecting at the time.

The Name of Jesus

St. Paul wrote that God gave Jesus "the name that is above every name, so that at the name of Jesus every knee should bend, in heaven and on earth and under the earth" (Philippians 2:9–10). That Jesus was a God-given name is revealed in the Gospels. According to the Gospel of Luke, an angel directed Mary to give her son this name. It is confirmed in Matthew's Gospel when an angel instructs Joseph to name the child Jesus.

In Aramaic, which has no "J" sound, Jesus' name would have been *Yeshua*, a common Jewish name at the time. It's akin to the name of Joshua, the great leader who succeeded Moses and led the people through Jericho into the Promised Land. Both names are short forms of *Jehoshua*, which means "Yahweh is his salvation." What then could have been a more appropriate

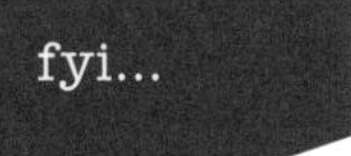

The monogram for Jesus, *IHS*, derived from the Greek spelling of Jesus, dates from the seventh century and was popularized by St. Bernardine of Siena. Later the letters were interpreted to stand for the Latin *Iesus Hominum Salvator* (Jesus, Savior of Mankind). This monogram surmounted by a cross and above three nails constitutes the logo of the Society of Jesus, or Jesuits, the largest male religious order in the Church:

for your spiritual health...

To honor Jesus you might adopt the custom of bowing the head at the name of Jesus and avoid using his name disrespectfully.

short prayer...

Simply saying the word *Jesus* is a powerful prayer. The Church encourages saying the name of Jesus at the hour of death. This is what St. Joan of Arc did. While being burned at the stake, in a loud voice she repeatedly called, "Jesus."

name than *Yeshua* for the savior of the world? Today we use the Latin translation of the Greek word for Yeshua, which is "Jesus" in English and Spanish (where it is pronounced "heyzoos").

When Jesus lived so many people had the same names that they were distinguished by linking them to their hometowns or their fathers. Jesus, then, would have been called Jesus of Nazareth as well as Jesus bar Joseph. "Bar" is Aramaic for "son of," and Joseph was the name of Jesus' earthly father.

Holy Name

Jews believed that names were closely identified with the people who bore them. Consequently, out of awe they never pronounced the word *Yahweh*, God's personal name, revealed to Moses at the burning bush. Instead, they used a substitute that we translate "Lord." Christians too acknowledge the unity of a person and his or her name and so are insulted when someone mocks our name. That is why it is truly sad that it has become common to use the name of Jesus casually and carelessly to express strong emotion (both positive and negative). The Church has long celebrated a day called the Holy Name of Jesus, which is an optional memorial on January 3.

There is also a litany, a long prayer with responses, in praise of the Holy Name of Jesus. And an ancient prayer gaining in popularity is the Jesus Prayer, which is repeated over and over: Lord Jesus Christ, Son of God, have mercy on me, a sinner.

What Did Jesus Look Like?

We have no image of Jesus as he really was because for the Jews images were like idols and therefore forbidden. (Deuteronomy 5:8 commanded, "You shall not make for yourself an idol, whether in the form of anything that is in heaven above, or that is on the earth beneath, or that is in the water under the earth.") Neither has anyone found a physical description of Jesus written by those who knew him. The Gospels are silent in this regard. Some people interpret the prophecy of the suffering servant to mean that Jesus was unattractive: "He had no form or majesty that we should look at him, nothing in his appearance that we should desire him" (Isaiah 53:2). Nevertheless, we can claim with Vasily Vasil Yevich Rozanov: "Jesus is certainly more beautiful than anything in the world or even the world itself. When He appeared, then, like the sun, he dimmed the stars."

Although we lack evidence of Jesus' physical appearance, we can make some educated guesses. Coming from a Mid-Eastern country, Jesus probably had the dark complexion and dark eyes of Arabs today. (One poet said he had his Father's eyes.) Hours under the hot Palestine sun would have kept Jesus tanned. Most Mid-Eastern men have hair that is thick, dark, and curly. Some propose that because Jesus was a descendant of David, who was a handsome man with auburn hair, Jesus might have inherited these traits. Recent scholarship indicates that men of his time (unless they were Nazarenes under vow) kept their hair rather short, not the flowing-over-the-shoulders style seen in most religious art depictions of Jesus. In fact, St. Paul states, "If a man wears long hair, it is

quick quote...

The name of Jesus is honey for the mouth, music for the ear, and gladness for the heart.

St. Bernard of Clairvaux

trivial tidbit...

The Society of the Holy Name of Jesus, or the Holy Name Society, active in many Catholic parishes, has for its primary purpose the promotion of love and reverence for the name of God and Jesus.

fyi...

A picture of Christ in the Vatican collection is the image of Edessa, called "Mandylion" by Orthodox Christians. One legend holds that the holy face was imprinted on cloth after Jesus visited King Agbar in Edessa in the first century. The earliest reference to this cloth is by St. John Damascene in the sixth century. The cloth vanished during the Crusades and again during the French Revolution. Many copies of the image were produced as icons. Some think that the original Mandylion is the Shroud of Turin folded so only the face shows.

degrading to him" (1 Corinthians 11:14).

Many Catholics, however, get their picture of Jesus from the image on the Shroud of Turin, the purported burial cloth of Jesus, or from the Veil of Veronica, the cloth that supposedly was used to wipe the face of Jesus on the way to the cross. Neither of these has ever been verified by the Church, although they are still a source of popular piety.

Whether Jesus had a beard is also debatable. The earliest depictions show him beardless, and some historians think that Jewish men of the time might not have worn a beard, especially when younger. On the other hand, a prophecy in Isaiah refers to soldiers "plucking my beard." Moreover, a beard was a sign of virility, and shaving it off was a way to humiliate captives and slaves.

When Christians first began to portray Jesus in art, they did so only in symbols: a lamb, a fish, and a shepherd. The earliest known picture of Jesus as a person, a grown man, dates back to 235 A.D. It was found by archaeologists in 1921 on a wall painting in a house church in Syria. This painting illustrates the healing of the paralytic as well as Jesus and Peter walking on the water. Jesus appears as a teacher with close-cropped hair. It wasn't until the mid-fourth century that Jesus was first shown with long hair parted in the middle and usually with a beard, perhaps modeled on the Greek and Roman gods. Eastern Church icons depicted Jesus in this style, which may have shaped the modern conceptions of him. Incidentally the earliest halos around Jesus' head appeared at 340 A.D. Halos as an artistic symbol were borrowed from the pagans, who drew them around their gods and deified emperors.

As for Jesus' build, a man who worked as a carpenter and in construction as he probably did, who could fast for days and pray all night, and who spent months living outside as he journeyed from town to town surely had a tough, muscular body and good health. The mysterious image imprinted on the Shroud of Turin is of a man about six feet tall. This height is considered tall for men of the first century. Jesus must not have been too tall, though, because he was able to slip into a crowd and disappear.

Through the centuries artists have portrayed Jesus to reflect their own culture and beliefs. You might see him depicted as resembling a Native American, a Japanese, a Kenyan, and even a woman. This variety in images serves to emphasize the universality of Jesus. He is truly a person for all peoples.

a cool website...

To view 100 images of Jesus through the centuries, go to www.religionfacts.com and click on "Jesus" and then on "Jesus Image Gallery."

Parents and Extended Family

The Church believes that Jesus is the Son of God, miraculously conceived in Mary (Miryam) by the power of the Holy Spirit with her consent. Mary, the Mother of Jesus, is therefore the "Mother of God," as the Church proclaims. Based on the story of the virgin birth, Jesus would have drawn all his humanity from his mother. Although Catholics believe God was the Father of Jesus, Mary's husband, Joseph (Yosef), was assumed by everyone at the time to be his physical father. It was Joseph who was the head of the household and who, as the legal father and guardian, brought up Jesus to be the man he was, taught him the Jewish faith, and trained him in his trade as a carpenter or construction worker. Religious art depicts Joseph as an old man. This may be because in the *Protoevan-*

trivial tidbit...

In the twelfth century, art began to depict Jesus as dead instead of alive on the cross. Recently, some crosses have begun to show the risen Christ on the cross. Technically, a cross with a corpus (body) on it is called a "crucifix."

gelium of James, an apocryphal (not canonical or official) gospel, Joseph claims, "I am an old man." This may have been an attempt to emphasize and make understandable Mary's virginity. Or, Joseph could have been a widower much older than Mary. But for the most part first-century Jewish men married around the age of twenty, and most likely Joseph and Mary were married when he was in his twenties and she was a young teen, as was the custom. We assume that Joseph died when Jesus was a teenager or young adult because Scripture doesn't mention Joseph after the story of Jesus being lost in the Temple at about age twelve.

Although the Gospels refer to Jesus' brothers (James, Joses, Judas, and Simon) and two sisters (unnamed), the Catholic Church holds that his mother, Mary, was always a virgin. Several possible explanations for the "brothers and sisters" in Scripture have been proposed. These words could be translated as "cousins," for Aramaic has no word for this. Or they could be understood in a general sense, as when a preacher addresses the congregation as "my brothers and sisters." The six "siblings" might have been Joseph's children from a previous marriage or children of other close relatives. If Mary actually had so many other children, then it's odd that as Jesus was dying he would entrust her to "the beloved disciple," someone outside the family.

Mary's parents are known as Joachim and Anne, even though they are not mentioned in the Bible. Their names are found in the *Protoevangelium of James*. Like most grandparents, they probably doted on Jesus. The Gospel of John mentions that "his mother's sister" stood near the cross. So perhaps Jesus had at least one aunt, or maybe this woman was Mary's cousin.

According to the Scriptures, Jesus never married or had children. Bachelorhood was rare in his culture, for the Jews believed in following God's command to Adam and Eve, "Go forth and multiply." But the single life is understandable for someone who wanted to give himself one hundred percent to a cause or work. Jesus chose to sublimate his sexual energy and focus on his mission. He is the prime example of his teaching that some forego marriage for the sake of the kingdom (see Matthew 19:10–12).

trivial tidbit...

In order to make Jesus an Aryan, the Nazis claimed that he was the son of a German legionnaire and Mary!

Family Tree

The Hebrews traced a person's lineage through the father. Scripture provides two genealogies for Jesus through Joseph. In the Gospel of Luke, the family tree of Jesus extends all the way back to "Adam, the son of God" (see Luke 3:23–38). The Gospel of Matthew presents Jesus' lineage back to Abraham, the ancestor of all Jews (see Matthew 1:1–16). This latter genealogy is constructed of three sets of fourteen generations: Abraham to David, David to the Exile, and the Exile to Jesus. In Hebrew thinking, fourteen was twice the perfect number seven. Also, in the Hebrew numbering system for letters, the letters in the name David add up to fourteen. Some of the names in the two Gospels' genealogies don't match. But both Luke and Matthew include King David, which was meant to emphasize that Jesus was of royal blood and of the tribe of Judah. Because Mary was related to the priestly family of Zechariah and Elizabeth, and priests

Jesus Christ is the center of everything and the object of everything, and he who does not know him knows nothing of the order of nature and nothing of himself.

Blaise Pascal

were Levites, some deduce that Mary belonged to the tribe of Levi.

The ancestors of Jesus—like many of ours—include some skeletons in the closet. For example, the childless widow Tamar posed as a prostitute so that she could bear a child by her father-in-law, Judah. Rahab, who assisted the Jews in conquering the Promised Land, actually was a prostitute. The widow Ruth was a Gentile who followed her mother-in-law's advice to place herself in a compromising position in order to snare a new husband. Solomon was David's son by Uriah's wife, with whom David committed adultery. And when Solomon became king, he let his pagan wives lure him away from the true God. The point of these stories, and the reason the Scripture writers included them, is that God acts through real people to produce the Messiah. If these flawed people had not acted when and as they did, there would have been no Jesus. And no Jesus means no salvation.

Native Country

Jesus spent his life in what is now called Israel when it was occupied by Rome, and apparently he never ventured more than several miles from it. In the first century the Romans named his country Palestine, perhaps after the Philistines, its former inhabitants. Today we call it the Holy Land because of its famous citizen. Israel was the Promised Land of Canaan to which Moses led the chosen people after they escaped from slavery in Egypt. The country was about the size of Rhode Island (150 long and 50 or 60 miles wide) at the time of Jesus and was divided into three main provinces: Galilee, Judea, and Samaria.

In the north was fertile Galilee, a small territory about fifty miles long and twenty-five miles across, where Jesus carried out most of his ministry. Galilee was clothed with wheat and barley fields, grapevines, fig trees, and olive trees. It alternated between two climates: a hot, dry summer and a cool, wet winter. In his teaching, Jesus drew his images from rural Galilee rather than from city life. He spoke of vineyards, sowers, mustard seeds, mother hens, treasures in fields, and yokes. Galilee was referred to as "land of the Gentiles" because many Gentiles lived there and because it was crossed by a main trade route. This foreign influence and the fact that Galilee was some distance from the Temple, the heart of Judaism, made Galileans rather laid back when it came to following the prescriptions of Jewish law. Galilee was the location of the village of Nazareth, known as Jesus' hometown, and also Capernaum, where Jesus lived during much of his ministry.

On the east border of Galilee was the Sea of Galilee, and therefore fishing was a major industry there. This sea is thirteen miles long and seven miles wide and lies 600 feet below sea level. It is also called the Sea of Tiberias and Lake Gennesaret (which means harp) because of its shape.

In the south of Palestine was Judah, the location of both Bethlehem, Jesus' birthplace, and Jerusalem, which was the capital known both as the Holy City and the City of David. This province was named for the tribe of Judah, which dwelt there until they were exiled in 587 B.C. Judah, a mostly rocky and dry land, was bordered by the Dead Sea on the east and the desert on the south. Greeks and Romans rereferred to

fyi...

Jerusalem is 2500 feet above sea level; hence the phrase "Go up to Jerusalem." The city Jesus knew is buried beneath twenty centuries of rubble about twelve feet under the present city. A wall with eight sets of gates surrounds Jerusalem, which is two and a half miles in circumference. The Golden (or Beautiful) Gate, on the eastern wall is traditionally considered the one Jesus would have entered through on Palm Sunday. Because Jewish tradition holds that the Messiah will pass through this gate, Muslims walled it up in the sixteenth century. Facing this gate on the Mount of Olives are Jewish tombs.

trivial tidbit...

In 1342, the pope made the Franciscan Order of Friars Minor the official custodians of the Holy Land. They safeguard the Christian presence there and care for the major shrines and biblical sites. Each year on Good Friday a collection is taken up worldwide to support them in this work.

a cool website...

Take a virtual tour of the Holy Land at www.ffhl.org, a site run by the Franciscans, who are entrusted with the care of the Christian places. Another tour is available at www.mustardseed.net.

Judah as Judea. Judeans looked down on Galileans as "country bumpkins."

Locked between Galilee and Judah lay Samaria, home to the Samaritans, who were longtime enemies of the Jews. The Sea of Galilee and the Dead Sea are connected by the Jordan River, which, because of its serpentine path, travels 166 miles to cover the 66-mile distance between the two seas. The Jordan River is the east boundary of Israel. Its name is from the Hebrew for "descend" because the river flows to the Dead Sea, which at 1,300 miles below sea level is the lowest point on the Earth.

Like other towns in those days, towns in Palestine were surrounded by walls for security and were accessible only through gates, which were locked every night and guarded.

Alexander the Great had conquered Israel in 66 B.C., and so Greek (Hellenist) influence permeated Palestine's culture and economic practices. In fact, the Jewish Temple was constructed with Greek columns, and the New Testament was written entirely in Greek.

Jesus' Hometown

Jesus was so identified with his hometown that he was referred to as "the Nazarene" (see Matthew 2:23; Mark 14:67, 16:6). Nazareth, a village in Galilee of about two hundred people, was so obscure that there is no mention of it in any documents other than Scripture. Galilean Jews with their northern accent were scorned by the Judeans, who had an expression "as stupid as a Galilean." When the apostle Nathanael first heard about Jesus being the one Scripture fore-

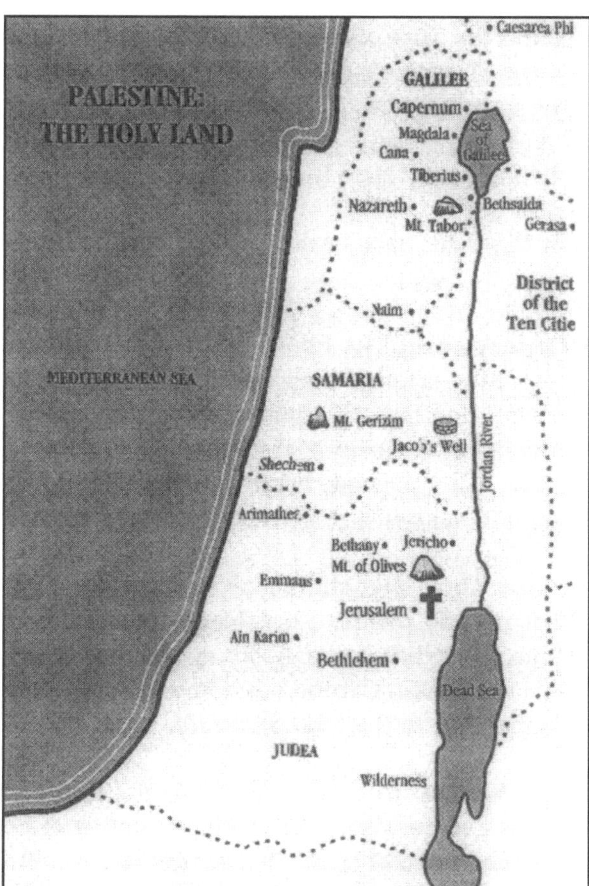

told, he scoffed, "Can anything good come out of Nazareth?" (John 1:46). Even in his origins, Jesus already aligned himself with the underdogs.

At 1250 feet above sea level, Nazareth offers a commanding view of the surrounding territory. From the hills of Nazareth, Jesus could see snowcapped Mount Hermon and, in the far distance to the west, the blue Mediterranean Sea. Because there were no electric lights, at night the starry sky must have been a spec-

Holy Land site...

Excavations in Capernaum under a fifth-century octagonal church uncovered a first-century house thought to be St. Peter's house where Jesus stayed. It is identified as such by Egeria, a fourth-century pilgrim. Fishhooks and graffiti seemingly left by second- and third-century Christians were discovered there. The large room (twenty feet by twenty feet) had been plastered three times, although no other Capernaum houses have been found with plaster. Jars and lamps were in this room, but no household pottery. These two facts suggest that this room had been an early house church. Today a modern Franciscan church stands over the site.

The Parable of the Two Seas

Two seas lie in Palestine. In the north is the Sea of Galilee. Its fresh, blue waters teem with fish; trees spread their branches over it and stretch out roots to sip its waters; along its shores children play. Jesus could look across its silver surface as he taught. People build their homes near it, and birds their nests; and every kind of life is happier because it is there. It's been called the most beautiful sea in the world. The Jordan River makes this sea with sparkling water from the hills.

The Jordan River flows on south into another sea. Here there is no splash of fish, no fluttering leaf, no song of birds, no children's laughter. Travelers choose another route. Dead trees coated with salt jut out of it. The air hangs heavy above it, and no creature drinks its brackish waters filled with mineral deposits. It is the lowest point on the earth's surface.

What makes the difference in the seas? The Sea of Galilee receives but does not keep the Jordan. For every drop that flows into it another drop flows out. The other sea gives nothing. It is named the Dead Sea.

(Author unknown)

tacular sight.

Jesus' base while he was ministering in Galilee, however, was not Nazareth but Capernaum. Matthew calls it "his own town" (Matthew 9:1). This fishing village on the shore of the Sea of Galilee was ideal for Jesus' work because it was on a main highway, the Via Maris. The black basalt synagogue built by a Roman centurion, where Jesus taught, is still slightly visible under the ruins of a fifth-century limestone synagogue.

Jesus' Language

Israel was a multilingual country at the time of Jesus. Recall that the inscription Pilate had posted on the cross ("This is the king of the Jews") was written in Hebrew, Latin, and Greek. Jesus would have been at least bilingual. His native tongue, the one he spoke at home, was Aramaic, the language of the Aramaens, Abraham's people. Jesus also would have used Aramaic in his ministry, because that is what all Jews spoke. However, Jesus would have had the thick accent of the Galileans: Aramaic is still spoken in isolated parts of the Mideast, and several Eastern rite Catholic and Orthodox churches use it in liturgy. Since the Hebrew Scriptures were written in Hebrew, Jesus must also have had command of that language. He probably knew a smattering of Greek too from engaging in commerce with the Gentiles in Galilee, and maybe he even picked up a little Latin from the Roman soldiers stationed in Palestine at the time.

trivial tidbit...

Galileans apparently dropped opening sounds, much like people who speak Cockney English do. A derisive joke from Jesus' time was about a merchant who taunted a Galilean customer, "You stupid Galilean, do you need something to ride on (*hamar*, 'a donkey') or something to make a dress with (*'amar*, 'wool'), or something for a Temple sacrifice (*immar*, 'lamb')?"

trivial tidbit...

To view or hear the Lord's Prayer in Aramaic, type "Lord's Prayer Aramaic" in any Internet search engine.

trivial tidbit...

"Shalom aleichem" (Peace be with you) was the usual Jewish greeting, along with a kiss on both cheeks instead of a handshake, in Jesus' time. The peace wished in *shalom* is tantamount to "fullness of life." A similar greeting, *"Assalamu alaikum"* is used by Muslims.

quick quote...

By a Carpenter mankind was made, and only by that Carpenter can mankind be remade.

Desiderius Erasmus

Jesus' Social Status, Education, and Work

The fact that Jesus' family didn't own their own land probably put them in the lower middle class. They were peasants, but they weren't necessarily poor. In other words, they were like most of the Jews in Israel at the time.

Beginning at age three, boys were taught at home by their fathers, so Joseph would have instructed Jesus. At age six the boys, but not the girls, went to the synagogue in their town, where they learned to read and write (although this wasn't mandatory until 65 A.D.). Their sole textbook would have been the Torah (the first five books of Hebrew Scripture, also called the Law). Jesus, therefore, was literate, but his mother, Mary, was not. Because Jesus had studied Hebrew Scripture intensely and had memorized it, he was able to quote and refer to it often as he taught.

Like his father, Joseph, Jesus was a blue-collar worker, a *teklon*. This Greek word means a worker not only in wood but in stone and metal. Thus, the two men were most likely not just carpenters but construction workers. Their job description would include making farm tools, furniture, and boats as well as helping to erect buildings in Nazareth and in nearby towns. Sephoris, for example, had been destroyed in 3 A.D. and was being rebuilt by Herod only two and a half miles away. Most likely Jesus and his friends and cousins would have worked on projects there. Construction was hard work, especially considering the crude tools that were in use and the hot climate. The hands of Jesus had to be rough and callused from wielding hammers and saws and shaping wood. He knew firsthand what it meant to earn his bread by the sweat of his brow.

When Jesus was in his thirties, he had a career change. He became a traveling preacher. He traded the security of a home with Mary and steady work for the uncertain life of the road. From then on he would never know where his next meal was coming from. Jesus journeyed from town to town, now and then with great crowds following him. Peter summed up these years by saying, "He went about doing good and healing all who were oppressed by the devil" (Acts 10:38). Jesus taught, healed, and announced the kingdom of God throughout Galilee and Judea, sometimes making a foray into neighboring regions such as Decapolis, a cluster of ten cities. He did this for at most three years until his death. During this time Jesus was supported by his disciples, in particular women followers who provided financial support for him and the apostles. In the evenings he relied on people's hospitality, slept outdoors, or found shelter in caves.

Although Jesus was called rabbi as a title of respect, he wasn't the kind of rabbi we know today. Originally the title rabbi meant "my great one." Only between 60 to 80 A.D. did "rabbi" become a technical term for someone authorized to teach. Neither was Jesus a Jewish priest but a layman. In his culture priests were from the tribe of Levi who were descended through Aaron, Moses' brother, and were in charge of Temple services and sacrifices.

trivial tidbit...

To walk thirty miles would take one full day. From Nazareth to Jerusalem was 65 miles.

fyi...

Pope Benedict XVI has written a two-volume work called *Jesus of Nazareth*.

A Quick, Creative Mind and Charismatic Personality

The Gospels give evidence that Jesus had a high IQ and a quick, razor-sharp wit. It requires extraordinary intelligence to weave the memorable stories he told,

quick quote...

[We have] very efficiently pared the claws of the Lord of Judah, turning him into a household pet for pale curates and pious old ladies.

Dorothy Sayers

to come up with the striking aphorisms that were second nature to him, and to field the attacks of his enemies with clever adroitness as he repeatedly did. Over and over the Gospels comment that people marveled at Jesus' teaching. As a man, Jesus wasn't omniscient, but he certainly was gifted.

Jesus is the best of what it means to be human, and he prompted people who encountered him to become their best selves as well. The fact that at Jesus' invitation people left their families, homes, and jobs to follow him into the unknown shows his charisma. Jesus' strong, magnetic personality drew hundreds of people to him when he taught or just walked down the road. The paparazzi of today would have had a field day with him. This ability to attract people enabled Jesus to accomplish much in a short period of time.

Jesus emanated power and authority and showed a bit of chutzpah, as when he argued with the Jewish leaders or drove the moneychangers from the Temple. He was passionate and capable of holy fury. Yet this man of steel was gentle and showed great tenderness. People, even sinners, felt safe and accepted in his presence. Children, too, who are usually cautious and shy with strangers, weren't afraid of him. And Jesus was affectionate in word and action. He called the paralytic "child," the woman who touched his cloak "daughter," and his disciples "children" and "little flock." Jesus embraced children, touched the sick, and wasn't embarrassed by a woman crying at his feet. Jesus often praised and affirmed people. His disciples, including the women who followed him, must have found Jesus charming.

Judging from Jesus' interaction with individuals

and his presence at parties and dinners, he was definitely a people person, someone who thrived on being with others. Jesus showed a keen sensitivity toward people, be it a blind beggar or a repentant apostle. He empathized with losers like the woman about to be stoned to death, Zacchaeus the despised tax collector, and the dying thief on the cross. He showed compassion for the suffering like the widow whose son had died, the paralyzed man who could never make it to the healing waters on time, and the blind beggar. A hallmark of his relationships is that Jesus was inclusive. He embraced everyone: Jews, Romans and Samaritans, men and women, rich and poor alike. This same universality and equality was to characterize his Church. In it "there is no longer Jew or Greek, there is no longer slave or free, there is no longer male and female; for all of you are one in Christ Jesus" (Galatians 3:28).

And Jesus obviously liked a good time: His critics accused him of being a glutton and a drunkard (Matthew 1:19). They objected to his hanging out with the "wrong" crowd. Jesus was a person others enjoyed being with. Theologian Edward Schillebeeckx pointed out that you couldn't be in his presence without feeling joy. On the other hand, Jesus had a kind of aura so that as he walked ahead of the crowd, "they were amazed, and those who followed were afraid" (Mark 10:32).

Special Friends

Like us, Jesus needed special friends. He singled out three of his apostles—Peter, James, and John—to be his companions at key times in his life. And accord-

fyi...

Jesus' struggle to overturn social trends that suppress people has led to two contemporary kinds of theology. Liberation theology, which is especially strong in Latin America, is centered on freeing the oppressed. Feminine (or feminist) theology works to change cultural tendencies that subjugate women or treat them as inferiors.

quick quote...

I believe there is no one lovelier, deeper, more sympathetic and more perfect than Jesus.

Fyodor Dostoevsky

quick quote...

When I try to bow to thee, my obeisance cannot reach down to the depth where thy feet rest among the poorest, and lowliest, and lost.

Source unknown

ing to the Gospel of John, he favored one called "the beloved disciple," who may or may not have been John himself. There were other people with whom Jesus could relax and be himself. He felt at home with Lazarus and his sisters, Mary and Martha, in Bethany. We know that "Jesus loved Martha and her sister and Lazarus" (John 11:5). Apparently none of the three was married, which suggests that they might have been teenagers. Bethany is a village outside of Jerusalem where Jesus often stayed. Its name means "house of the poor," which is appropriate; for Jesus aligns himself with the poor. Last but not least, from the loyalty of Mary Magdalene at the crucifixion and Jesus' appearance to her first after the resurrection, we can infer that he had a distinct friendship with her.

A Heart for the Vulnerable

It's said that the moral test of a society is how it treats its most vulnerable members. That also holds true for individuals. Jesus passes this test with flying colors. Reaching out with compassion and help to the poorest, most isolated, most defenseless people in society was arguably the dominant motif of his public ministry. In Jesus' culture this group included widows, children, and Samaritans. Jesus was definitely on the side of the weak. His loving care encompassed all types of misfits: not only the crippled, the diseased, and the insane, but also sinners, crooks, sluts, and bums. Jesus noticed these poor, most of his miracles were worked for them, and he taught others to care about them. Today he carries out this work through the members of his Church all over the world.

Jesus' Sense of Humor

Although there is no hard evidence in Scripture that Jesus laughed, how could he not help but smile at seeing the height-challenged dignitary, Zacchaeus, perched in a tree, peering through the leaves to get a glimpse of him? It's also easy to imagine that Jesus laughed heartily at the looks on the faces of the seasoned fishermen when at a "carpenter's son's" direction they lowered their nets and pulled them up loaded with fish, or when Peter tried to walk on the water but began to sink like a stone.

No doubt some of Jesus' illustrations in teaching were delivered with a grin and made people laugh. For example, there's his depiction of a camel trying to squeeze through the eye of a needle as the image of a rich person entering into the kingdom of God. Then there's the image he used of the overly zealous Pharisees straining out gnats from their food but then swallowing camels. Even a few miracles have an element of fun, such as Peter finding money to pay a tax in a fish or devils being sent into pigs and running off a cliff. Also, it's a playful person who gives his friends nicknames. Jesus dubbed James and John "the Sons of Thunder" and Simon "the Rock." Perhaps the ability to play is what Jesus meant when he said that "unless you change and become like children, you will never enter the kingdom of God" (Matthew 18:3).

trivial tidbit...

The picture "Laughing Jesus" by Ralph Kozak and others like it combat the myth that Jesus was always somber.

quick quote...

No one else holds or has held the place in the heart of the world that Jesus holds. Other gods have been as devoutly worshipped; no other man has been so devoutly loved.

John Knox

For insight into the relevance of the kingdom of God to our lives today, read Gregory Pierce's fine book *The World as It Should Be: Living Authentically in the Here-and-Now Kingdom of God*.

trivial tidbit...

In Matthew's Gospel, the kingdom of God is called the kingdom of heaven (or more literally "the kingdom from the heavens") because Matthew was a Jew, and Jews avoided using the name of God.

Jesus' Mission: The Kingdom of God

The predominant focus of Jesus' ministry was proclaiming and inaugurating the kingdom of God. In this kingdom, God's will is done and goodness reigns. Consequently it is a utopian kingdom of wholeness and freedom, characterized by peace, love, and joy. The evils of sin, injustice, hate, and violence have no home in it.

Jesus summoned his followers to live as kingdom-minded people. He taught about this kingdom, using stories to describe it, and he ushered it in by his saving acts. The kingdom was present in Jesus himself and in his ministry. Whereas faithful Jews prayed for a Messiah who would establish an earthly kingdom, Jesus the Messiah taught Christians to pray to God "your kingdom come…on earth as it is in heaven" (Matthew 5:10). He saw God's kingdom as a spiritual reign. This kingdom, in Jesus' mind, is already among us and within us, yet it will not come to completion until some unknown time in the future. He tells his followers, "Do not be afraid, little flock, for it is your Father's good pleasure to give you the kingdom" (Luke 12:32). In the Gospels, Jesus always proclaimed the kingdom, never himself. In fact, in the beginning of the Acts of the Apostles, Luke says that after his death and resurrection, Jesus "presented himself alive to them by many convincing proofs, appearing to them over the course of forty days and speaking about the kingdom of God" (Acts 1:3). Only later did the proclaimer become the proclaimed.

2 Son of God: Emmanuel

A little girl was drawing a picture at the kitchen table. Her mother asked, "What are you doing?" and she responded, "I'm drawing a picture of God." "You can't do that, honey," the mother said with a chuckle. "No one knows what God looks like." Undaunted, the girl replied, "They will when I'm through."

Most human beings yearn to know what God is really like. Because of the revelation of Jesus, we Christians believe we know for certain that God is close to us, concerned about us, and, indeed, active in our lives. In Scripture we read, "Long ago God spoke to our ancestors in many and various ways by the prophets, but in these last days he has spoken by a Son" (Hebrews 1:1). John's Gospel echoes this when it says, "It is God the only Son, who is close to the Father's heart, who has made him known" (John 1:18). For us, when looking at Jesus we behold the face of God, see God in action, hear God, and, consequently, come to know what God is like. Jesus is *Emmanuel*, "God with us," as an angel told St. Joseph.

In John's Gospel when Philip asks to see the Father, Jesus replies, "Whoever has seen me has seen the Father.... The words that I say to you I do not speak on my own; but the Father who dwells in me does his works. Believe me that I am in the Father and the Father is in me" (John 14:9–11). That is, Jesus is God. Theologians teach that Jesus is the same (*homo*) substance (*ousia*) as God. He is somehow a divine person who has become a human being like us. Jesus is much more than a prophet who speaks for God; through the eyes of faith he is God speaking directly to us.

He is the image of the invisible God, the firstborn of all creation.

Colossians 1:15

The people of Israel were accustomed to using the title "son of God" in reference to angels, to kings, and sometimes to Jews as a whole. Today we Christians consider ourselves to be sons and daughters of God. With Jesus, however, this expression assumed a whole new meaning. We believe that Jesus is literally the "only begotten" Son of God, that he has a unique relationship with the Father, similar to that between a parent and an only child.

The Gospel of Mark recounts that during the agony in the garden Jesus addressed God as *Abba*. This is the only instance in the Gospels where Jesus uses this Aramaic word for "father." Some scholars think that *Abba* is a more personal term, comparable to "Father dear" and with overtones of intimacy, respect, and trust.

Divine and Human Natures

We Christians believe that in Jesus the triune (three persons in one) God entered our history as a human being. Think about that for a moment. As the flesh-and-blood Jewish man named Jesus, God was able to delight in creation the way we do. God gazed on vivid orange sunrises over the Sea of Galilee, inhaled the wholesome scent of freshly-baked bread, knew the soft embrace of a mother's arms, experienced the satisfaction of quenching thirst with a drink of cold water on a hot day, beheld the beautiful faces of children, and enjoyed the camaraderie of good friends. Christians believe Jesus was God-Man—true God at the same time that he was a true man. That is why Jesus is one person with two natures. (*Person* means who someone is; *nature* means what someone is.)

Catholics do not believe that Jesus somehow "became" God gradually as he grew up. Neither do we believe that he "achieved" his sonship by being "adopted" by God as an award for a heroic life. We believe that Jesus actually is the Second Person of the Blessed Trinity, the only Son of God. The way St. John put it in his glorious opening to his Gospel was this: "In the beginning was the Word, and the Word was with God, and the Word was God. He was in the beginning with God. All things came into being through him, and without him not one thing came into being" (John 1:1–3). As God, then, Jesus is pure, uncreated spirit. He is omniscient (all-knowing), omnipotent (all-powerful), eternal (having no beginning or end), immutable (unchanging), and equal in perfections (all-good, all-wise, all-merciful, all-just) with the Father and the Holy Spirit.

On the other hand, Jesus was a real human being; he wasn't just pretending or some kind of spirit made to look like a man. "The Word became flesh, and lived among us" (John 1:14). Jesus had a flesh-and-blood body, five senses, emotions, sexuality, imagination, curiosity, and a sense of humor. He really felt hunger and thirst, pain, sadness, joy, and love. He also learned. St. Luke tells us that as a young boy, Jesus "increased in wisdom and in years, and in divine and human favor" (Luke 2:52).

Jesus was clearly dependent on others, including his parents. In many ways his divine powers were suspended, or at least unused. Although at times Jesus appeared to foresee future events, for example, he apparently didn't know everything: He revealed that only the Father knew the day of the second coming

trivial tidbit...

Jesus is a common name among Spanish-speaking people. Some other names that have their origin in the names for Christ are *Christian, Christopher* (which means "Christ-bearer"), *Christine, Immanuel* or *Emanuel* (which means "God with us"), and *Salvador* (which means "Savior"), along with their many variations.

quick quote...

A man who was merely a man and said the sort of things Jesus said would not be a great moral teacher. He would either be a lunatic—on a level with the man who says he is a poached egg—or he would be the devil of hell. You must make a choice. Either this man was, and is, the Son of God; or else a madman or something worse.

C.S. Lewis

(see Mark 13:32), appeared to be challenged and changed by his encounter with the Syrophoenician woman in Tyre (see Mark 7:24–30), and had many other encounters that showed his humanity, vulnerability, and humility. Moreover, Jesus clearly had the perceptions of a first-century Jew, some of which we now know were false. He probably literally believed, for example, that the first five books of the Bible were written by Moses himself, that David wrote Psalm 110, and that the story of Jonah was historical. He may well have believed that the sun revolved around the Earth, or that the Earth was flat. Catholics now know from modern science and biblical scholarship that none of these can be true, but because Jesus was human and lived in a certain time and place, he couldn't have known otherwise.

Just as we do, Jesus had to grow in knowledge and self-awareness. He also experienced temptation, but he withstood it. Scripture says that Jesus "in every respect has been tested as we are, yet without sin" (Hebrews 4:15), which means that he also did not experience guilt and remorse. Because of his sinlessness, Jesus could challenge his enemies, "Which of you convicts me of sin?" (John 8:46). Thus Jesus, the perfect human being, is a model for all of us of what it means to be genuinely and completely and perfectly human. He is love incarnate.

Some Early Church Teachings about Jesus

For centuries after the death of the last disciples who knew Jesus, Christians wrestled with their understanding of Jesus. The first seven ecumenical Church councils, in fact, were called primarily to resolve questions about Jesus. The early Church defined that Jesus is truly human and truly divine at the Council of Chalcedon in 451. St. Ephrem explained that in Jesus the two natures are combined just as two pigments are combined inseparably to form a new color on the artist's palette. How can a person be fully God and fully man at the same time? This is a mystery beyond our comprehension. Theologians call the existence of two natures in Jesus the *hypostatic union*, a term based on the Greek for "person."

During persecutions, Christians used the sign of a fish as a secret means of identification. The letters in the Greek word for "fish" (ICHTHYS) were an acronym, the initial letters of these words in Greek: "Jesus Christ, Son of God, Savior."

The relationship between Jesus' humanity and divinity generates a host of intriguing questions that theologians have been grappling with for ages. Did Jesus know he was the Messiah? Did he know he was God? If so, when did he realize this? Since Jesus was God, did he know the future? How did he experience the presence of the Father? You will not find the definitive answers to these questions and others like them in this or any other book.

The early Church did, however, condemn certain beliefs about Jesus as heresies. While the word *heresy* comes from the Greek for "choice," to Christians it stands for a belief in opposition to an established and widely accepted Church teaching. Here are a few of the heresies about Jesus:

- *Arianism,* taught by a bishop named Arius in the fourth century, held that Jesus was not of the same "substance" as the Father and that Jesus was created by the Father at a particular point in time and therefore was not truly God. At the ecumenical council of Nicaea in 325 A.D. the

fyi...

The Nicene Creed originally stated that the Holy Spirit "proceeded from the Father." To this the Western Church added the word *filioque* ("and the Son") in order to stress that the Son and the Father are equal. The Eastern Church saw this expansion as heresy. The dispute was a factor in the Great Schism of 1054 that split the Church into Roman Catholic and Eastern Orthodox and has yet to be resolved.

Church condemned Arius' teaching and taught that Jesus Christ was "consubstantial" or equal in substance with the Father.

- *Nestorianism,* promoted by Nestorius, the then patriarch of Constantinople, held that Christ was two persons, one human and one divine and that Mary was the mother only of the man Jesus, not the mother of God. The third ecumenical council at Ephesus in 431 A.D. proclaimed that the two natures were combined and that Jesus Christ is one person, who is the Son of God, and that Mary truly is the Mother of God by virtue of her conception of the Son of God as her human/divine son.

- *Docetism* was the belief that Jesus' body was only an illusion because God could not have become man and remained God. Its name comes from the Greek word *dokeo* that means "to seem." The Council of Chaldedon in 451 A.D. taught that Jesus is truly human and truly divine at the same time.

- *Monophysitism,* taught by the monk Eutyches in the fifth century, held that the human nature in Jesus simply disappeared when God's Son assumed it. Therefore Christ has only one nature, a divine one. This heresy's name is from the Greek for "one nature." It also held that Christ's body was different in substance from ours. The Council at Chalcedon in 451 A.D. affirmed that Jesus Christ has two distinct natures, one human and one divine, that come together in one person.

- *Monothelitism* was the belief that Jesus had only one will, which was divine, and lacked a human will. This was rejected by the Council of Constantinople in 680 A.D.
- *Gnosticism* was the belief in hidden knowledge revealed only to a few. Gnostics thought that the material world was evil, and therefore God would not have become man. This heresy was popular for many centuries in the early Church and was the basis for other heresies. Early saints and theologians, such as St. Justin and St. Irenaeus, refuted Gnosticism, and several early Christian writings, including the Gospel of Thomas, were excluded from the Bible because they contained traces of it.

big book search...

The theology of Jesus was developed by St. Paul in his letters and is found in a nutshell in Colossians 1:15–20. Read this passage.

A Unique Spirituality

No one can completely fathom the spirituality of Jesus, but the Gospels provide clues. For one thing, as would be expected, Jesus had an extraordinary, intimate relationship with God the Father. Jesus had complete trust in the Father's providence and taught others to depend on the Father's love and care. Basically Jesus was a happy person because he was anchored in the love of the Father.

Jesus clearly fostered his relationship with the Father through prayer. Jesus prayed before major events in his life and was known to spend the night in prayer. He sometimes prayed spontaneously. Most importantly for us, Jesus was ever attuned to the will of the Father. He had come to carry out the mission of the Father, and he did so faithfully. At the end of his life, Jesus surrendered himself to the Father: "Father, into

Sin is any act or omission that alienates us from God, other people, and our own best selves. It creates a state of unbalance and turmoil in our lives and in the world. Catholics distinguish between mortal (or serious) sin and venial (or lesser) sin. Social sin is an evil condition that a group is responsible for creating and sustaining.

your hands I commend my spirit" (Luke 23:46).

Why Did the Second Person of the Trinity Become a Human Being?

The Church has long held that the original sin of human beings caused their estrangement from God and that because of his incredible love for us, God the Father sent his Son to save us from sin and death. At the Easter Vigil we hear sung in the *Exsultet*, "O happy fault…which gained for us so great a Redeemer!" Through his life, death, and resurrection, Jesus atoned for all sins, reconciling us with the Father and making eternal life a possibility for us again. This teaching is presented by Paul, the earliest New Testament writer. Alluding to the original sin of Adam and Eve, he wrote: "Just as one man's trespass led to condemnation for all, so one man's act of righteousness leads to justification and life for all" (Romans 5:18).

It was St. Anselm, Archbishop of Canterbury in the eleventh century, who spelled out why our redemption required a God-man. Only God is perfect enough to make up for sin, he said, which is an unfathomable crime against the all-holy God. Therefore the redeemer had to be divine. Yet it was human beings who sinned, and so logically a human being had to make reparation for the sins of all. Love for us motivated the Father to act and the Son to willingly sacrifice himself.

You may remember learning that even if you were the only person in the world Jesus still would have come to earth to save you. God loves each of us that much. Because of Jesus' selfless act, humankind has been reconciled with God once again and given the

The Blessed Trinity

What we Catholics call the Blessed (or Holy) Trinity is a strict mystery, which means it can never be understood by human beings. Yet we still try to explain it. According to a legend, St. Patrick used a three-leaf clover to teach about the Trinity. Other analogies are the three forms of water (gas, solid, liquid) and the three parts of an egg (shell, albumin, yolk). Tertullian, an early Christian apologist, compared the Trinity to a plant. The Father was the deep root, the Son the shoot that breaks forth into the world, and the Spirit that which spreads beauty and fragrance, fructifying the earth with flower and fruit. St. Augustine renamed the Father, Son, and Spirit as "the Lover, the Beloved, and Love."

There is a great story about St. Augustine and the Trinity. Supposedly he was walking along the beach in North Africa and encountered a young boy who was taking a cup of water from the Mediterranean Sea and then running back and pouring the water into a hole he had made in the sand. After watching the boy make several trips, Augustine said to him, "You will never be able to move all the water from the sea into that hole." The boy looked at the Father of the Church and said, "And you will never be able to understand the Trinity."

The Church teaches and we pray in the Creed at Mass that God the Son is generated (begotten) by the Father and that the Holy Spirit proceeds from both of them. However, Catholics also believe that all three persons of the Trinity are eternal and have equal powers, but that they are distinct "persons"—perhaps not persons like we humans are persons, but unique and separate as we are. Although the Trinity always acts together as one God, we humans attribute certain divine acts to each person. We say that the Father is the Creator of the universe, the Son is the Redeemer of the world, and the Holy Spirit is the Sanctifier, who makes us holy.

Christ is God, or he is the world's greatest imposter.

Dorothy Day

opportunity of sharing in divine life. As St. Athanasius put it, "He was made human so that we might be made divine." That is why we say that Jesus is the mediator between the human race and God.

The Humility of God

One theory for explaining why Lucifer and the angels he led turned against God is that they refused to accept that God would become human. They found this idea of almighty God becoming a creature of flesh and blood abhorrent. We, on the other hand, are so familiar with the concept of the incarnation that we tend to forget what an incredible gesture this was on God's part. St. Paul describes it like this: "He emptied himself, taking on the likeness of a slave" (Philippians 2:7). Cardinal John Henry Newman refers to Jesus as "omnipotence in bonds." In a whimsical way poet George Herbert captures the debasement involved in God's lighting on our planet:

> The God of power, as he did ride
> In his majestick robes of glorie
> Resolv'd to light; and so one day
> He did descend, undressing all the way.

So what is God really like? Catholics answer that question by saying that God must be Jesus-like, because Jesus is the most perfect revelation of God. No wonder Jesus is a towering figure in human history! In him, we see the kind of God we all would want: compassionate, just, powerful, tender, merciful, approachable, and above all loving. This is what the Gospels, the record of Jesus' life, make crystal clear. He is truly *Emmanuel*, "God with us."

3 The Way: Early Writings about Jesus

Jesus called himself "the Way" (John 14:6) because he is the way to the Father's house. His earliest disciples were known simply as followers of "the Way." (They weren't called *Christians* until much later, in Antioch, which is in present day Turkey.) You would think that Christ, the most significant person in history, the one who teaches the human race the way to happiness, would have left plenty of footprints when he walked our earth. This was not the case.

Imagine that some thirty years after your death someone sets out to write your biography. From the pictures and writing and testimony of people you left behind, would your biographer know the real you, what you were thinking, and why you acted as you did? Would the documentary evidence and people's memories of you give the biographer a complete, consistent record of what you did and said on different occasions? Of course not. We know how widely people's accounts of the same event can differ and how people can have different impressions of the same person. We also know that people of good will can interpret written documents in ways that come to completely opposite conclusions. Consider then the challenge of gaining true, accurate knowledge of Jesus, especially since he lived in an era before video cameras, tape recorders, newspapers, the Internet, and so forth. Not to mention that most people were illiterate at the time he lived!

quick quote...

Let us remember that when we have traveled all ways, we shall come to the End of all ways, who says, I AM THE WAY.

St. Ambrose

In fact, there are some people who argue that Jesus never existed or at least that we cannot prove he did. However, it is safe to say that more words have been written *about* Jesus than any other person in history. So what evidence do we really have about Jesus and his message?

Ancient Secular Writings

Jewish references to Jesus in the first and early-second century are nonexistent, except for a couple of mentions in the writings of a Jewish historian of the time, Flavius Josephus. This may be because records were destroyed in the fall of Jerusalem in 70 A.D.

Born in 37 A.D., Flavius Josephus fought the Romans in Galilee and then switched sides. He moved to Rome, where he wrote two major works on the history of the Jews. In his twenty-volume *Jewish Antiquities*, there is a passage where he mentions Jesus, but it appears to have been embellished over the years by Christian copyists. Here is one version that is considered to be unaltered:

> At this time, lived Jesus, a wise man who performed good deeds; his virtue was recognized. Many Jews and people of other nationalities became his disciples. And Pilate sentenced him to death on the cross. But those who had become his disciples continued to preach his doctrine. They reported that he had appeared to them three days after his crucifixion and that he was alive; accordingly he was perhaps the Messiah, concerning whom the prophets have recounted wonders.

Josephus also speaks of the stoning of "James, brother of Jesus who is called the Christ."

Other secular documents of the time mention Jesus. About 73 A.D., a Syrian named Mara bar Sarapion wrote to his son from a Roman prison, where it seems he was facing execution. In the letter he observes that wisdom doesn't safeguard against persecution and refers to three wise men who were unjustly killed: Socrates, Pythagoras, and an unnamed "wise king" of the Jews. Mara claims that these men live on; the Jewish king lives "because of the new law he had given."

There are other minor references to Jesus. Pliny the Younger, a governor in Asia Minor, wrote a letter about 111 A.D. to the Emperor Trajan in which he mentions the sect that "assembled before daylight on a fixed day and sang hymns to Christus as God." The Roman historian Tacitus (about 115 A.D.) wrote that Nero tortured "the people called Christians." He explained, "This name was derived from Christus, who, under the reign of Tiberius, had been put to death by Pontius Pilate." And the historian Suetonius in *The Twelve Caesars* (about 120 A.D.) reported that Claudius had expelled Jews from Rome in 49 A.D. because they "caused continual disturbances at the instigation of Chrestus."

Lucian of Samosata, a second-century Syrian satirist, derided Christians and their founder. In his "Death of Peregrine" he reflects what seems to have been his era's common perception of Christians:

> The Christians, you know, worship a man to this day—the distinguished personage who intro-

fyi...

In the Mediterranean world, writing was done on papyrus made from the stem of the papyrus, a reed in the Nile Delta in Egypt. The stem was stripped, and the sticky pith inside was sliced into strips. These were laid next to each other, and another layer was laid across them. The strips were pounded together and dried. A round object such as a seashell was used to smooth the papyrus. Writing was done on the side with the horizontal strips. By 800 A.D., papyrus was mostly replaced by parchment made from animal hide.

fyi...

Famous movies about Jesus include *King of Kings* (1961), which made history by showing his face rather than only his hands and backs; *Jesus Christ Superstar* (1971) based on an opera by Andrew Lloyd Weber; *Jesus of Nazareth*, which appeared as a television mini-series in 1977; *The Gospel of John* (2003), a beautiful portrayal of his life; and *The Passion of the Christ* (2004).

> duced their novel rites, and was crucified on that account.... You see, these misguided creatures start with the conviction that they are immortal for all time, which explains their contempt of death and voluntary self-devotion which are so common among them; and then it was impressed on them by their original lawgiver that they are all brothers, from the moment that they are converted, and deny the gods of Greece, and worship the crucified sage, and live after his laws.

Both Tacitus and Suetonius, writing at the end of the first century, mention prophecies about a leader or leaders rising from the East. Tacitus wrote in his *Historiae*: "Most were convinced that the ancient books of the priests predicted that, around this time, the East would grow more powerful. And that the rulers of the world would emerge from Judea." Similarly, Suetonius says in his *Life of Vespasian*: "Throughout the East, an idea was gaining currency: the consistent and very ancient view that it was to be written in the world's destiny that from Judea would emerge the rulers of the world."

A passage in the fourth *Ecologue* of the Roman poet Virgil, written in 40 B.C., is viewed as propaganda for Octavius Caesar, but from a Christian perspective it is a prophecy about Jesus:

> We have reached the last era in the oracle of the Sibyl of Cumae: the long sequence of the ages starts afresh. The Virgin comes to dwell with us, and the rule of Saturn is restored. The first born of the new age is already on his way from high heaven. A new-born child born in the reign of

the Emperor Augustus shall end the iron race and shall raise a race of gold for the entire world.

These ancient writings don't prove much about Jesus. They certainly would not be enough to convince anyone to follow him or to think he was important, much less that he was the Son of the one, true God. Believing that Jesus is God is only possible with the eyes of faith, eyes that are helped by the written testimony about Jesus that his followers left behind. We Christians call this testimony the "New Testament," which makes up the second part of the "Bible" or the "Sacred Scriptures." (The first, and much longer, part of the Bible is what Christians refer to as the "Old Testament," which is Hebrew Scriptures with a few additional books and material.)

trivial tidbit...

Gospel is from the Old English "good spell," which is a translation of the Greek *evangelium* (good news), the source of our word *evangelist*.

Earliest Scripture References to Jesus

St. Paul is known as the "Apostle to the Gentiles." His letter to the Thessalonians, probably the first of his letters, was written around 51 A.D. and is the earliest Christian document in the Bible, even preceding the Gospels. Paul greets the Church "in God the Father and the Lord Jesus Christ," and he thanks them for their "hope in our Lord Jesus Christ." So Jesus is already clearly accepted by Christians even by that time as being equal to God. In this letter Paul sets forth the Christian belief that Jesus, God's Son, will return to earth someday. He exhorts the Thessalonians to be holy before God the Father "at the coming of our Lord Jesus with all his saints" (1 Thessalonians 3:13). Paul concludes his letter, "The grace of our Lord Jesus Christ be with you" (1 Thessalonians 5:28).

Paul's letters, however, do not tell much about Jesus'

In the second century, St. Irenaeus argued for keeping the number of Gospels at four, saying that there are the four corners of the world, the four winds, and the Church stands on the four pillars of the Gospels. He bluntly stated, "Those who say the Gospels should be more or fewer in number are futile, ignorant, and presumptuous."

To correct a mistake in a Scripture book or to add a comment, copyists over the centuries made notes called glosses in the margins of the text. One challenge Scripture scholars face is deciding whether or not these glosses are part of Scripture.

life and ministry in Palestine. He quotes no parables and describes no miracles. But then, Paul's experience of Jesus was mainly limited to one life-changing encounter with the Risen Lord. Nevertheless, we are largely indebted to Paul for helping shape the theology of Christ through his preaching and letters.

First Accounts about Jesus

During the life of Jesus and after he died and rose, news about him spread by word of mouth. Over and over his teachings and stories about his deeds were told, especially when Christians gathered for the Eucharist. If they were lucky, they heard the apostles and other eyewitnesses relate their experiences with Jesus.

You've probably played the game Telephone, in which a message is whispered from one player to another and all laugh at how different the final message is. Therefore, you can understand how stories about Jesus could have been altered. In time, as converts increased, as eyewitnesses died, and as heresies multiplied, it became obvious that permanent written records were needed. Besides, apparently Jesus wasn't coming back as soon as the first disciples expected. So about thirty-five or forty years after Jesus died, memories of his life began to be preserved in writing.

Luke tells us in the first sentence of his Gospel that a number of people undertook to write accounts of Jesus' life. Four of these accounts were accepted by the Church as divinely inspired, or canonical books, and are now the Gospels of the New Testament. Other accounts have come down to us as "apocryphal," or non-canonical gospels. Some of these are the Gospel of the Egyptians, the Gospel of Thomas, the Gospel of Peter, the Gospel of James, the Gospel of Nicodemus, and even the Gospel of Judas.

Three criteria for determining what Gospels to include in the New Testament were association with the apostles, faithful reflection of Christian teachings, and use of the reading in early church liturgy.

Some apocryphal writings that were not accepted into the canon are quite bizarre. The *Protoevangelium of James* presents Jesus as striking a playmate dead for jostling him. It also tells the charming, but unlikely, story of Jesus making clay birds that come alive and take flight. It's no surprise that this Gospel did not make the cut. In 150 A.D., the present books of the New Testament were already listed in various church documents, and the list was confirmed at the Council of Rome in 382 A.D. The Council of Trent in 1546 solemnly defined the canon, or list, of the books in both the Old and New Testament and decreed that they were divinely inspired, which means ultimately authored by God.

The *Didache* from second-century Syria, also called *The Teachings of the Twelve Apostles*, is the oldest actual copy of a Christian document we have. Described as a training manual for non-Jewish recruits, the Didache contains instructions for catechesis on baptism, fasting, prayer, the Eucharist, tithing, and leadership. It reflects the belief in Jesus as the Lord, the God of David, and the Son of God. Early fathers of the Church witness to the same conviction. St. Irenaeus, in *Against Heresies*, says that St. Clement of Rome (about 96 A.D.) referred to Jesus as the Lord. St. Ignatius of Antioch (107 A.D.) and Melito of Sardis (120 A.D.) also affirm both the humanity and divinity of Jesus.

quick quote...

All the way to heaven is heaven because he said, "I am the Way."

St. Catherine of Siena

trivial tidbit...

In 1945, in a tomb near Jerusalem, E.L. Sukenik, a professor at Hebrew University, discovered two ossuaries (boxes for human bones) that were carbon dated to 50 A.D. On them were charcoal graffiti of four crosses and the phrases "Iesous iou" and "Iesous aloth." The first phrase is understood as a prayer to Jesus for help, the second a request that Jesus would raise the person whose bones the ossuary held.

Did Jesus Really Do or Say It?

Some scholars today distinguish between the historical Jesus who lived in Palestine and the Jesus of faith as his followers perceived him after the resurrection. There is a movement to use historical-critical methods to discern as far as possible exactly what Jesus did and said as a man on earth. This effort is called "the quest for the historical Jesus" and was begun in the eighteenth century by the German philosopher Hermann Samuel Reimarus. Albert Schweitzer joined in the quest in 1906 and quite put an end to it by concluding that the new biographies of Jesus were simply a reflection of the scholars who wrote them. But then in the 1950s and 1960s the German theologian Rudolf Bultmann and others contributed ideas that gave rise to a second and a third quest for the historical Jesus.

The Jesus Seminar, founded in California in 1985, involves about 200 scholars. Its purpose is to determine the authentic sayings and deeds of Jesus by a historical-critical method. The group voted on sayings using colored beads with these meanings: *red* (Jesus did say the passage, or something very much like it), *pink* (Jesus probably said something like it), *grey* (the idea is probably from Jesus, but he may not have said it) and *black* (Jesus most likely did not say it). The Seminar concluded that of 500 sayings they studied, 18% are authentic. They also said that in their opinion about 16% of the events in Jesus' life are reliable. As you can guess, the Jesus Seminar is controversial. One criticism is that relatively few members are New Testament experts. Also, the members aren't allowed to assume the divinity of Jesus or the possibility of miracles. A benefit of the Seminar is that the quest for the historical Jesus is an ecumenical and international pursuit.

Here are criteria that scholars use to determine whether or not they think Jesus himself might have said it:

◆ *Multiple attestations.* The matter is present in the Gospels several times. The fact that the account of the multiplication of loaves and fishes appears six times, for example, indicates that this event or something similar must have happened.

◆ *Embarrassment for the Church.* The material reflects weakness in Jesus or the apostles such that authors and editors would not have included it unless it actually occurred. Examples are Jesus needing two attempts to cure a blind man, Peter's denials of Jesus, and perhaps even the fact that Jesus appeared first to Mary of Magdala rather than one of the male apostles.

◆ *Irony.* The saying or story is a surprising reversal, an impossibility, or a paradox, such as Jesus' command to love our enemies and his parable in which a Samaritan, the despised enemy of the Jews, turns out to be the hero.

◆ *Orality.* A short, clever, or provocative saying, such as "turn the other cheek," would more likely have been preserved accurately because the accounts were handed down orally.

◆ *Discontinuity.* The act or words are a break with tradition, such as Jesus' prohibition of all oaths. The validity of this criterion is questioned because it's difficult to tell to what extent Jesus was a product of his culture.

◆ *Coherence.* The passage is in sync with what we know about Jesus. For example, although the parable of the Prodigal Son appears only in Luke's gospel, it certainly jibes with Jesus' life and teachings.

Can the Gospels Be Trusted?

The Gospels were written early enough that they could depend on eyewitnesses as a source. Granted, mistakes might have crept into the stories about Jesus by oral repetition. However the Jews belonged to a highly oral culture. They were used to repeating stories and memorizing material. The several versions of events that have come down to us in the different Gospels are remarkably similar.

At a later stage, when these accounts were rewritten, it could be that copyists and editors introduced changes and mistakes and embroidered upon facts. The earliest whole surviving copies of the Gospels date to the fourth century, but they are closer to their originals than most ancient documents are to their originals. Consequently, fewer mistakes or changes would have entered into them. In addition, when our Gospels of today are compared to ancient manuscripts of them that have been discovered recently, there are relatively few differences.

It is pretty much undeniable that Jesus lived in Palestine in the first third of the first century A.D.; was known as a teacher, a prophet, and a worker of wonders; was crucified by the Romans, died, and was buried. His disciples encountered him as risen from the dead. Details in the Gospels may contradict one another, but the heart of the matter remains. All in all, the Gospels show conclusively that Jesus was not a concoction of the apostles' imagination but rather a real, historical, extraordinary person. Besides, for Catholics, Jesus is not so much a person in the past but a living, acting presence we encounter in our lives every day and in a special way in the Eucharist.

One drawback to written records of Jesus as opposed to a video-recording is that they lack the tone of voice, facial expressions, and gestures that accompanied what he said and which might have influenced his meaning.

quick quote...

Nothing so demonstrates God's positive attitude towards the human race as embracing my humanity.

St. Bernard of Clairvaux

4 The Truth: The Four Gospels

Jesus tells Pilate, "For this I came into the world, to testify to the truth." And Pilate cynically replies, "What is truth?" (John 18:37–38). He doesn't know that the man before him once defined himself as the truth: "I am the way, and the truth, and the life" (John 14:6). Jesus is truth, the opposite of all that is artificial and false. He is the answer to our human thirst to know what is real, the thirst that drives our quest for knowledge and makes being lied to so repulsive. The more we know Jesus, the more we possess the truth.

Virtually everything we know about Jesus is mined from the Gospels of Matthew, Mark, Luke, and John. These books differ from one another and at times contradict. The reason is that the writers did not draw up accurate historical documents as we know them. Rather, they produced testimonies of faith in the risen Christ. Moreover, they shaped the facts and their unfolding not only according to Jewish literary styles but with their respective audience in mind. Each evangelist (Gospel writer) had a specific intention in writing, and that intention wasn't to give us a complete biography of Jesus. In addition, the evangelists were writing from the other side of Easter. Their accounts were colored by what they knew about Jesus then: namely, that he was Lord and God.

The task of the evangelists can be compared to creating a mosaic of Jesus.

Pope Leo XIII in his 1893 encyclical *Providentissimus Deus* encouraged biblical study. Then in 1943, Pope Pius XII in the encyclical *Divino Afflante Spiritu* opened the door for the Church to read Scripture not literally but taking into account literary forms, the original languages, and the discoveries of history and archaeology. The Second Vatican Council document *Dei Verbum* (On Divine Revelation) of 1965 further promoted biblical study.

The story units about Jesus, called *pericopes*, and his sayings are like the colored tiles the Gospel writers had to work with. Each evangelist shaped these tiles uniquely and then arranged them differently, using his choice of grout (transitions) to hold them together. These are the main images of Jesus as each Gospel portrays him:

- Matthew: The Jewish Messiah
- Mark: The Suffering Servant
- Luke: The Savior
- John: The Son of God

Although there are various theories about the sequence of the Gospels and their sources, it's now widely agreed that Mark's Gospel was the first one written (even though Matthew's appears first in the New Testament) and that Matthew and Luke relied on Mark as a starting point. These three Gospels are called *Synoptic*, which means "same view," because they are similar in content and in the ordering of events. Sometimes they even use the exact same words. It's thought that Matthew and Luke also made use of a collection of sayings that scholars call "Q," for the German word *quelle*, which means "source." A few scholars propose that there was an earlier Gospel of Matthew in Aramaic that the Synoptic evangelists also drew from, but this has never been proven.

The fourth Gospel, the Gospel of John, was composed later than the Synoptics, when Christian theology was more developed. It is in a class all its own. Reading parts of John, especially the opening, is like reading a mystical book of poetry.

If the Gospels are Sacred Scripture inspired by God, then God speaks directly to us in them. The Second Vatican Council's *Constitution on Divine Revelation* teaches, "In the sacred books, the Father who is in heaven comes lovingly to meet his children and talks with them." (21) Jesus is present in the Gospels in a special way. That is why at Mass before listening to the proclamation of the Gospel we joyfully sing "Alleluia" (Praise the Lord), and we stand at respectful attention.

The Gospel of Mark: Christ in Action

This Gospel, the first and the shortest, is believed to date back to 65–70 A.D. Tradition holds that the author is John Mark, the son of a woman at whose house Christians gathered for prayer according to Acts 12:12. He also accompanied his cousin Barnabas and the apostle Paul on missionary journeys. Mark was Peter's interpreter in Rome and perhaps recorded Peter's memories of Jesus' life. One reason for this conclusion is that Mark's narrative includes details not in other Synoptics, an indication that it is an eyewitness account. For example, Jesus took Peter's mother-in-law *by the hand*, James and John left their father in the boat *with the hired servants*, and the multitude sat on the *green* grass in *hundreds and fifties*. Lastly, this Gospel alone omits Jesus promising or bestowing upon Peter the primacy (chief leadership) in the Church. This could be because Peter was too humble to talk about his special appointment and responsibility.

Mark wrote his Gospel for Gentile converts in Rome and adapts it to them in several ways. He inserts Latin words (*centurion, legion, Caesar, denarius*)

trivial tidbit...

The John Rylands papyrus, acquired on the Egyptian market in 1920, is the oldest extant fragment of the New Testament. It dates from about 130 A.D. and contains John 18:31–33 and 37–38 in Greek.

big book search...

Read a Gospel in one sitting. You might choose Mark, the shortest. Or read only the boldface headings in a Gospel and then reflect on the impact of the whole.

Symbols of the Evangelists

The four symbols for the evangelists are carved into lecterns and depicted in religious art. In a vision the prophet Ezekiel saw God's throne resting on cherubim with four faces: that of a lion, an ox, a man, and an eagle (Ezekiel 1:5–10). These four creatures also appear in John's vision of heaven (Revelation 4:6–7). How were these symbols and evangelists paired? One explanation is that it was based on how the Gospels begin:

Mark opens with the voice of John
roaring in the wilderness,
so his symbol is the lion.

Matthew begins with
the human genealogy of Jesus,
so his symbol is the man.

Luke starts with the priest Zechariah
offering sacrifice, so his symbol is the ox,
a sacrificial animal.

John opens with sublime, theological thoughts
(the Divine Word that existed in the beginning with God),
so his symbol is the eagle that soars high and according
to legend is the only creature able to look into the sun.

Another explanation is that the symbols stand for the way the Gospels present Jesus. Mark shows Jesus as king, so his symbol is the king of beasts (lion). Matthew points to the human nature of Jesus, so his symbol is a man. Luke focuses on Jesus as priest and sacrifice, so his symbol is an ox. And John stresses the divine nature of Jesus, so his symbol is an eagle.

and defines Jewish terms that the Romans wouldn't understand, such as *defiled* (not washed) and *Day of Preparation* (before the sabbath). When Aramaic is used, Mark translates it (*talitha cum, abba,* and *ephaphta*). Realizing that the Gentiles would be unfamiliar with Jerusalem, he explains that the Mount of Olives is across from the Temple. So that the Gentiles could better identify with his Gospel, Mark mentions that Simon of Cyrene was the father of Alexander and Rufus because Rufus was a Roman Christian whom his Roman readers might know. Since Hebrew writings wouldn't mean much to the Gentiles, Mark mentions only one Old Testament prophecy. Also, in Mark's Gospel Jesus travels mostly in Galilee, the "land of the Gentiles."

Mark's Gospel begins with the baptism of Jesus and says nothing about Jesus' birth and childhood. One-fourth of the book is about Jesus' miracles, for Mark wants his readers to know that Jesus' power proves he is God. To emphasize this, Mark frequently punctuates his writing with words like "astonished" and "amazed." Mark's writing is fast-paced and action-packed. The words "immediately" or "at once" occur forty-two times. Instead of using subordinate clauses, the sentences are joined by *and*, the way a child tells a story, creating a breathless effect. Mark presents Jesus as a man of action: In his Gospel Jesus delivers only two discourses (long talks). Furthermore, Mark frankly shows Jesus with emotions and the apostles with flaws. The fact that his stories are the most unpolished of the four Gospels is a hint that it is the earliest Gospel.

In Mark's Gospel the divine-human identity of

fyi...

The complete Gospel of Thomas was discovered in a jar in Nag Hammadi, Egypt, in 1945, along with other early Christian writings. It is a collection of 114 sayings attributed to Jesus, which scholars think might be a section of Q. In verse 77 Jesus says, "All has come from me, and the all has returned to me. Split a piece of wood, and I am there. Lift a stone, and you will find me there." Other sayings are similar to those in the Synoptic Gospels.

quick quote...

Ignorance of Scripture is ignorance of Christ.

St. Jerome

trivial tidbit...

The Gospel of Mark has only 661 verses. It is sometimes described as a passion narrative with a long introduction.

Jesus is known by demons, but not by people and not entirely by the disciples before the resurrection. Rather, Mark shows us the suffering Jesus as well as the suffering his disciples could expect. Often in this Gospel Jesus doesn't want people to know he is the Messiah. This could be because they have the wrong idea of the Messiah or because Jesus doesn't come into the fullness of being the Messiah until his death. His command to people not to tell that he does the works of the Messiah, which is characteristic of Mark, is called the "messianic secret." Mark might have used this as a device to explain to his Gentile audience why the Jews as a whole didn't automatically acknowledge Jesus as their Messiah.

The Gospel of Matthew: Christ the Teacher

Matthew's Gospel is so carefully planned and constructed that it is like architecture. For centuries Matthew was thought to be the first Gospel, and it was read and quoted more than the others. Now we think that this Gospel was written about 85 A.D. in Antioch, the capital of Syria, and not by the apostle Matthew but perhaps by one of his disciples. Unlike Mark, Matthew wrote for Jewish Christians in Palestine. By this time Christians were no longer viewed as a Jewish sect and were banned from the synagogues. In addition, Gentiles were becoming Christians without having to follow the Jewish traditions. Shaken by these two new situations, the Jewish Christians needed to be affirmed in their belief that Jesus was really their Messiah. To accomplish this, Matthew wrote a definitely Jewish document sprinkled with no fewer than forty-five Old Testament prophecies and quotations. As the first book in the New Testament, the Gospel of Matthew makes a good bridge between the Old and New Testaments.

Matthew begins by tracing Jesus' genealogy back to Abraham. Then because Moses was the Jews' great prophet, teacher, and lawgiver, Matthew presents Jesus as the new Moses—a great prophet, teacher, and lawgiver. Just as when Pharaoh kills the Hebrew baby boys only Moses is saved, when Herod kills all male babies in Bethlehem only Jesus is saved. Moses flees from Egypt to Israel. Similarly, the Holy Family flees to Egypt and then returns to Israel from Egypt. Like Moses, who doesn't eat or drink for forty days and nights on the mountain, Jesus fasts forty days in the desert. Where Moses goes up a mountain to receive the Law, Jesus ascends a mountain to give his new law, including the Beatitudes. In Matthew, Jesus is called rabbi or teacher dozens of times.

The Jews believed that Moses wrote their Law, the first five books of the Bible. This may be why Matthew builds his Gospel around five discourses that contain Jesus' teaching. In Matthew's Gospel, Jesus explicitly upholds the Law of Moses instead of abolishing it. However, by his words and example he teaches inward goodness over mere external observance.

Because Matthew's Gospel is heavy with discourse, it has fewer miracles. Perhaps in order to make up for this omission, Matthew doubles people. There are two blind men, two beggars, and two demoniacs. Despite the lack of individual miracle stories, Jesus definitely is introduced as the Son of God by Matthew when he repeats the grand sweeping statement

The Gospels were written in Greek, which had no breaks between words or sentences. The chapter divisions were created in 1205 by Stephen Langton, a professor in Paris who became Archbishop of Canterbury. The verses were determined in 1551 by Robert Stephanus, a book printer in Paris. A common story is that Stephanus marked the verses while riding to Lyons on horseback, and that is why they occur at odd places. However, his son attested that his father had worked on them at inns during breaks in his journey—so there's no excuse for such erratic work!

quick quote...

Luke is the recorder of Christ's loving-kindness.

Dante

big book search...

Because of its themes and subjects, Luke has been called the gospel of mercy, of women, of prayer, of the poor, of the Holy Spirit, and of joy. We might also call it the gospel of meals, for there are ten dinners in Luke. Skim the Gospel of Luke finding reasons why it deserves each name listed here.

that *all* who came to Jesus were healed, some merely by touching him.

Matthew mentions the "kingdom of heaven" fifty-two times. Matthew wants to convince his Jewish audience that Jesus inaugurated a new Israel, a new kingdom, which was to come "on earth as it is in heaven" (Matthew 6:10). In doing so he offers a picture of Jesus who brings forgiveness of sins and good news to the poor and oppressed in this life, as well as entrance into heaven through his Church.

The Gospel of Luke: The Compassionate Christ

The French writer Ernest Renan called the Gospel of Luke the most beautiful book in the world. Written somewhere between 70 and 90 A.D., this Gospel is actually the first of a two-part volume. Part two is the Acts of the Apostles. Luke was a doctor, a disciple of St. Paul, who refers to him as "Luke, the beloved physician" (Colossians 4:14) and one of his "fellow workers" (Philemon 1:24). Luke is thought to be a well-educated, widely traveled Gentile and has the reputation of being an artist. In his Gospel, Luke also paints with words in a polished, literary style that creates warm, human stories. Luke's whole Gospel is built on the framework of Jesus' journey up to Jerusalem.

A Greek himself, not a Jew, Luke wrote for the Gentile converts in Greece. His main theme is that salvation is not only for Jews but for everyone and especially for the poor. He demonstrates that Christianity is a new world religion and that Jesus is the new Adam, the center of history. Luke wants to persuade his readers that Christians can be good citizens of the Roman Empire. To do this, he presents Jesus not as an instigator of unrest but as a humanitarian teacher. He portrays Pilate as an agreeable fellow, not a cruel tyrant. In making overtures to the Gentiles, however, Luke is at times antagonistic toward Judaism.

The Gospel of Luke is special in other ways. Luke's focus is not so much the *parousia*, the coming of Christ at the end of the world, but how to live as a Christian today. In his Gospel, Jesus is powerful from all aspects: prophet, healer, and savior. He is the merciful one begotten by God and appointed by God to save all from oppression. Half of the Gospel of Luke is unique. It contains six miracles that are not in other Gospels: the miraculous catch of fish, the widow of Nain's son, the man with dropsy, the bent over woman, the ten lepers, and the servant's ear. Moreover, Luke has eighteen parables not found in the other Gospels, including some favorites such as the Good Samaritan and the Prodigal Son. Also, it is Luke we have to thank for the three canticles prayed in the Liturgy of the Hours (Divine Office): Zechariah's "Benedictus" (Luke 1:68–79), Mary's "Magnificat" (Luke 1:46–55), and Simeon's "Nunc Dimittis" (Luke 2:29–32). These gems are all in the infancy narratives, which are stories about Jesus' conception and birth. Some people surmise that Luke must have heard these intimate stories personally from Mary.

According to tradition, Luke painted several icons of Mary holding the Baby Jesus. Two of these can be seen in Jerusalem and Rome. A legend holds that one icon was painted on wood from a table that Mary and St. John ate on.

trivial tidbit...

Scripture was originally written on sheets of papyrus glued together to form long pieces called scrolls that were then wound around a stick. By the late first century, sheets of papyrus were stitched together and placed between wooden or leather covers. This book form (called a codex) replaced scrolls.

quick quote...

Above all it's the Gospels that occupy my mind when I'm at prayer; my poor soul has so many needs, and yet this is the one thing needful. I'm always finding fresh lights there, hidden and enthralling meanings.

St. Thérèse of Lisieux

The Gospel of John: Christ the Eternal Word

The last Gospel is the Gospel of John, probably written in Ephesus somewhere between 90 and 100 A.D., when much of our current understanding of Jesus had been formulated by the early Christians. The purpose of this Gospel is stated in John 22:30: "That you may come to believe." John's Gospel is quite different from the Synoptics. For one thing John omits 90% of their material. Furthermore, John uses elegant, lofty language and centers on Jesus' cosmic role of redeeming humanity rather than on his earthly mission of healing and teaching. This Gospel contains no moral teaching, such as the Beatitudes, other than love as the predominant Christian characteristic.

Traditionally it's been thought that this fourth Gospel was written by the apostle John, who was presumed to be "the beloved apostle" referred to only in this Gospel. Most likely it was written by the disciples of John—unless he lived to be a centenarian! In any case, the author was Jewish and well-educated. His audience was the Greek converts at Ephesus at a time when Christians had to defend the faith. He teaches that belief in Jesus leads to eternal life, and he tells how Jesus announces the coming of the Holy Spirit, the Comforter. John stresses Jesus' presence with his Church, through which he continues his work until he comes again in glory.

Scholars distinguish two sections in John. The first is the Book of Signs, which contains seven miracles (called signs by John), each symbolic. The second is the Book of Glory, which covers Jesus' dialogue with the disciples at the Last Supper as well as his death and resurrection.

The Gospel of John is laced with a high theology, which stresses that Jesus is the Son of God, a title that occurs twenty-eight times. The author's motive could have been to counteract heretics who at the time he was writing were teaching that Jesus wasn't divine. John starts by describing Christ as the Word (Logos) with God from all eternity. In this prologue, to promote the idea that Christ ushered in the new creation, he uses words that echo the creation story in Genesis: "In the beginning," "light," and "darkness." Light and darkness continue to appear as a theme in this highly poetic and symbolic work, as seen in these examples:

- Nicodemus comes to Jesus at night.
- The man born blind comes to see the light.
- Jesus calls himself the light of the world.
- After Judas leaves the Last Supper, John comments, "And it was night."

The sacraments are another theme in John: Jesus teaches Nicodemus about being born again of water and the spirit (Baptism); the first miracle is worked at a wedding (Marriage); Jesus promises the Holy Spirit (Confirmation); and he appears to his apostles Easter night and bestows on them the power to forgive sins (Holy Orders and Reconciliation). Although John doesn't recount the institution of the Eucharist at the Last Supper as the Synoptics do, he presents this sacrament at length in connection with the multiplication of loaves in chapter 6.

John's Gospel is a maverick in other ways. It describes a two- or three-year ministry for Jesus, where

trivial tidbit...

The opening verses of John's Gospel (John 1:1–14) might have been an early Christian hymn. In former days this passage was prayed as "the Last Gospel" after every Mass.

trivial tidbit...

Some speeches in John are duplicated, perhaps because the original author heard St. John explain something in two different ways and decided to include both.

Jesus = God

John reinforces the Son of God theme whenever Jesus says, "I am," which is tantamount to saying, "I am God." God's personal name revealed to Moses is Yahweh, which is translated "I am who I am." Therefore, by repeatedly using "I am" statements, John hammers home his message that Jesus and God are one. Here are the seven statements where "I am" on the lips of Jesus points to his divinity:

- "I am the bread of life" (6:35).
- "I am the light of the world" (8:12).
- "I am the gate" (10:7, 9).
- "I am the good shepherd" (10:11).
- "I am the resurrection and the life" (11:25).
- "I am the way, and the truth, and the life" (14:6).
- "I am the true vine" (15:1).

In addition to these statements, which all link Jesus with a life-giving image, there are times when he simply declares, "I am." For example, Jesus claims, "Before Abraham was, I am" (8:58).

The "I am" statements in John parallel statements in Isaiah 40–55, where God establishes his identity for his people.

the Synoptics describe everything as happening in a single year. The "kingdom of God" is mentioned only once in John, although he uses other images for the rebirth of creation. The cleansing of the Temple occurs not at the end of Jesus' ministry (as it does in the Synoptics) but at the beginning, which provides a reason for the Jewish leaders' antagonism toward Jesus early on. Only a few events in John are set in Galilee, and there are no entertaining parables, only allegories and metaphors. In John it is the Jews, not the Romans, who are responsible for Jesus' death (probably to make Christianity more appealing to the Gentiles). Also, John uses the broad term "the Jews" in the passion account instead of "some Jewish leaders." As a result, John's version of the crucifixion has given impetus to anti-Semitism over the centuries, even though John makes it clear that all the original disciples were Jewish, as was Jesus himself.

John concludes his Gospel with: "There are also many other things that Jesus did; yet if every one of them were written down I suppose that the world itself couldn't contain the books that would be written" (John 21:25). Nevertheless, as Cardinal John Henry Newman wrote: "When we contemplate Christ as manifest in the gospels…then we shall believe in him with a conviction, a confidence, and an entireness which can no more be annihilated than the belief in our senses."

big book search...

Find other places where Jesus declares, "I am": John 8:24, John 8:28, and John 13:19.

quick quote...

Scripture enables us to know the heart of God through the word of God.

St. Gregory the Great

Harmonizing the Gospels

Scripture harmonizing means picking and choosing from the four Gospels to piece together a complete story of Jesus' life. Scholars frown on this practice because it destroys the integrity and unity of each individual Gospel. Harmonizing is comparable to constructing a picture of Jesus by combining the body of Michelangelo's Jesus in the "Pieta," the head of Jesus in El Greco's "Crucifixion," and the eyes of the Divine Mercy portrait. (It is true that this book presents a somewhat harmonized picture of Jesus, but it often notes significant differences in the Gospel accounts. In addition, for many passages it provides the Scripture references for all four Gospels.)

5 The Nazarene: A First-Century Man

In his book *To Know and Follow Jesus: Contemporary Christology*, Thomas Hart offers a delightful, hypothetical alternate version of the Caesarea Philippi conversation: Jesus asked his disciples, "Who do you say that I am?" They reply: "You are the Revealer. You are the absolute, unsurpassable victory of God's self-bestowal. You are the Second Person of the Blessed Trinity. You are the unbroken contact with the Ground of Being. You are the man for others. You are the Word Incarnate. You are the proleptic manifestation of the eschaton."

And Jesus, somewhat befuddled said, "What?" He apparently did not recognize himself in all the highfalutin theological language.

When Jesus lived in Nazareth, long before theologians analyzed and explained him, he was an ordinary day laborer in what was considered a hick town. Like his first-century neighbors, Jesus didn't know that the world is round, that germs cause sickness, or that new human life resulted from the union of sperm and an egg. As a child Jesus ran and played with his cousins and their friends. He went with his mother, Mary, to the village well and to market. When he grew older, Jesus was a bigger help to his mom and dad, working in the fields and in the carpentry shop. He accompanied them to social events, danced at weddings, and at harvest times stomped grapes and squeezed olives. After Joseph died, Jesus supported

On the side of a hill in Nazareth there is a site called Nazareth Village, which is a model village and a working farm on twenty acres. Visitors can experience a first-century house, a synagogue, a stone quarry, a carpenter's shop, an olive press, and first-century foods. People in costume and real live donkeys and sheep contribute to the realistic effect.

his mother, continuing to make yokes, benches, and wooden beams for the neighbors and occasionally going out of town to help with building projects.

All of his life, Jesus was a man of his times. To understand him and his teachings, it helps to be familiar with the context of his life: his culture, traditions, way of life, and the political situation at the time.

Jesus' Village

Today about 74,000 people live in Nazareth, a lot more than the maybe thirty or so families who called it home in Jesus' day, but still a small town. Nazareth was an agricultural community with grapes, olives, and grain planted on terraces cut into the slopes surrounding the village, which was likely guarded by watchtowers. The village population didn't increase much in those days because there was only one spring of water. Six miles from Nazareth was a main trade route the Romans called *Via Maris* that connected the Mediterranean coast and Damascus. From Nazareth you could see the large city of Sepphoris.

Life in Nazareth in the first century was simple and rough compared to our civilization. For some reason God, whose ways are not our ways, chose to become a human being there and then. Archaeologists, historians, and Scripture scholars alike shed light on what Jesus' life must have been like.

In some ways Nazareth today is much the same as when Jesus labored under its sun and walked its dusty paths. Archaeology is giving us clues to everyday life in Nazareth through excavations. One example lies beneath the convent of the Sisters of Nazareth, where an ancient house and a burial site have been discovered. Some conjecture that a tomb there is St. Joseph's. In December 2009, archeologists in Nazareth announced that they had unearthed a first-century house next to the Basilica of the Annunciation, the traditional site of Mary's home. They found a wall, a hewn pot, a cistern, and a courtyard, along with shards of vessels. From obscurity, Nazareth has become one of the most recognized villages, thanks to its native son Jesus.

A Typical Nazareth Home

A typical house in Nazareth was about ten-feet square. It was built out of rock held together with mud and straw. In Israel the rock was usually white limestone, but in Galilee many houses were built of black basalt from the Sea of Galilee. The floor was dirt pounded down. The roof was made of wooden beams woven with branches and packed with clay. An outside staircase or ladder led to it. This flat roof was fine for drying clothes or fruit and, on hot nights, for sleeping. For safety, a low wall was built around the roof.

Inside the house there was one room that had a raised platform in the back where everyone in the family slept and ate. Animals, such as the family goat or donkey, shared the house. There were either no windows or high, small ones. Light shone through the one open wooden door, which would be barred at night. Clay oil lamps set high on ledges or on stands also provided light. These lamps were molded all around, leaving a hole for oil and a spout for the wick. (You can see how the woman looking for her lost coin would have had a difficult time in the dim room.) There was a depression in the earth floor where a fire

fyi...

In Loreto, Italy, from at least the fifteenth century, pilgrims have visited the Holy House of Loreto, which tradition holds is the house of the Holy Family in Nazareth. Angels supposedly transported the house there from Palestine after stays at two other sites. The cottage is enclosed within an enormous basilica. The Litany of Loreto, which is composed of titles of Mary, is named for this site.

trivial tidbit...

In 2007, Christian groups called "For Nazareth Foundation" aimed to build the world's largest cross in Nazareth in order to help its citizens. The cross is planned to be 197 meters high with 7.2 million tiles, inscribed with a name chosen by a donor. According to the plan, at the intersection of the crossbeams 15 stories high there will be a vast church.

could be made for warmth, but most cooking was done on an oven outside the house.

The room was simply furnished: mats stuffed with wool for beds, a mat for eating, perhaps a table and benches, a loom for weaving, and a grinding stone for meal. Water pots, jars for flour and olive oil, baskets, and cooking utensils were kept on ledges or on the floor.

Because there was no electricity, people went to bed early. Without television, movies, and video games, they had to devise their own entertainment. They told stories, sang, danced (men and women separately), and played games. The men wrestled. While picturing Jesus dancing and wrestling may seem strange to some, it's really what would have happened.

The house opened onto a courtyard. Most people had small plots of land and maybe a cave nearby to store grain. Cisterns dug in the ground collected rainwater. There was no plumbing, so waste materials were buried.

As commanded by God in the Torah, a mezuzah was attached to the right doorpost of the house. This was a small box containing a parchment inscribed with Deuteronomy 6:4–9 and 11:13–21, which includes the verses called the Shema (Hear): "Hear, O Israel: The LORD is our God, the LORD alone. You shall love the LORD your God with all your heart, and with all your soul, and with all your might." On the back of the parchment was "Shaddai," a name for God. The Jews touched the mezuzah and then kissed their fingers as they entered, comparable to the Catholic custom of blessing ourselves with holy water as we enter a church.

Food and Drink

People in Israel ate two meals, one in the morning and one in the evening. But on the Sabbath they had only one meal, at noon. Seated cross-legged on the ground, they ate off metal plates with their fingers because there were no forks or spoons. They scooped up soups and bean or lentil stews with a flat piece of wheat or barley bread, which was the staple. Cheese, yogurt, fresh or pickled olives, cucumbers, onions, pomegranates, figs, nuts, and grapes completed the meal. Once in a while there would be dried fish, but meat was a luxury. Honey substituted for sugar. The diners drank their beverage—milk, water, or red wine—from metal cups with no handles. For festive meals the Jews imitated the Greco-Roman custom of eating while lying on couches or cushions.

People grew their own food. They also went to the market outside the city walls every day because there was no refrigeration. Chores for women like Jesus' mother, Mary, included grinding grain on a millstone; baking round, flat cakes of bread on an oven outside; and fetching water from the well. Clothes were washed by pounding them with a stone at the spring.

The yarmulkes (small circular hats) worn by Jews today did not originate until the third or fourth century, so Jesus wouldn't have worn one.

Men's Clothing

An Israelite man wore a long cotton or wool tunic seamed around the waist and cinched with a belt or girdle into which he tucked his money, tools, and knife. John's Gospel remarks that Jesus' robe when he died was seamless. This was apparently a rather new style. For work, a man would tuck the bottom of the tunic into the girdle, from which came the expression

When Judas the Galilean led a rebellion about 6 B.C., protesting a census and a tax, the Roman Empire leveled the city of Sepphoris in Galilee, crucified 2,000 men, and sent 3,000 into exile.

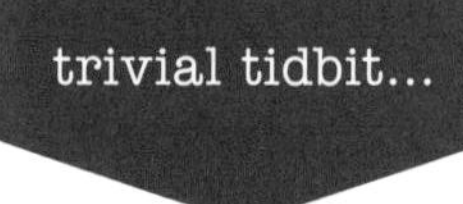

Jesus often traveled by boat on the Sea of Galilee. The seventy-six references to the sea, fishing, and sailing in the Gospels indicate that water activities played a large part in his life.

"to gird up your loins." Over the tunic a man wore a heavy cloak made of goat hair, camel hair, or wool. He could wrap this around himself for sleeping. In those days there was no such thing as nightwear. Under the tunic a man wore a loincloth. On his head, as protection from the hot sun, was a white cloth secured by a band across the forehead, rather like our sweatbands today. His sandals were leather, held on by a thong that ran between the first two toes.

Transportation

People usually walked even great distances, sometimes joining caravans for safety. They might be fortunate enough to ride a donkey, which could cover twenty miles a day. Some travelers owned a camel, which was faster. Although Roman soldiers had horses, the Jews did not. Traveling was not a joy. Roads were not always clearly marked, it was often scorching hot, and taxes had to be paid as the travelers passed through different districts. To make matters worse, there was the constant threat of bandits. Along the way, inns provided shelter (and prostitutes), but travelers often slept in the open.

Roman Occupation

The situation in Jesus' country was volatile. In 63 B.C., Rome had conquered Palestine and made it part of its Syrian province. When Jesus was born, the head of the Roman Empire was Caesar Augustus, Julius Caesar's grandnephew and adopted son. Coincidentally, this emperor ushered in the era of Pax Romana ("Roman peace"), while Jesus came to establish everlasting peace for the whole world. In 14 A.D., the stepson of Augustus, Caesar Tiberius, inherited the throne and ruled until 37 A.D.

Herod the Great had been appointed to govern Israel. Besides being only half Jewish, Herod was a puppet king controlled by Rome, and therefore most Jews hated him. Herod attempted to improve his relations with the Jews by rebuilding the Temple. Known for this and other gargantuan building projects, he is even more remembered for his cruelty. At one time he had the Roman eagle placed on a Temple gate. Some Jews protested this idolatry, and Herod ordered them burned alive. When Herod suspected that his favorite of ten wives and two of his sons were plotting against him, he had them murdered. Herod did, however, abide by the Jewish dietary laws, refraining from pork. This gave rise to a wry saying enriched by a play on words in Greek: It is better to be the pig (*hus*) of Herod than to be his son (*huios*).

After Herod the Great died in 4 B.C., his territory was divided among three of his sons, who were all named after him. Herod Philip II was given the region east of Galilee. Herod Antipas inherited Galilee. (During Jesus' trial, Pilate sent Jesus to Herod Antipas, because as a Galilean Jesus was under his jurisdiction.) Herod Archelaus acquired Judah and Samaria. When he proved to be inept, antagonizing the Jews, Rome replaced him in 6 A.D. by a string of Roman procurators (like appointed governors) who were responsible for keeping peace and procuring taxes. The most famous of the fourteen procurators was the fifth one, Pontius Pilate, who governed from 26 A.D. to 36 A.D. and condemned Jesus to death.

Jewish rebellions made the Romans wary of and

fyi...

The Zealots overthrew Rome in 66 A.D., and Israel was independent again until Rome destroyed Jerusalem in 70 A.D. and built the city Aelia Capitolina over it. At a last stronghold, the fortress Masada, a thousand Jews committed suicide rather than submit to Rome. In 132 A.D., the Jews rebelled again under the leadership of Ben Kochba. This time after vanquishing the Jews, Rome banished them from Jerusalem.

quick quote...

It is Jesus Christ alone we must present to the world. Outside of this, we have no reason to exist.

Pope John Paul I

harsh with the Jewish people. To the Romans who worshiped myriad gods, the Jews were strange people and rather like atheists since they believed only in one God. But Rome was usually respectful of them. It did not require military service of the Jews, because of their religious objection to serving alongside Gentiles. Roman troops circumvented Jerusalem when their banners depicted the emperor, which Jews considered idolatry. Naturally the Jews resented the presence of Roman troops as well as Roman laws and taxes. A further insult was that Roman soldiers could force Jewish men to carry a burden for them for up to a mile. Mile markers along roads helped determine the distance.

Money

In Palestine there were Roman, Greek, and Jewish coins in circulation. Israelites paid taxes to Rome and to Herod. In addition, every male twenty years and older had to pay a half-shekel tax for the upkeep of the Temple. They also had to offer the first fruits of their crops and to pay an annual tithe of 10%. All of these taxes amounted to as much as 35% of their income. At the Temple only Jewish coins were accepted for paying taxes and purchasing sacrifices. Therefore moneychangers sat in the Court of the Gentiles, regulating the rate of exchange and tacking on an arbitrary charge for their service.

Marriage

Jews were very sociable and loved celebrations, as many of Jesus' parables attest. Marriages were cause for rejoicing and could mean a whole week of feasting and dancing. The father of the groom approached the prospective bride's father and offered a "bride price" for her. The couple was betrothed for a year, a relationship as binding as marriage but without cohabitation. On the wedding day, the groom came for the bride in procession and escorted her to his house.

short prayer...

Lord, one more day to love you. (Blessed Charles de Foucauld)

Funerals

When someone died, even poor families hired flute players and professional mourners to wail outside the home. Mourning lasted for seven days, but because there was no embalming in hot Palestine, by Jewish law the body had to be buried within twenty-four hours, unless it was the Sabbath. The poor were buried in the ground, but others were interred on ledges in caves enclosed by a large stone. After a year or so, when a body had decomposed, the bones were collected in a limestone ossuary to make room for another body.

Women's Place

The Jews regarded women not only as inferior but also as dangerous sources of temptation. In Israel, as in other cultures both then and now, women were powerless second-class citizens. They were possessions first of their fathers and then of their husbands. Women could not serve as witnesses in a court of law. Husbands could divorce their wives even for a minor matter such as a badly prepared meal. All they had to do was to say "I divorce you" three times, and the marriage was over. On the other hand, rarely could wives divorce their husbands. Women were not educated and were not even required to pray! In the Temple they were confined to the Women's Court, and in

quick quote...

I just sat there and thought of Our Lord, and his visit to us all those centuries ago, and I said to myself that my great luck was to have had him on my mind for so long in my life!

Dorothy Day

synagogues they were seated separate from the men. In public, women had to be veiled and were to walk a distance behind their husbands.

In contrast to these kinds of prevailing customs, Jesus was a champion of women. He treated them with respect, gentleness, and sensitivity. To the amazement and sometimes dismay of some Jews, Jesus spoke to women, healed them, defended them, and treated them as intellectual equals. He accepted women as his disciples, traveled with a mixed group of unrelated men and women (something unheard of), and chose Mary of Magdala to be the first witness of his resurrection. His mother, of course, was a remarkably brave and holy woman. Jesus empowered and ennobled women, never oppressed or patronized them.

Early Holy Land Pilgrims

Three early pilgrims give us insights into the Holy Land sites today. St. Helena was the mother of Constantine, the emperor who made Christianity an official religion of the Roman Empire. At an advanced age, Helena made a pilgrimage to the Holy Land before she died about 327 A.D. Later, a legend developed that Helena had discovered the true cross. According to the story, she found three crosses and the one that cured a sick woman by its touch was judged to be the cross of Jesus.

The Bordeaux Pilgrim is an anonymous Jewish Christian from Bordeaux, France, who left a chronicle of his pilgrimage to Jerusalem about the year 333. He saw Jerusalem's early basilicas and refers to many traditions that have come down to us.

A woman named Egeria made a four-year pilgrimage to the Holy Land about 381–384 and described her travels in a long letter to her friends back home. The middle of the letter has been preserved. In it, Egeria mentions holy sites and liturgical practices in Jerusalem.

6 Yeshua: A Jew

Marc Chagall, a Jewish artist, painted a disturbing crucifixion scene in which Jesus is depicted as a Jew, garbed in a prayer shawl and surrounded by Holocaust images. While this is an unusual image, it should not surprise us, for Jesus lived and died a good Jew. His parents were devout Jews, and he grew up learning the stories and songs of his people from them. Jesus professed the Jewish faith of his ancestors, followed Jewish laws, had Jewish thought patterns, and for the most part observed Jewish customs. Christianity, which began with Jesus, is deeply rooted in Judaism, so much so that the original disciples were first considered to be a sect of Judaism. Jesus did not overthrow Judaism; he built on it. He declared that he came to fulfill the Law (the teachings in the Torah that Jews lived by) not abolish it (see Matthew 5:17). To understand Jesus and his teachings then, we need to look at the religion that shaped him.

Jewish Prayer Life

All of Jewish life at the time of Jesus was centered around prayer and liturgical feasts. Like other Jewish men, Jesus would have prayed the *Shema*, the main Jewish prayer, twice a day, once in the morning and again at night. He also prayed another blessing before meals and possibly an early version of the Eighteen Benedictions used by Jews today. As a Jewish man, Jesus wore a rectangular white prayer shawl that had fringe or tassels at the four corners, as prescribed by God for all men in Numbers 15:58. A blue thread in each tassel represented God.

The arrangement of the threads and knots added up to 613, the number of Jewish laws. At prayer, men would drape this garment over their heads, creating their own tent where they would meet God, as Moses had conversed with God in the Meeting Tent. When some men prayed, they strapped phylacteries to their forehead and left arm. These were small, square, leather cases containing four Scripture passages, including the Shema. Phylacteries were also called *tefillin*, which means "prayers." Jesus criticized the Pharisees who wore ostentatious large ones and long fringes.

The Book of Psalms in Hebrew Scripture was the main prayer book of the Jews. Many of these prayer songs were attributed to Jesus' ancestor King David. They expressed the relationship of the people to God. Some psalms are messianic and prophetic, pointing to a future king who will rule at the end of the world. Matthew, intent on demonstrating that Jesus is the promised Messiah, referred to twenty-one psalms in his Gospel. St. Augustine, fifth-century bishop of Hippo in North Africa, explained each of the 150 psalms in light of the mystery of Christ. Jesus prayed the psalms and quoted them.

For the Jews the Sabbath began at sundown on Friday and continued through sundown on Saturday. The Sabbath was a day of strict rest and prayer when services were held at the local synagogue. As a child, Jesus went with his parents to the synagogue in Nazareth. Later, as a young man, he attended synagogue services with his apostles. Thirty-nine kinds of work were banned on the Lord's Day, including tying or untying a rope, lighting a fire, and using medicine. You can see then why the scrupulous Pharisees were

for your spiritual health...

One way to pray the psalms is to pray them with the mind of Christ, conscious of what they must have meant to him. Try it.

The Lord's Prayer bears a striking resemblance to some Jewish prayers. For example, Kaddish, a Jewish prayer of praise that Jesus must have prayed, begins, "Exalted and sanctified is God's great name...and may he establish his kingdom."

angry when Jesus cured on the Sabbath. He did so because he thought and taught that promoting life was more important than even the Sabbath.

Jewish Customs

Many Jewish customs had to do with washing. Before praying in the Temple, men and women, including Jesus, took baths in *mikvahs*, which were large pools of water (well water, spring water, or rainwater) surrounding the Temple. This was not for the sake of hygiene but as a means of ritual purification. Coming in contact with something "unclean"—an animal that was declared unclean, a corpse, a leper, or a Gentile—meant that one couldn't enter the Temple until being totally immersed in a mikvah. This ritual bathing was also required for women after menstruation and childbirth and for men after nocturnal emissions. Also, before eating, Jews washed their hands according to a set ritual. And on entering a house after a journey on the dirt roads, a person's feet were washed. Large jars of water stood by the door for this purpose. Jesus, as a practicing Jew, followed these customs, but apparently not entirely. At least once, Pharisees questioned why the disciples did not wash their hands in the ritual manner before eating (see Matthew 15:2).

Jesus also abided by the Jewish dietary customs such as not eating meat and dairy products together in the same meal and draining meat of all blood before cooking it. Certain food was forbidden. Jews ate only animals that chew their cud and have cloven hoofs (no pork), and only seafood that have fins and scales (no lobster or shellfish).

trivial tidbit...

Archaeologists have located one hundred mikvahs near the site of the Temple in Jerusalem, which the Romans destroyed in 70 A.D. These pools are rectangular, about six-by-nine feet and range from four to eight feet deep. Steps lead down into them.

trivial tidbit...

It's estimated that in Jesus' day some 18,000 lambs were sacrificed in the Temple because of the influx of Jews for Passover. According to a reputable scholar, 180,000 Jews could be in Jerusalem for Passover.

Jewish Feasts That Jesus Celebrated

The three major Jewish feasts were Passover, Pentecost, and Tabernacles. These are called "pilgrimage feasts," because males over the age of eighteen who lived within twenty-five miles of Jerusalem were obliged to journey to the Temple to celebrate them. The Gospels refer to Jesus being present in Jerusalem for these feasts, even though it was a three-or-four-day journey from Galilee to Jerusalem.

✦ *Passover* or *Pesach* – This feast celebrates the Israelites' escape from Egypt. In the Torah, God commanded that Passover be observed each year. A special meal of lamb, unleavened bread, bitter herbs, and four cups of wine was shared, and the Exodus story retold. Jesus would have eaten this meal with Mary and Joseph, his extended family, and his friends. Perhaps at least once he was the youngest child at a Seder meal and got to ask the question reserved for that child, "Why is this night different from all other nights?" Passover was followed by a week of the Feast of Unleavened Bread, when bread without yeast was eaten as it was on the night of the Exodus.

✦ *Pentecost, Feast of Weeks,* or *Shavuot* – Originally this was the feast of the first fruits of the harvest and occurred fifty days after Passover. Two loaves of bread made from wheat were offered in the Temple, and farmers brought the first fruits of their crops there. After the time of Jesus this feast became a celebration of God giving the law to Moses.

✦ *Sukkot, Tabernacles,* or *Tents* – Sukkot means "booth." After the fruit crops had been harvested, the Jews built booths (tents) out of boughs to represent the huts they had lived in during the Exodus. It's probable that some years Joseph and Jesus worked on their hut together and lived in it with Mary during the seven days of this thanksgiving celebration.

The Jews at the time of Jesus also celebrated these two high holy days:

✦ *Rosh Hashanah* – This was the Jewish New Year celebrated in the seventh month. It opened a ten-day period of repentance and prayer that ended with Yom Kippur. To announce Rosh Hashanah, the high priest would blow the shofar (ram's horn) in the Temple.

✦ *Yom Kippur* – This Day of Atonement, the most solemn day of the year, came ten days after Rosh Hashanah. It was the one day when the high priest entered the Holy of Holies, where he sprinkled the blood of a bull sacrificed for the sins of the people. It was also the only occasion when the name of God was said in prayer, but only by the high priest, who pronounced it ten times.

Jesus observed two other Jewish feasts:

✦ *Hanukkah* or *Dedication* – This eight-day celebration in December is in memory of the rededication of the Temple in 164 B.C. after the Israelites, led by Judas Maccabee, overthrew the Assyrians, who had profaned the Temple. Hanukkah is also called the Festival of Light. The Talmud (Jewish writings from rabbis) tells of a one-day supply of oil for the Temple's eternal flame miraculously lasting for eight days. This story gave rise to the custom of lighting eight Hanukkah candles, one each night. Because of the legend that during their oppression the Jews gathered

quick quote...

Jesus Christ will be Lord of all, or he will not be Lord at all.

St. Augustine

for prayer under the pretense of gambling, on this feast children were given money and played with a dreidel, a top with a letter on each of its four sides that together form an acronym for "A great miracle happened there." Perhaps Jesus the carpenter carved dreidels for children.

✦ *Purim* – This holiday celebrates Queen Esther's heroic deliverance of the Jews from slaughter in Persia. The name Purim is derived from the word for lots because the wicked Haman cast lots to determine the day on which the Jews were to be destroyed. On Purim the Old Testament Book of Esther, which recorded this event, was read; and children wore costumes and gave gifts to the poor.

The Jewish Temple

The mainstay of Jewish religion was the Temple, where the Jews believed God was present. It was the only place where sacrifices and sin-offerings were carried out (not in the local synagogues, for example). Temple duties involved 25,000 priests. To the consternation of the Jews, Jesus foretold the destruction of this Temple. He saw himself as replacing the Temple as the way for us to encounter the Father, for he was God present on earth and the sacrifice of his life was a perfect sacrifice that atoned for all sin for all time.

The first Temple had been built by King Solomon to house the Ark of the Covenant, the wooden chest that God instructed Moses to make during the Exodus and where God dwelt with the Israelites. This Temple stood for four hundred years until it was ransacked by the Babylonians in 587 B.C. and burned ten years later. At that time the Ark of the Covenant disappeared.

trivial tidbit...

The Jews removed their sandals before going into the Temple. They entered through gates.

After the second Temple was destroyed, sacrifices were no longer part of Jewish religion. On the other hand, Christianity perpetuates the sacrifice of Jesus through the celebration of the Eucharist.

When the Jews returned from exile in Babylon, they built the second Temple in 515 B.C. Then in 19 B.C., Herod decided to have this Temple rebuilt, a project that took about eighty years to complete—throughout Jesus' lifetime. It employed 18,000 workers. The result was a magnificent structure, a fitting tribute to God, with its imported white marble and its gold-plated walls that shone in the sun. The stones in the retaining or platform walls, built to expand the natural plateau, were immense; one measured 46 x 10 x 10 feet and weighed about 415 tons. In 70 A.D., ten years after the Temple was finished, this wonder of the world was destroyed by Rome, despite orders that had been given to spare it.

Synagogues

Synagogues were the houses of prayer for the Jews at the time of Jesus. Inside was a cupboard that held the Torah, the first five books of the Bible. The services consisted of singing of psalms, prayers, Scripture readings, teachings, and blessings. After the age of thirty, any Jewish man was allowed to read and teach in the synagogue. This afforded Jesus the opportunity to proclaim the kingdom of God to many people.

Jewish houses of worship are still called synagogues today, although—much like Christian churches—most of them are much larger and more ornate than they would have been in Jesus' time.

Jewish Groups

In the first century, Judaism was a "salad bowl" of different kinds of people. Jesus was in contact with several groups of Jews.

trivial tidbit...

Today a gold-domed mosque (the Dome of the Rock or Mosque of Omar) dominates Jerusalem. It is believed that this mosque, built in 688 A.D., stands where the Temple once was. Inside the mosque is a large stone, supposedly Mount Moriah, where Abraham almost sacrificed his son and where Mohammed was taken up to heaven. The mosque is presumed to be the former site of the Holy of Holies, and for that reason Jews do not set foot in it.

The Temple Herod Built

The Temple itself was not that big: 115 feet long, 35 feet wide, and about 50 feet high. It had three sections: the vestibule, the Holy Place, and the Holy of Holies (where the Ark of the Covenant was originally housed). The Holy Place was a large room with high windows. It contained the altar of incense, the table of showbread (twelve loaves of unleavened bread as an offering), ten lamp stands, and other items for worship. This room was separated from the Holy of Holies by two veils. A seven-foot staircase led into the Holy of Holies, a completely dark room paneled in cedar and gold. The only person allowed to enter this room was the high priest and only on Yom Kippur when he offered incense and sprinkled the blood of a sacrifice. The Holy of Holies was empty except for a stone to hold the censer.

Outside of the Temple proper was the Court of the Gentiles, a 35-acre court, the size of twenty football fields. It was surrounded by almost a thousand thirty-seven-foot-tall pillars set in double or triple rows under porches. This enormous plaza was open to anyone, including what were called "the God-fearers," those Gentiles who wanted to worship the Jewish God but had no desire to become circumcised Jews and eat only kosher food. The Court of Gentiles was where teachers like Jesus spoke, beggars asked for alms, and moneychangers carried on their business. Beyond this court, Gentiles were banned on pain of death. Fourteen steps led to the Women's Court, where the Levitical choir (priests) sang and where thirteen trumpet-shaped chests for offerings were located. From there, fifteen steps took male Jews to the Court of the Israelites. Surrounding the Temple was the Court of Priests where the Altar of Holocaust was located. Twelve steps led from the Court of Priests to the Temple. Its huge main door, carved from olive wood, took twenty men to open. A ten-foot-high fence surrounded the inner sanctuary. Along the eastern side of the Temple was a covered colonnade called Solomon's Porch.

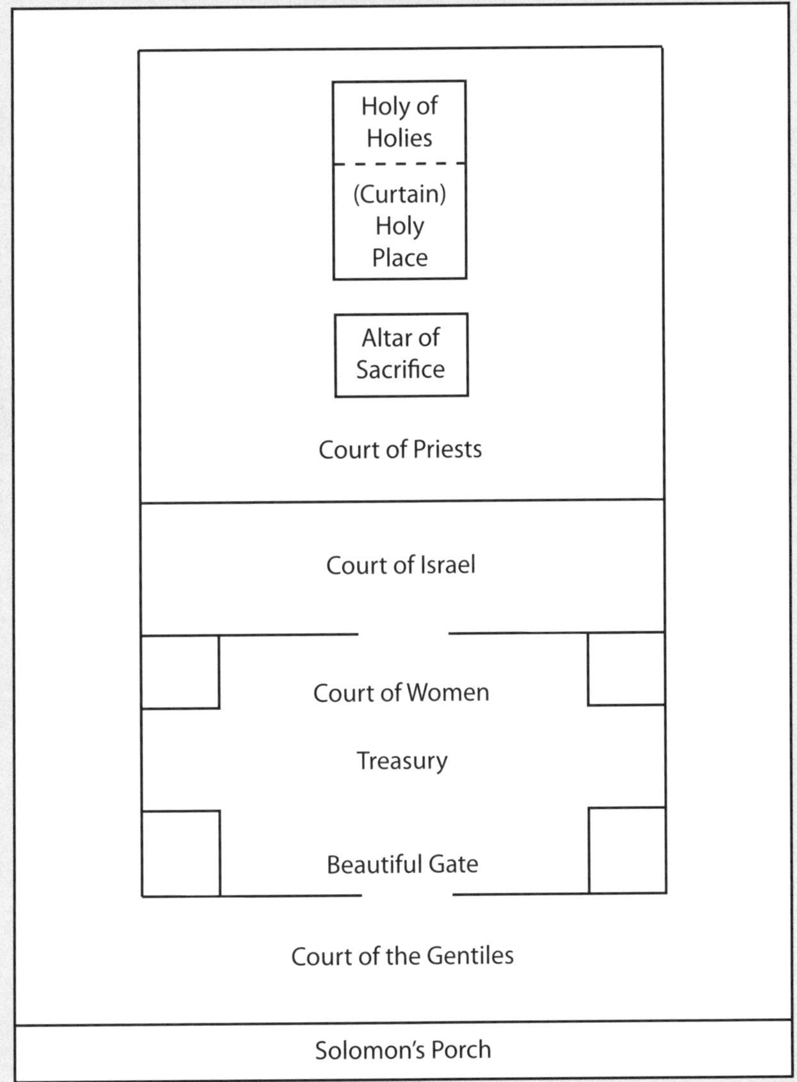
Herod's Temple
Western Wall
Holy of Holies
(Curtain) Holy Place
Altar of Sacrifice
Court of Priests
Court of Israel
Court of Women
Treasury
Beautiful Gate
Court of the Gentiles
Solomon's Porch

fyi...

Jews today revere the Western Wall of the Temple platform, a foundation wall, as their holiest site. It is also known as the Wailing Wall because Jews from all over the world come there to pray and grieve for the destruction of their Temple. Visitors write prayers on slips of paper and tuck them into its crevices. Periodically these are buried. In September of 2007, archaeologists discovered in a suburb of Jerusalem what they think was the quarry for the Temple.

✦ The Pharisees, the largest division, was composed mostly of middle-class laymen. The word *Pharisee* meant "set apart" or "separated." This devout group came into being about 2 B.C. for the purpose of preserving Judaism from the influence of Greek culture. They were known for their love of the Torah, the Law. The stricter among the Pharisees devised 613 regulations, which enumerated some 1,521 ways the Sabbath could be broken. The Pharisees also believed in some Jewish oral tradition that included belief in angels, the resurrection, and the last judgment. The Gospels tend to paint the Pharisees as enemies of Jesus. He scolds them for their outward show of faith and their rigidity. Keep in mind that when the evangelists wrote, Christians had been banned from the Temple and synagogues and were being persecuted by the Jewish leaders. Consequently, the evangelists didn't have much love for the Pharisees. It was the Pharisees though who, after the destruction of the Temple in 70 A.D., preserved Judaism and the Old Testament. Two Pharisees presented in a good light in Scripture are Nicodemus and Paul. And in Mark's Gospel, assumed to be the first one written, the Pharisees aren't implicated in the death of Jesus at all.

✦ The *Sadducees* were the Jewish aristocracy, a wealthy priestly class who served in the Temple. Members were high-priestly families, lesser priests, and other persons of rank. Concerned with ingratiating themselves with the Roman officials, they were lax in observing the law and rejected the Pharisees' additions to the Torah and belief in angels, resurrection, and reward and punishment. After the fall of Jerusalem, the Sadducees disappeared.

◆ The Jewish governing body, or supreme council, was the *Sanhedrin*, a group of seventy-one Jewish men. The high priest was the spiritual leader of Judaism and regarded almost as a king. At the time of Jesus, Caiaphas was the high priest, but his predecessor and father-in-law, Annas, still had clout. The Sanhedrin was composed of priests from the priestly families in Jerusalem and elders from other leading families in the city. Sadducees predominated. The Sanhedrin could make legal decisions in both religious and secular affairs. It had the power to accuse and convict, except in cases where Rome made the final decision, such as the decision to put Jesus to death.

◆ *Scribes* were lawyers, the professional teachers and interpreters of the law. They supported and sometimes belonged to the Pharisee party. Some scribes were members of the Sanhedrin. The scribes were highly respected and often addressed as Master and Teacher, which in Hebrew is *Rabbi*.

◆ Two other religious groups in Palestine at the time of Jesus were the *Zealots* and the *Essenes*. The philosophies of these two groups were completely opposite. The Zealots sought to overthrow Rome by violence. They spearheaded the revolt in 66–70 A.D. that resulted in the fall of Jerusalem and the destruction of the second Temple. During the time of Jesus, however, this group was not yet organized. In Luke, one of the apostles was Simon the Zealot. The Essenes, on the other hand, withdrew from the "corrupt" society of the cities to live a spiritual life in villages and the desert. Most were ascetics and lived like celibate

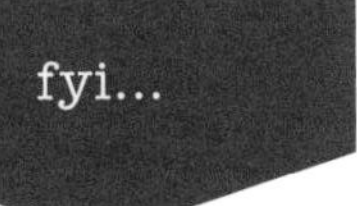

Jesus' thinking was more compatible with that of the Pharisees than with that of the more conservative group at the time, the Sadducees.

Holy Land site...

Roman coins have been found dated 29 A.D. and 31 A.D. and bearing the name of Pontius Pilate. Also, in 1961, archaeologists discovered in a step of an amphitheater in the city of Caesarea Maritima an inscription on stone that was originally part of a nearby temple. The Latin reads, "Pontius Pilatus, Prefect of Judea, has dedicated to the people of Caesarea a temple in honor of Tiberius."

monks, although a few married. They lived in communities, sharing their possessions and performing penance as they awaited the coming of two Messiahs: one priestly and one royal. This Jewish sect believed in the immortality of the soul and final reward and punishment. Scripture doesn't mention the Essenes, but the Dead Sea Scrolls are widely assumed to have been their work and therefore shed more light on them. Some think that John the Baptist was an Essene.

◆ The *Samaritans*, who lived in Samaria between Galilee and Judea, believed that their lineage traced back to Joseph and Benjamin, Jacob's favorite sons. They were descendants of the Jews who, during the Babylonian Exile, had been left behind and had intermarried with non-Jews, which was an abhorrent crime in the eyes of "pure" Jews. After the Exile, the Jews spurned the Samaritans' help in building the second Temple. Animosity between the two groups escalated, and the Samaritans built their own temple on Mount Gerazim around 330 B.C. It's thought that this temple was destroyed about 129 B.C. The Samaritans viewed the Torah as the only inspired books, excluding the prophets and other books of Hebrew Scripture. The Jews regarded the Samaritans as ritually unclean; and when traveling between Galilee and Jerusalem, they avoided passing through Samaria.

◆ Another Jewish faction mentioned briefly in the Gospels were the *Herodians*. Scholars theorize that they were Jews who were in support of the original King Herod the Great and/or one of his sons.

To our knowledge, Jesus didn't belong to any of these Jewish groups. Moreover, the Jewish leaders considered him quite unorthodox. Jesus, though, was a full-blooded Jew. That is why anti-Semitism by Christians is especially heinous. It means turning on our Lord and Savior's own people.

trivial tidbit...

As of 2008, there were only 710 Samaritans identified in the world, most of them living near Mount Gerazim, their holy mountain.

The Dead Sea Scrolls

In 1947, in a cave at Qumran in the West Bank near the Dead Sea, a Bedouin shepherd accidentally discovered a collection of scrolls written between 200 B.C. and 68 A.D. Between 1947 and 1956 eleven caves in all yielded scrolls, which appear to have been a kind of library of the Essenes. Most scrolls were written in Hebrew with quills on either papyrus or leather. Altogether there are about 600 scrolls and fragments, and about one-fourth of these are biblical. The scrolls include biblical commentaries and writings pertaining to the Essene life. Although the scrolls do not mention Jesus, they have been a tremendous aid in learning about Jewish culture and religious thought during his time. The Dead Sea Scrolls contain some of the oldest copies we have of the Old Testament: all of Isaiah and fragments of most other Hebrew Scripture books. Prior to their discovery, our oldest texts dated from the ninth century. In Jerusalem, the Shrine of the Book museum was built to house the scrolls. Its roof is shaped like the lid of the jar that held the first scroll found.

7 Son of David: History of His People

To really know Jesus, you have to know the story of the Jewish people. (Some wit referred to the Christian adoption of Hebrew Scriptures as the greatest corporate takeover in history!) The Hebrew Scriptures are the sacred texts that Jesus, as a practicing Jew, would have read, pored over, and prayed.

The story of Israel is primarily a love story, one that is our story as Catholics too. It's all about God's tremendous love for us, as it traces the unfolding of God's rescue plan after the fall of Adam and Eve. Jewish history begins with the call of one man, Abram, and his wife, Sarai, in about 1850 B.C.

Abraham and Sarah

Jesus' people were originally called "Hebrews," a name whose original meaning is obscure. Stories about their origin were handed down from generation to generation, until they were finally written down in the book of Genesis. At the time of Abram and Sarai, all people believed in multiple deities, some of whom demanded human sacrifice. Suddenly, in the town of Ur in Mesopotamia, the one true God revealed himself to a man named Abram, and changed his name to Abraham, which means "father of many nations," and his wife's name to Sarah. God made the old and childless Abraham an incredible promise: His descendants would be as numerous as the stars in the sky, a mighty nation in which all nations would find blessing.

fyi...

As was the custom at the time, the barren Sarah at first gave Abraham her maid Hagar to produce a son for him. Hagar bore a son named Ishmael. Then, after Sarah gave birth to Isaac, she forced Abraham to banish Hagar and Ishmael from their camp. Ishmael became the forefather of the Arab nations. Thus Jews, Muslims, and Christians all share Abraham as a common ancestor.

trivial tidbit...

Testament (as in Old Testament and New Testament) is another word for *covenant*. The New Covenant was instituted by Jesus at the Last Supper and sealed with his blood.

Abraham believed this promise and acted upon it, leaving his home to find a new land in Canaan, a land God promised would belong to him and his descendants. Miraculously, he and his aged wife, Sarah, did have one son, Isaac.

Abraham's faith was unwavering, even in the face of a horrific command. At God's bidding, Abraham was willing to sacrifice even his son, although this was a painful request that didn't make any sense if he was to have descendants. Abraham passed this test with flying colors, and God provided a ram for sacrifice in place of Isaac. This story also taught the Hebrews that, unlike pagan gods, their God did not require human sacrifice.

God and Abraham entered into a covenant, or bond, in which God promised Abraham the land of Canaan. This covenant was sealed with the blood of animals. The sign of this special covenant with God was circumcision for him and his male descendants, which is still practiced by Jews today.

Isaac and Rebecca

Isaac and his wife Rebecca had twins, Jacob and Esau. God's promise was passed on through Jacob, the younger son, who tricked his father into giving it to him. Jacob, whose name God changed to Israel, sired twelve sons, each of whom became the head of a tribe of Israel. The promise then was passed on through his eldest son, Judah, from whose name the words *Jew* and *Jewish* are derived.

Another of Jacob's sons, Joseph, was his father's favorite. His jealous brothers attacked and sold him into slavery in Egypt. However, because of Joseph's ability to interpret the Pharaoh's dreams, Egypt survived a famine and distributed food to other peoples, including the Israelites. Joseph and his family were reunited and reconciled, and the Israelites migrated from Canaan to Egypt.

Over a period of some three hundred years, however, the Egyptians forgot their debt to Joseph and enslaved his people. Then, about 1280 B.C., God called forth a man named Moses to lead the Israelites to freedom back in Canaan. Moses confronted the Pharaoh, aided by God's power and a series of ten plagues that culminated in the death of the firstborn among the Egyptians. To protect the Israelites from death, Moses directed them to slaughter a lamb on the day of the tenth plague and mark their doors with its blood. They were to eat the lamb and bread with no yeast while standing, ready to run.

The Exodus was the highpoint of Jewish history, and Moses is the greatest Jewish hero. He led the Israelites through the Reed Sea, fed them with manna and quail, obtained water, and spoke to God for them. In the desert God gave Moses the Ten Commandments and instructed him to build a chest called the Ark of the Covenant to hold the tablets. God made a covenant with the Israelites: He would be their God, and they would be his people, as long as they did everything he commanded.

After forty years of wandering in the desert, the Israelites, under the leadership of Moses' successor, Joshua, infiltrated and conquered Canaan, the Promised Land. At first the tribes of Israel were a loose confederation, like the original thirteen colonies of the United States. For about two hundred years, judg-

trivial tidbit...

On his deathbed Jacob prophesied that his son Judah would be a lion honored by his brothers. Jacob foretold, "The scepter shall not depart from Judah, nor the ruler's staff from between his feet, until tribute comes to him; and the obedience of the peoples is his" (Genesis 49:10). This is understood by Catholics as a prophecy of the Messiah.

big book search...

Read the exciting story of the beginning of the Exodus in Exodus 1:1–2:18. Or watch the classic movie *The Ten Commandments,* starring the late Charlton Heston as Moses.

es, such as the mighty, longhaired Samson and the prophet Samuel, ruled certain tribes and led them to victory over their enemies. Around 1020 B.C., Samuel anointed Saul as the first king of Israel. His successor, King David, son of Jesse, ruled from 1000 to 961 B.C. He was the peerless king who united Israel and established Jerusalem as its capital and the holy city by bringing the Ark of the Covenant into it. David's son Solomon, known for his wisdom, built the first Temple in Jerusalem and increased Israel's greatness and wealth. But foolishly he permitted the worship of false gods.

After King Solomon died in 922 B.C., the kingdom split into the north and the south. In 722 B.C., Israel, the northern kingdom, fell to the Assyrians and became the "ten lost tribes" of Israel. In 587 B.C., Judah, the southern kingdom, where only the tribes of Judah and Benjamin lived, fell to the Babylonians. The Jewish people were exiled to Babylon. Forty years later, Cyrus, ruler of Persia, after having conquered Babylon, allowed them to return home and build a new Temple.

When the Persians in turn were conquered by Alexander the Great in 332 B.C., the Greeks took over the land and renamed it Judea. Then in 322 B.C., Egyptians inherited the land and ruled it until they were defeated in 198 B.C. by the Syrians. The Syrian king Antiochus Epiphanes not only suppressed religious activities but desecrated the Jewish Temple by erecting a statue of Zeus there and sacrificing a pig to it, an event known in Jewish history as "the abomination of desolation." In 163 B.C., the Jewish Maccabee family led a rebellion and was victorious. The Jews enjoyed independence for 100 years until Pompey made Judah a Roman province in 63 B.C. Understandably, they deeply resented being ruled once again by pagans in their Promised Land and resisted in many ways.

The Romans destroyed Jerusalem in 70 A.D. and again in 135 A.D. Until 1948, the Jews did not have a nation of their own and lived in what they called the *Diaspora*, which means "Scattering."

The Messiah

God had promised David that his kingdom would have no end: "Your house and your kingdom shall be made sure forever before me; your throne shall be established forever" (2 Samuel 7:16). Many Jews interpreted this to mean that a king born in David's line would establish Israel as a mighty nation and endure to the end of time, thus fulfilling the promise made to Abraham. Jesus was a Son of David because his father Joseph belonged to the house of David. However, he did not meet the qualifications of the Messiah, at least as most of the people at the time (and perhaps today) understood them. Instead of overthrowing the Romans and making Israel a military power, Jesus was killed by the Romans, with the complicity of the Jewish religious leaders of his time.

After the exile in Babylon, however, some Jews read prophets like Isaiah and began to believe that the Messiah would be a king who would have to suffer and would bring people under the reign of God peacefully. Others expected a messiah-priest. Some people anticipated two messiahs, one religious and one military, and some just gave up hope completely. A few self-proclaimed messiahs arose over the centuries, but were short-lived. However, a small group of Jews, despite their suffering, continued to hope and pray for the Messiah and faithfully lived by God's laws. These pious Jews are known as the *anawim*.

The Old Testament tells what the Messiah is, and the New Testament tells who he is.

Source Unknown

Jesus warns his followers not to follow false messiahs. He never directly proclaims himself to be the Hebrew Messiah or the Son of David. However, he admits to the Samaritan woman that he is the long-awaited Messiah. And when Pilate asks if he is king, Jesus replies, "You have said it." On occasions when people want to crown Jesus king, he eludes them. And when people identify him as the Messiah, he tells them not to talk about it, probably because he knows he isn't the violent political and military messiah they expect. At last, when Jesus is on the cross, he is publicly identified as the king of Jews by the sign above his head. However, it is not the kingdom of David but the kingdom of God that Jesus inaugurated by his life, suffering, death, and resurrection.

Types or Figures of Jesus

Certain people, objects, and events in the Hebrew Scriptures bear a resemblance or connection to Jesus and his life. They can be viewed as foreshadowing him. Here are a few of the more obvious types:

- *Adam* was the first human being and the father of the whole human race. Jesus is the new Adam, the first man of the new creation. He was the firstborn from the dead who gave us spiritual life. From Adam's side came forth Eve, the mother of the human race. Similarly, from Jesus' pierced side out of which flowed blood and water came forth the Church, the spiritual mother of all.

The Jesse Tree

A favorite Advent custom is the Jesse Tree, a tree decorated with symbols of Old Testament people and events and topped by a symbol of Christ. It takes its name from Jesse, the father of King David, and from Isaiah 11:1: "A shoot shall come out from the stump of Jesse, and a branch shall grow out of his roots." The tree can be a live or artificial pine tree, a large limb set in plaster of paris, or a tree cut from a large piece of felt or simply drawn on paper. The symbols could be made out of clay, construction paper, or objects. Here are Jesse Tree symbols and the people they represent:

- apple with two bites out of it *(Adam and Eve)*
- ark or rainbow *(Noah)*
- bundle of wood or ram in bush *(Abraham and Isaac)*
- ladder *(Jacob)*
- pitcher *(Rebecca)*
- well or coat of many colors *(Joseph)*
- burning bush or tablets of the Law *(Moses)*
- lamb on the altar *(Paschal lamb)*
- sword *(Judith)*
- sheaf of wheat *(Ruth)*
- root, stem, and flower or shepherd's staff *(Jesse)*
- harp, key, or crown and scepter *(David)*
- Temple or scale of justice *(Solomon)*
- whale *(Jonah)*
- scroll *(Isaiah)*
- six-pointed star and chain *(Esther)*
- baptismal shell *(John the Baptist)*
- carpentry tools—hammer, saw, chisel, angle, plane *(Joseph)*
- lily, crown circled by stars, or decorative M *(Mary)*
- city of Bethlehem or rising sun *(Jesus)*

The *O antiphons* are Advent's brighest jewels. These are seven prayer songs that each begin with *"O"* and invoke Christ under a title from Isaiah's prophecies. Each antiphon has a call to the Messiah under a title, an expansion of that title, and an appeal beginning with *come*. An antiphon is sung before the Magnificat in the Liturgy of the Hours and as the Gospel acclamation from December 17 to 23. The verses of the song "O Come, O Come, Emmanuel" are the O antiphons.

✦ *Abel*, the son of Adam and Eve, offered an acceptable sacrifice to God. Jesus offered the perfect sacrifice on the cross. Abel was murdered by his brother Cain. Jesus was killed by people he considered to be his brothers and sisters.

✦ *Noah* built the Ark that saved people from the flood. The Ark is a symbol of the Church, because Jesus is a savior of us all through the waters of Baptism.

✦ In the time of Abraham a mysterious priest named *Melchisedek* offered bread and wine. He is a figure of Christ, our high priest, who offers sacred bread and wine in the Eucharist.

✦ Like *Isaac*, Jesus was beloved by his father. He was innocent and yet willing to be sacrificed.

✦ *Joseph* was sold into slavery by his brothers for twenty pieces of silver. Jesus was sold by Judas for thirty pieces of silver and suffered because of sins committed by us, his brothers and sisters. Like Joseph, who forgave his brothers and fed the world during a time of famine, Jesus forgives us and nourishes us with his own body and blood.

✦ The prophet *Moses* led the chosen people from slavery to the Promised Land. When we were enslaved by sin and death, Jesus broke the hold of evil over us.

✦ *Joshua*, who led the people into the Promised Land, also prefigured Christ, who leads us into the kingdom of God.

◆ *David*, who overcame the giant Goliath with five stones and a slingshot, is like Jesus, who conquered Satan by his five wounds. As the greatest king of Israel, David prefigures Christ, King of the Universe.

◆ The prophet *Jonah*, who was trapped in the great fish for three days, is a figure of Jesus, who was in the jaws of death for three days.

◆ *Judith* and *Esther*, two Jewish women who courageously saved their people, are also types of Christ, who saved humankind.

In addition to people, certain things in the Old Testament are types of Jesus:

◆ The night the Israelites escaped from Egypt they were protected from the death of the firstborn by sacrificing a lamb and marking their doorposts with its blood. This *paschal lamb* foreshadowed Jesus, whose blood saved us from eternal death.

◆ In the desert, the Israelites ate *manna*, the "bread from heaven." It is a figure of Christ, who nourishes us on our journey of faith with the sacred host that is himself.

◆ When the people were bitten by snakes in the desert, they looked upon a *brazen serpent* on wood that Moses held up and were saved. This is a foreshadowing of Jesus, who was lifted up on the cross to save us from evil. Jesus referred to Moses and the serpent when he instructed Nicodemus in John 3:14.

trivial tidbit...

The oldest representation we have of Mary and Jesus is a third-century fresco in the catacomb of Priscilla in Rome. It shows Mary and her baby beside the prophet Balaam, who is pointing to the star mentioned in his prophecy.

Scholars identify 109 distinct Old Testament prophecies that Jesus can be said to have fulfilled.

Hebrew Prophecies

Often in Jewish history God has raised up prophets to speak to his people. Usually they exhorted the Israelites to turn back to God after they sinned, but sometimes the prophets' words could be read as portents about the Messiah to come:

- One of the earliest was *Balaam*. He predicted, "A star shall come out of Jacob, and a scepter shall rise out of Israel" (Numbers 24:17).
- Much later, *Amos* called the people to social justice and a faith that goes beyond rituals.
- *Isaiah* told them of the holiness of God and that the Messiah would be a suffering servant.
- *Jeremiah* spoke of the new covenant that was to be written on the hearts of the people.
- *Ezekiel* urged the people to hope even when they were in exile, for God would revive them like dry bones being clothed in flesh again and coming to life.

8 Son of Mary: Birth

After being coaxed, a toddler was telling her priest-uncle the Christmas story. When she got to the part where Jesus was born, the little girl burst into giggles, spun around gleefully, ran around the room, and buried her head in a pillow on the couch. The uncle's comment: "What better response to the Good News of Jesus' birth!"

When we Catholics ponder the incarnation, it's not surprising if, like this girl, we can't contain ourselves. God's breaking into our history to save us in a very personal way is a cause of joy for all creation. We look to the Gospels for a deeper understanding of this great mystery.

The Infancy Narratives

The Gospel of Mark begins with the preaching of John the Baptist. The Gospel of John opens with the Word existing before time began and then jumps to the preaching of John the Baptist. It's the Gospels of Luke and Matthew that contain the accounts of Jesus' birth and are the wellspring of our beloved Christmas symbols. But remember, the Gospels were not intended to be historical documents but testimonies of faith. Moreover, the Gospels were written backwards. Once Jesus' followers realized who he was, they told the story of his life in terms that highlighted his divinity and mission. This is especially true in the infancy narratives, the Gospel stories of Jesus' conception and early life. Luke and Matthew wove together prophecies, oral traditions, and the literary conventions of ancient

The Scriptures say that God "overshadowed" Mary, recalling the cloud over the Ark of the Covenant in the desert and the cloud that filled Solomon's Temple that were signs of God's special presence. Mary is the new Ark of the Covenant, the new temple that housed our God.

hero stories to skillfully craft the Christmas stories we've grown up with. Was Jesus born in Bethlehem? Did angels appear to shepherds? Did a star show kings from the East the way to Jesus? Did Herod slaughter children in search of the newborn king? No one knows how much of the infancy narratives are historical. The significance of these stories lies in the fact that they teach eternal truths. The end result of the evangelists' art is that these birth narratives are the Good News in miniature. They present Jesus as the Son of God, the Savior, the long-awaited Messiah.

Birth Announcements (Luke 1:5–38, 57–66; Matthew 1:18–25)

In the literary genre of biography of heroes, the birth of the hero is often announced. For example, in Scripture, Samson's birth was foretold by an angel. God also revealed to Hannah that she would have a son, Samuel. The infancy narrative of Luke opens with two unusual announcements that mirror each other: John the Baptist's birth is announced to his father, Zechariah. And Jesus' birth is announced to Mary. John's birth is miraculous because his mother, Elizabeth, was too old to have children. Jesus' birth is miraculous because Mary conceived him not by a man but by the overshadowing of the Holy Spirit.

The priest Zechariah and his wife Elizabeth were relatives of Mary. Perhaps Elizabeth was Mary's cousin, but Aramaic had no word for "cousin." One day Zechariah is chosen by lot to offer evening incense in the Holy Place of the Temple. As he performs this once-in-a-lifetime privilege, Zechariah is surprised by an angel who delivers the incredible news that he and Elizabeth will have a son, whom he is to call John. Because he questions this message, Zechariah is struck dumb. Nine months later Elizabeth gives birth to a son. At the baby's circumcision when relatives debate what to name him, Zechariah writes, "His name is John." At that, the man regains his power of speech. He uses his voice in a prayer of praise named the *Benedictus* from its opening words, "Blessed be the Lord, the God of Israel." The prayer continues: "He has come to his people and set them free. He has raised up for us a mighty savior, born of the house of his servant David" (Luke 1:68–69). In this prayer, Zechariah predicts his son's job description: "You, my child, shall be called the prophet of the Most High; for you will go before the Lord to prepare his way, to give his people knowledge of salvation by the forgiveness of their sins" (Luke 1:76–77).

John the Baptist was to pave the way for Jesus by baptizing and preaching. His ministry would be like an overture to the symphony of Jesus' life. Perhaps no one in the Gospels is portrayed as more important to Jesus' mission than is John the Baptist.

Six months after the announcement to Zechariah, the angel Gabriel, in the guise of a young man, appears to Mary, a thirteen-year-old Jewish girl in Nazareth, a tiny village in Galilee. Mary is already "espoused" to Joseph, a carpenter, who is described in Scripture as a "righteous" man. Gabriel hails Mary as "full of grace" and announces that God has chosen her to bear a son to be named Jesus, who will be "the Son of the Most High" and a king who will "reign forever." In other words, her son will be the long-awaited Messiah. Mary asks how the angel's words are possible,

quick quote...

The purpose and cause of the incarnation was that He might illuminate the world by His wisdom and excite it to the love of Himself.

Peter Abelard

Holy Land site...

The Basilica of the Annunciation was built in Nazareth in the 1960s, erected over the grotto of the Annunciation, believed to be the site of Mary's childhood house. The building's dome is an upside-down lily. Inside the Basilica the walls are lined with images of Mary from many countries and cultures. In the grotto there is an altar inscribed with the Latin words for "Here the Word was made flesh."

since she is a virgin. Gabriel replies that the power of the Holy Spirit will overshadow her and her child will be the Son of God. Mary accepts God's proposal, calling herself the handmaid of the Lord. Perhaps she places her hand on her chest and bows, the Mid-Eastern gesture that signified complying with someone's will. The incarnation takes place: God becomes human; the Word becomes flesh. The angel also gives Mary the happy news that Elizabeth is six months pregnant.

At Mary's "Let it be," God enters her womb and becomes a human embryo. Floating in amiotic fluid, Jesus develops as all babies do. From a mass of cells his heart takes shape and his limbs grow. His facial features form, and he begins kicking inside Mary. Since Catholics believe that Jesus carried only Mary's DNA, we believe he greatly resembled her, the woman who bravely agreed to let him be made from her flesh and blood. There had been miraculous births before, where women past the age of childbearing gave birth, but the birth of Jesus from a virgin is unique. It paved the way for another unheard of "birth," the resurrection of Jesus.

Joseph's View

Matthew reveals the annunciation from Joseph's perspective. Although Scripture doesn't include a single word that Joseph said, from his actions we can infer that he was a devout, dependable man of integrity, someone who proved equal to the mission of protecting and providing for God's Son and his mother.

Mary's pregnancy had to be a shock to Joseph as well as a mystery. No doubt he spent sleepless nights

Mary, the Mother of Jesus

Mary was one of the *anawim*, the faithful Jews who waited in hope for the Messiah. She became the first to hear the Good News of salvation. Because God chose her to be the mother of his Son, from the moment Mary was conceived she was preserved from all sin, both original sin and personal sin, a privilege we Catholics call the Immaculate Conception. Accustomed to living fully attuned to God, when Mary was called to her unique and awesome role, she responded yes to God immediately. Her immense faith in God as she walked into the unknown serves as a model for all people. This holy young woman was the right one to be entrusted with the care and nurturing of the God-man, who grew up to resemble her in more ways than just physically. Jesus cherished Mary as much as any person cherishes his or her mother. Today we view Mary as the ideal woman, mother, and disciple. Best of all, we look to her as loving mother to us, who are the brothers and sisters of her son, Jesus.

She is not only mother of God but Mother of the Church. Each time we pray the Hail Mary, we honor Mary by echoing the words of Gabriel and Elizabeth, and we recall the great mystery of the incarnation.

The letters of Maria are found in this Marian monogram:

quick quote...

Where did your Christ come from? . . . From God and a woman. Man had nothing to do with him.

Sojourner Truth

a cool website...

St. Joseph Oratory in Montreal is the largest church in Canada. Learn its interesting history by going to www.saint-joseph.org and clicking on "English."

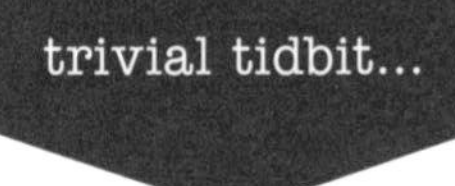

The Magnificat echoes the prayer of Hannah in 1 Samuel 2:1–10. Read it aloud.

wondering how his bride-to-be, who was so kind and loving, could have been unfaithful to him. Betrothal in Jewish society was equivalent to marriage, except that the couple still lived apart and did not have sex. The penalty for adultery was stoning to death. After agonizing over the situation, Joseph decides to divorce his fiancée quietly. Only then does he have a dream in which an angel, probably Gabriel again, informs him that Mary's child is the Son of God and that he should marry her and name the child Jesus. Joseph receives messages in dreams as the patriarch Joseph of the Old Testament did. So both Josephs were dreamers, and both were critical to salvation history.

A Visit as Christbearer (Luke 1:39–56)

Mary, pregnant with Jesus, immediately goes on a ninety-mile journey south to Ein Karem in Judea in order to assist her relative Elizabeth. Her motive is charity, for she knows that Elizabeth, a much older woman, will need help. Perhaps Mary also is impelled by the desire to share her good news...or possibly she is trying to avoid the inevitable town gossip about her pregnancy. The trip is arduous, often uphill on stony paths under the hot sun—no easy task for someone experiencing morning sickness.

At Zechariah's house, Mary enters and greets Elizabeth. On hearing Mary, Elizabeth exclaims, "Blessed are you among women, and blessed is the fruit of your womb," words immortalized in the Hail Mary prayer. Enlightened by the Holy Spirit, Elizabeth realizes that Mary is bearing the Messiah. She asks, "How is it that the mother of the Lord comes to me?" Then Elizabeth reveals that at the sound of Mary's voice,

St. Joseph, Husband and Father

A legend recorded in the apocryphal *Proto-evangelium of James* tells how Joseph was chosen for his awesome role in salvation history. Supposedly when Mary, who had made a vow of virginity, was to be married, the high priest based the search for her husband on the verse, "A shoot shall come out from the stump of Jesse.... The spirit of the Lord shall rest on him" (Isaiah 11:1–2). He assembled men descended from Jesse and had them bring their staffs. Joseph came but, perhaps assuming he was too old to participate, he did not present his staff. When no man's staff blossomed, Joseph's was discovered. His staff had blossomed and a dove settled on it. Scripture that describes the just man as blossoming like the lily (Hosea 14:6) is also applied to Joseph. For these reasons, he is often depicted with a lily, a symbol of perfection and purity.

Joseph's feast day is March 19. He has a second feast day on May 1, when he is honored as patron of working people. Because Joseph was such a good father to Jesus, he has received the title Patron of the Universal Church. And because we assume he died with Mary and Jesus at his side, Joseph is also the patron of a happy death.

Holy Land site...

Atop a hill in Ein Karem stands the beautiful Church of the Visitation with a striking mosaic of the event on its façade. Inside the church on the front wall is a lovely fresco of Mary meeting her relative Elizabeth. The Church of John the Baptist is in the center of town. It encloses a grotto in which a star marks where John the Baptist supposedly was born.

John the Baptist is the only saint other than Mary whose birthday is celebrated. The Church observes it as a solemnity on June 24, six months before Christmas.

the baby in her womb jumped. John the Baptist presumably recognized that the Savior was present and reacted with joy. He leapt just as King David once leapt and danced before the Ark of the Covenant. Tradition holds that at that moment John was freed from original sin.

Mary bursts into the Magnificat, a hymn that praises God. In it Mary foretells that all will call her blessed, describes God's kingdom as a kingdom of reversals in which the powerful are brought down and the lowly are lifted up, and states that God has kept his promise to Abraham. Clearly this whole episode of the visit points to the divinity and messiahship of Jesus.

Three months later, presumably after John was born, Mary makes the long journey back to Nazareth to await with Joseph the birth of her own son.

The Birth of Jesus (Luke 2:1–7)

The Christmas story that is celebrated and retold each year through Christmas cards, carols, and pageants, is painted beautifully and simply by Luke. The Roman emperor, Augustus, decrees that all should go to their hometown for a census. Because Joseph is a descendant of David, he must travel more than ninety miles south to Bethlehem, where David was born. Although Mary is nine months pregnant, she goes with Joseph, either because she has to or because of her love for him. And so the newlyweds travel to Bethlehem. This sets the stage for the fulfillment of the prophecy of Micah, which says that the ruler of Israel, the Messiah who will bring peace, will be born in Bethlehem.

Some scholars think that the Bethlehem in the

Gospel refers to a town in Galilee named Bethlehem. Others speculate that the Gospel writers merely told their story to underline Jesus' connection with King David and to correspond with Micah's prophecy. Again, these are not historical documents. They are stories of faith. Theologian John Shea says that atheists and agnostics are people who "can't hack metaphor." The main points of the birth narratives are that the infinite gulf between humans and God has been breeched, that God has joined with the poorest of the poor, and that peace will ultimately win out in our world. The rest may be symbolic of these truths.

According to Luke, so many people are crammed into Bethlehem for the census that poor Joseph can't locate a suitable inn, much less a maternity ward. To Joseph's dismay he has to be satisfied with sheltering his pregnant wife in a lowly place, probably a cave where animals are kept, and there that night Mary gives birth to Jesus. Mary wraps her baby in swaddling clothes, the binding cloths that made sure infants grew straight, and she lays him in a hay trough that we've come to call a manger. It is fitting that this child who would someday call himself the bread of life was born in Bethlehem, which means "house of bread," and be placed in a feeding box for animals. By showing Jesus homeless and cribless in the first moments of his life, the nativity story poignantly illustrates that he identifies with the poor. God could have elected to be born into a wealthy, prestigious family and be surrounded by all the comforts and trappings of the well-to-do but did not choose that path.

Although in the carol "Away in a Manger" we sing "no crying he makes," Jesus, who was like us in all

big book search...

Read Micah 5:2–5, the prophecy that links the Messiah to Bethlehem.

quick quote...

Artists give Mary a donkey on the way to Bethlehem; the Gospels do not.

Martin Luther

Jesus' Birthday

The date of Jesus' birth is completely unknown. The early Christians were so fixated on his death and rising that they seemed to pay no attention to the details of his birth. In addition, back then people didn't celebrate heroes' birthdays but their death days. Because the nativity stories involve Herod, who died in 4 B.C., it's thought that Jesus was born about 6 B.C. Dionysius Exiguus, the sixth-century monk whose work was the basis for the Gregorian calendar, miscalculated the years. So although he meant to divide time before and after Jesus' birth, he was off a few years. To complicate matters, Luke mentions that the census was taken when Quirinius was governor of Syria, but Quirinius didn't rule until 6 A.D. Scholars struggle to explain this discrepancy but, again, for people of faith it matters little.

Why is Christmas celebrated on December 25? At first countries commemorated the nativity on different days. As early as 336 A.D., however, it was observed in Rome on December 25. When Pope Sixtus III in 435 presided at the first Christmas midnight Mass, the date became set. Many theories have been proposed to explain the date. One of them is that the Jews thought that creation occurred on March 25, so it followed that Jesus, who inaugurated the new creation, would be conceived on March 25 and be born nine months later. Another theory is that Jesus died on March 25

trivial tidbit...

In the United States more than two billion Christmas cards are sent each year. The custom originated in 1843 in England, when Sir Henry Cole sent friends cards depicting good deeds. Louis Prang, a painter, first made cards in the United States and held annual contests for designs.

quick quote...

What good is it if Mary gave birth to the Son of God centuries ago, if I do not also give birth to the Son of God in my time and culture?

Meister Eckhart

and, because prophets lived complete years, he must have been conceived on that date. It's also possible that December 25 was chosen to counteract the feast of the Roman sun god Apollo and the Persian sun god Mithras, who were celebrated on this day.

December is actually a cold winter month in Bethlehem. Therefore the census would not have been taken then, nor would there have been sheep in the fields at night. Yet December 25 is symbolically fitting for Jesus' birthday because according to the Roman calendar it was the winter solstice, the shortest and darkest day of the year, when the sun is reborn. In the late third century the Emperor Aurelian made December 25 a festival of the invincible sun. This title fits Jesus, who is called the "sun of justice" (Malachi 4:2). Also, Zechariah in his *Benedictus* describes Jesus in terms of the sun: "The dawn from on high shall break upon us, to shine on those who dwell in darkness and the shadow of death, and to guide our feet into the way of peace" (Luke 1:78–79). Christmas Mass is traditionally celebrated at midnight, perhaps because of this passage: "For while gentle silence enveloped all things, and night in its swift course was now half gone, your all-powerful word leaped from heaven" (Wisdom 18:14–15).

trivial tidbit...

Some scholars think that it was more likely spring, the lambing season, when Christ, the lamb of God, was born.

fyi...

For a deeper and more thorough understanding and appreciation of Mary of Nazareth, read *The Catholic Companion to Mary* by Mary Kathleen Glavich.

Holy Land site...

The Basilica of the Nativity on Manger Square in Bethlehem dates back to 530 A.D. It is built on the site of the first church there, which was constructed in the first half of the fourth century. The entrance to the basilica was walled up almost completely by the crusaders to prevent invaders on horseback from entering. Today a four-foot-high doorway requires visitors to bend low, an apt symbol of humility, as they approach the site of Jesus' humble birth. In a cave in the lower level, a silver star marks his birthplace, and nearby is the presumed site of his manger.

things but sin, was a real human baby. So not only did he cry on being born like the rest of us, but he was fed with Mary's milk, had to be burped, and needed his diaper changed. No doubt Mary sang Jewish lullabies to put him to sleep. And Joseph, like so many other new dads, probably spent hours pacing the floor with Baby Jesus.

The Shepherds (Luke 2:8–20)

The first people to hear the news of Jesus' birth were shepherds, who were not only poor but were considered rascals and liars. They were low class, smelly, and avoided by polite society. What's more, they didn't observe all the Jewish regulations. In other words, shepherds were just the sort of people Jesus would associate with later on—the lowly ones he came to raise up. He would even call himself the good shepherd.

While the shepherds are watching their flocks during the night, suddenly a majestic angel stands before them and they are bathed in light. The angel tells them not to be afraid and then relays what he calls "good news for all the people." He says, "To you is born this day in the city of David a Savior, who is the Messiah, the Lord." He informs the shepherds that they will find the child wrapped in bands of cloth and lying in a manger. In a flash many angels are with him. Astounded at the great God becoming a child, they proclaim, "Glory to God in the highest heaven, and on earth peace among those whom he favors!" We echo these words today in the Gloria prayer during the Eucharist on Sundays and feast days.

After this spectacular vision, the awestruck shepherds confer and decide to find the child. They hurry to Bethlehem, abandoning their sheep. On locating Mary and Joseph with the baby, to everyone's amazement, the shepherds breathlessly explain what the angels had revealed to them about the child. Then the shepherds return to their flocks praising God. Luke tells us that Mary treasured the shepherds' words and pondered them in her heart. No doubt these words were reassuring to her because there is no record that she had any contact with angels herself from the time Gabriel left her. She might have wondered if this strange birth really was all God's doing. Several other unusual occurrences in the early life of Jesus would also confirm for Mary that her son was no ordinary human being.

Oddly, the Puritans who came to Plymouth in 1620 banned the celebration of Christmas in some colonies in an attempt to purify the church. To them, external trappings such as Christmas trees, decorations, and gifts detracted from the true meaning of the mystery. Today, of course, Christmas is celebrated in grand style, and although consumerism is in full force during this season, most people know that Christmas is the time to remember the greatest gift of all: the Father's gift of the Son.

The custom of three-dimensional nativity scenes originates with St. Francis of Assisi, who in 1223, in the town of Greccio, created the first crèche. To promote devotion to the Babe of Bethlehem, he had a manger with hay set up on a mountainside and procured a real ox and an ass. On Christmas Eve people carrying candles and torches thronged to the scene. There, Francis read the Gospel and preached about the nativity, his face streaming with tears of joy.

fyi...

At the pope's Christmas midnight Mass in Rome this proclamation is sung: "Many centuries since the creation of the world...13 centuries after the march out of Egypt...in the year 752 of the foundation of Rome...in the year 42 of the empire of Caesar Augustus... Jesus Christ, eternal God and Son of the eternal father...having been conceived by the power of the Holy Spirit...after nine months...was born in Bethlehem of Judea of the virgin Mary and made man."

Christmas Carol Origins

◆ *O Come, All Ye Faithful:* John Francis Wade, a Catholic musician in England, wrote this favorite carol in the eighteenth century.

◆ *Silent Night:* The traditional story is that the Catholic priest Joseph Mohr wrote the lyrics and Franz Gruber wrote the music one Christmas Eve in Austria when the church organ was broken. John F. Young translated the words into English.

◆ *Joy to the World:* Isaac Watts, a prolific hymnist, wrote the words in 1719 in England, and Lowell Mason arranged the music.

◆ *O Little Town of Bethlehem:* Phillips Brooks, an Episcopalian bishop of Massachusetts, wrote the words in 1867. Two years earlier he had been inspired at a Christmas Eve service in the old church in Bethlehem. Brooks's organist, Lewis H. Redner, set the words to music on Christmas Eve, 1868.

◆ *Away in a Manger:* was first published by James R. Murray in 1885 in a Lutheran Sunday School book. The author of "Away in a Manger" is, however, unknown, although the third stanza seems to have been added by Dr. John McFarland in 1904. Occasionally the tune is attributed to Martin Luther, though this appears to be erroneous. The confusion may have arisen out of the fact that "Away in a Manger" was subtitled "Luther's Cradle Hymn" in the 1885 publication.

✦ *O Holy Night:* The music was composed by Adolphe C. Adam in France in the early nineteenth century and is said to have been the first music broadcast by radio. The words were written in 1847 by Placide Cappeau, a French poet.

✦ *The First Noel:* This English carol possibly dates from the early thirteenth century.

✦ *Hark! The Herald Angels Sing:* The lyrics were written by Charles Wesley, brother of John Wesley, the founder of Methodism. The melody familiar today is from Felix Mendelssohn's cantata "Festival Song," which was composed to commemorate Gutenberg's printing press.

✦ *The Little Drummer Boy:* This popular carol, composed by Katherine K. Davis in 1941, is based on a Czech folk tune.

Holy Land site...

Not far from Bethlehem is the tent-shaped Shepherd's Field Church, which commemorates the angels' visit to the shepherds. Bright frescoes of nativity scenes cover its walls. Nearby, shepherds still tend their sheep. Greek Orthodox Christians have their own Shepherd's Field, which is built over a cave-church founded by St. Helena in 325.

quick quote...

Jesus Christ, the condescension of divinity, and the exaltation of humanity.

Phillips Brooks

9 Son of Man: Early Life

The infancy narratives cover events that occurred soon after Jesus' birth, as well as one story from when he was twelve. Other than this, we're left to assume that Jesus developed like any other Jewish boy. He drank his mother's milk and then learned to eat solid food. He crawled and then with his parents' help took his first steps. He cooed and cried and one day said his first word, probably the Aramaic for "Mommy" or "Daddy." Under his parents' tutelage Jesus learned how to put on his sandals, practice Jewish etiquette, play well with others, and share his toys. He also learned to pray and began to follow the Jewish religion. Jesus, son of Mary, was a true son of man.

Jesus called himself that—"son of man"—in the Gospels more than any other title. In Matthew he does so thirty-two times. *Son of man* is an ambiguous expression. It can simply be another way of saying "a human being." It can also substitute for "I" or "me," the way "yours truly" functions for us. Most intriguing though, in the prophetic book of Daniel the son of man stands for a royal, messianic person who is to come. How Jesus used the expression is debatable and may encompass all three meanings, depending on the circumstances.

Eight Days Old (Luke 2:21)

In keeping with Jewish law, eight days after Jesus was born he was circumcised and shed his blood for the first time. If the ceremony was like today's, then Joseph held

Jesus on his lap and prayed the ritual prayers while the circumciser carried out the painful surgery. To the Jews, circumcision was a sign of their covenant, their bond, with the one true God. It made Jesus a member of God's chosen people. On this day baby boys also received their name. Mary and Joseph named the baby "Jesus," as the angel had prescribed. Then the family celebrated with friends and relatives.

trivial tidbit...

The Feast of the Holy Family is observed on the Sunday between Christmas and New Year's Day. In years when these two days fall on Sundays and there's no Sunday between them, the feast is on Friday, December 30.

Forty Days Old (Luke 2:22–38)

Forty days after the birth of Jesus, Mary and Joseph traveled six miles north to Jerusalem to consecrate Jesus to God at the Temple in a ritual known as the Presentation. The Jews were required to pay a priest five shekels of silver to "buy back" their firstborn sons from God. This practice is rooted in the Exodus story in which the firstborn sons of the Israelites were not killed when the Angel of Death passed over Egypt. The Presentation is the first time that Jesus enters the Temple, the site of some key events in his life.

Luke combines the Presentation with Mary's purification. A woman was considered unclean forty days after bearing a son and eighty days after bearing a daughter. (Hmmm!) Then the mother was reinstated by offering a lamb and a bird or, if the family couldn't afford that, two birds. Mary sacrifices two birds, a sign that the Holy Family was not well-to-do.

An old man named Simeon was one of the *anawim*, the humble, faithful people who trusted in God's promise of a savior. The Holy Spirit had revealed to Simeon that he would not die until he beheld the Messiah. On the day that the Holy Family comes to the Temple for the Presentation of Jesus, the Holy

Spirit inspires Simeon, apparently a layman, to go there too. When Mary and Joseph enter the Temple, Simeon approaches them and takes the baby Jesus in his arms. He praises God and prays what the Church now prays every day during Night Prayer: "Master, now you are dismissing your servant in peace, according to your word; for my eyes have seen your salvation, which you have prepared in the presence of all peoples, a light for revelation to the Gentiles and for glory to your people Israel" (Luke 2:29–32). These words are a hint to the first Jewish Christians that their Messiah's saving acts will reach beyond the borders of Israel to the whole world.

Naturally Mary and Joseph are amazed at Simeon's words and probably heartened. Simeon blesses them, but then the mood changes. He looks at Mary and pronounces a sad prophecy. The old man predicts that her child is destined for the rise and fall of many in Israel and will be "a sign that will be opposed," so that the inner thoughts of many will be revealed. Mary also will be touched by sorrow. Addressing her, Simeon foretells, "A sword will pierce your own soul too." This prediction will be fulfilled sevenfold as Mary suffers the consequences of being the Savior's mother. We Catholics remember her suffering to this day in the devotion of the Seven Sorrows of Mary.

Simeon had no sooner spoken than the eighty-four-year-old prophetess Anna appears on the scene and somewhat dispels the shadow of doom. She too belongs to the *anawim*. A widow after only seven years of marriage, she now lives in the Temple, praying and fasting night and day. Praising God, Anna undertakes the delightful task of spreading the good

trivial tidbit...

Byzantine Catholics call the feast of the Presentation the feast of the Encounter with Simeon.

trivial tidbit...

A delicate flower with six white petals is named Star of Bethlehem.

news of Jesus' arrival to others who are awaiting the Savior of the world.

A Heavenly GPS to Bethlehem (Matthew 2:1–23)

Matthew includes a fascinating story about Jesus' infancy not found in Luke. It unquestionably identifies Jesus with Moses, the great Hebrew prophet and leader who was spared from slaughter at birth and who came to Israel out of Egypt. According to Matthew, wise men in the East spot a new star, which to ancients signaled the birth of a king or other major event. The wise men make the first Christian pilgrimage. Seeking the new King of the Jews, they follow this star that rose in the East to the city of Jerusalem. Many attempts have been made to explain the star scientifically. Most often it is thought to have been a conjunction of Jupiter with the star Regulus or with Saturn or Venus. (The planet Jupiter is named for the king of gods, and the name Regulus means king.) But there's no reason why the Bethlehem star couldn't have been a supernatural phenomenon. It is linked to the prophecy of Balaam: "A star shall come out of Jacob" (Numbers 24:17).

When Herod gets wind that men from the East are inquiring in town about the new king, he is frightened, along with everyone else in Jerusalem. He consults all the chief priests and scribes and asks them where the Messiah is to be born. They quote Micah 2:6, "And you, Bethlehem, in the land of Judah, are by no means least among the rulers of Judah; for from you shall come a ruler who is to shepherd my people Israel." Then Herod secretly summons the wise men and asks when they saw the star. He directs them that when they find out where the new king is, they should return to inform him of the place so that he too can do him homage. The wise men aren't wise enough to see through this duplicity. That Herod doesn't also charge his soldiers to search for the king suggests that this story is symbolic.

The wise men continue to follow the star until it stops over the house in Bethlehem where the Holy Family lives. (A star would be above the whole town and so couldn't designate one house, unless it was a falling star that landed on its roof—another indication that Matthew is using figurative language.) The visitors are overjoyed that their quest is ended. The wise men have found Wisdom incarnate. They enter the house, fall prostrate, and pay homage to Jesus, the newborn king. Some scholars think that Jesus might have been two years old by then. Opening their treasure chests, the wise men take out gold, frankincense, and myrrh and offer them to him. These are expensive and strange gifts for an infant, but they make sense in view of their symbolism: gold for a king, frankincense for a priest, and myrrh (used to embalm) as a sign of Jesus' passion and death. That night the wise men are warned in a dream not to return to Herod, so they go home via another route.

The significance of this story is that Jesus came not only for the Jews, but for Gentiles too. He is Savior of the whole world. Roman Catholics celebrate the event on the feast of the Epiphany on the Sunday after the first Saturday after Christmas. Originally both the nativity of Jesus and the visit of the wise men were celebrated on January 6. *Epiphany* means "manifes-

quick quote...

Every authentic believer is always on a journey in his personal itinerary of faith and, at the same time, with the little light that he carries in himself, can and must be of help to those he finds at his side and who perhaps have difficulty finding the road that leads to Christ.

Pope Benedict XVI

fyi...

An Epiphany custom is to bless houses and write in chalk across a doorsill the magi's initials between the digits of the year. For example, in the year 2012 this would be 20 + C + M + B + 12.

tation." At first the Eastern Church commemorated several manifestations on this day, including the one at the wedding at Cana, but today on Epiphany it mainly celebrates the baptism of Jesus.

Identity of the Wise Men

In Greek versions of the Bible the wise men are called *magi*, that is, priests of the Persian religion Zoroastrianism and experts in astrology. Our word *magic* is derived from that title. The magi could have come from Persia; some say from China. Because three gifts are mentioned, it's been assumed that there were three wise men, but there could have been more. Since the eighth century the Church in the West has called the wise men Caspar, Melchior, and Balthasar, as a sixth-century manuscript named them. In time, to show universality, the wise men came to be portrayed as a European, an Asian, and an African, although none of this is in the Bible.

Why do we sing "We Three Kings" instead of "We Three Magi"? The wise men evolved into "kings" around 450 A.D. because of Isaiah 60 and Psalm 72, which describe kings coming from far countries with gifts for the new Jewish king. Camels became figures in nativity sets because they too are mentioned in Psalm 72.

In the year 66, close to the time Matthew was being written, magi from the East visited the Emperor Nero and did him homage. In the same year Halley's comet appeared. It's possible that the evangelist Matthew creatively intertwined these two events in a story to teach religious truths about Jesus, that is, that the real "King of the World" was Jesus, not Caesar.

trivial tidbit...

When the Persians invaded Bethlehem in 614 A.D., they did not destroy the Basilica of the Nativity, possibly because on one of its mosaics were magi garbed in Persian clothes.

Refugees in Egypt

After the wise men depart, Joseph too has a dream. In it an angel commands him to flee to Egypt until further notice because Herod is seeking to kill Jesus. Joseph arises, wakes Mary, and conveys the frightening message. They hurriedly pack and head out into the night, fleeing for the holy child's life. Matthew comments that this is to fulfill Hosea 11:1, "Out of Egypt I have called my son." The trip is a long one. Egypt, in Africa, is about a hundred miles from Bethlehem. If the family traveled to Alexandria, where Jews were settled, that meant an additional two hundred miles.

When Herod realizes that the wise men aren't coming back, he is furious. He orders his soldiers to kill all children in and around Bethlehem who are two years and under, calculating from the time the wise men said they first noticed the star. These first martyrs probably number about twenty. We call them the "Holy Innocents" and celebrate their feast on December 28. There is no other historical reference to this slaughter, and many scholars view it as a literary device Matthew uses to align Jesus with Moses and the ancient Hebrews, who escaped Pharaoh's killing of the firstborn males. The atrocity, however, is plausible, because it is in accord with Herod's reputation as a monster.

The apocryphal gospels tell incredible stories of the flight into Egypt. Palm trees bend to give their dates to the Holy Family; on seeing Jesus, robbers are in

trivial tidbit...

Today shrines and churches mark places in Egypt where the Holy Family supposedly visited. Tours trace their route, and legends are linked to certain cities. For example, the one legend says the Holy Family rested in Zeitoun; another says that in Cairo idols came crashing down as the three passed by.

awe and do not harm the travelers; and even lions and leopards along the way adore Jesus. In one account the family is magically transported to Egypt in no time. In reality, the three refugees no doubt endure the scorching desert sun, dust, insects, hunger, and fatigue. Some nights they sleep outside without shelter. And all the while, Mary and Joseph are filled with anxiety at the threat of Herod's soldiers in hot pursuit.

In Egypt the Holy Family finds a safe haven with other Jewish refugees and stays perhaps three years. When Herod dies, an angel delivers the news to Joseph in a dream and directs him to take his family back to Israel. Joseph packs up again and heads for Judea, until he hears that Archelaus, a despot nearly as cruel as his father, Herod, rules there. Still another dream alerts Joseph to the danger in Judea, and so he settles in Nazareth in Galilee. It may seem odd that Joseph wouldn't have headed directly for his and Mary's hometown in the first place. Perhaps Joseph really was thinking of moving closer to the "big city" of Jerusalem, or maybe this was just part of the story that Matthew was weaving to make other points that had nothing to do with "history" as we conceive it today.

For example, this story of the flight into Egypt demonstrates that young Jesus is one with the poor. He is oppressed (singled out by the king to be murdered no less); and he becomes a refugee, a foreigner in a foreign land. But his coming out of Egypt also identifies him with his people, the Israelites, who were brought out of Egypt to Israel.

A Normal Boy

God chose to have his Son grow up as a member of a family. However, nothing is told in the Scriptures of Jesus' life as an infant and child in Nazareth. Naturally, Mary and Joseph tickled and cuddled him, rocked him to sleep, and taught him to walk and talk. Some art from long ago depicts homey scenes such as Joseph carrying Jesus piggyback and Jesus helping Mary with the cooking. One picture even shows Mary spanking Jesus! Probably as a young child Jesus played with rattles and other wooden toys made by Joseph. His education was either conducted by Joseph and other village men, or he attended class at the synagogue. When Jesus grew older, he played games and wrestled with the other boys in the neighborhood. Along with other villagers he helped bring in harvests. Soon Joseph started instructing him in the art of carpentry.

A Precocious Lad in the Temple (Luke 2:41–52)

The Gospels resume the story of Jesus' life when he is twelve, on the brink of attaining the age of majority, which for a Jewish boy at the time was thirteen. At that age a boy was considered responsible for keeping the commandments. However, in Jesus' time the Jewish rite of passage known today as the *bar mitzvah* wasn't practiced yet. The earliest references to it come from the sixth century.

Being devout Jews, Mary and Joseph make the trip each year to Jerusalem for the Passover, although they aren't obliged to do so because they live so far away. When Jesus is twelve, he accompanies them for the festival, presumably for the first time. There, like a typical

fyi...

St. Anthony of Padua, a Franciscan who died in 1231, is often shown holding the Christ child, who is standing on a Bible. This depiction springs from a legend that one night the saint was observed in his brightly lit hermit cell talking with the child Jesus. St. Anthony was a great preacher of the Gospel, especially of the Incarnation, so the Bible and child are fitting symbols for him.

Holy Land site...

In Nazareth, near the Basilica of the Annunciation, is the Church of St. Joseph. Inside the church, stone steps lead down into a cavern reputed since the seventeenth century to be St. Joseph's workshop.

adolescent, the boy Jesus makes an impulsive decision, seemingly oblivious to the effect it would have on his parents. Fascinated by the religious discussions at the Temple, he misses the departure of the caravan.

On the way home, Mary and Joseph assume that Jesus is with others in the caravan. They travel for a whole day before starting to look for him among their relatives and friends. When they realize that Jesus is nowhere to be found, they trek back to Jerusalem alone and search for him. For three days Mary and Joseph are worried sick as they retrace their steps, knock on doors, and ask, "Have you seen our twelve-year-old son Jesus?" Finally they go to the Temple and, lo and behold, there Jesus is, sitting surrounded by teachers. He is listening to them and asking them questions. To the teachers' amazement, this country boy with a "hillbilly" accent shows an understanding far beyond his years. Jesus' appearance as a child prodigy in this account gives a clue to his real and ultimate identity.

Mary and Joseph are astonished to see their son engaged in discussion there. As any mother would do, Mary scolds Jesus, "Child, why have you treated us like this? Look, your father and I have been searching for you in great anxiety." Jesus' reply is his first recorded words. They are an enigma that puzzles Mary and Joseph: "Why were you searching for me? Did you not know that I must be in my Father's house?" Nevertheless, the three leave Jerusalem and wend their way back to Nazareth, where, after his frightening and mysterious escapade, Jesus is obedient to his parents. The omnipotent God submits himself to two of his creatures.

This story definitely highlights the divinity of Jesus.

He is in the Temple again, and he calls it his Father's house. In addition, his knowledge of religion is extraordinary for one so young. Yet the story ends with Jesus' obedience. Luke comments that Mary ponders all these things in her heart, as we too do.

The only scriptural information about the rest of Jesus' life in Nazareth is that he grows "in wisdom and in divine and human favor" (Luke 2:52). That is why Jesus' years in Nazareth are called his "hidden life." They serve as a thirty-year novitiate, preparing him for his life's main work. During this time, with his parents' help, Jesus was schooled in the customs of his culture and in the history and laws of his religion. Sometime during these years Joseph died, either of natural causes or perhaps in a construction accident. Jesus must have felt his death keenly. This strong, quiet man chosen by God to be his earthly father had been his protector, provider, and role model. Certainly Joseph helped shape Jesus' image of God as his *Abba*, or Father.

In Nazareth, Jesus was a common laborer, the village carpenter. At first he worked at Joseph's side and then, after Joseph died, Jesus most likely took over the business and supported himself and his mother. We can imagine him sawing wood, pounding nails, and measuring beams while singing or whistling a Hebrew song. Periodically someone would come by to hire him for a job or ask for a favor. Children would gather at the doorway or play in the sawdust. Maybe Mary would drop in to see what he was working on or to bring a snack. By being a workman for most of his life, Jesus emphasized for us the dignity of manual labor.

trivial tidbit...

At the top of a hill in Nazareth is the Basilica of Jesus the Adolescent, which affords a panoramic view of the town and the hills of Galilee. The Salesians, a religious order, run it as well as an adjacent school for boys.

Jesus, Mary, Joseph!

The experiences Jesus had in his family and in the neighborhood during his so-called hidden life helped make him the human being he was. They also were a fertile source of ideas for his teaching. Finally, when Jesus was around thirty, an age when other men were married and had families of their own, Jesus closed up shop, hugged his mother good-bye, and set off on his mission. He was to proclaim and inaugurate the kingdom of God, on earth, as it is in heaven.

10 Messiah: Start of His Ministry

In 2002, Pope John Paul II presented the world with new mysteries for the rosary that focus on highpoints in Jesus' public life. He called them the "Luminous Mysteries" or the "Mysteries of Light." The third mystery of light is Jesus' Proclamation of the Good News of the Kingdom of God. This is the essence of the mission of Jesus. In him the hopes of God's people have been fulfilled. Their Messiah has arrived. Jesus is the great prophet who calls his people to a conversion of their hearts and offers them a radical vision of the world as it could be. God's kingdom—or divine reign of peace, justice, and love—is a present reality, inaugurated by Jesus himself. But this kingdom has also not completely arrived yet, as we who live in this world torn by violence know all too well. The fullness of God's kingdom is slated for the future at a time even Jesus did not know. This now-but-not-yet kingdom is the core message that Jesus delivered, both in word and deed.

Baptism: The Decisive Hour

Jesus' cousin, John the Baptist, was half a year older than Jesus and had been living an ascetic life in the wilderness when God's word came to him, compelling him to preach (see Matthew 3:1–17; Mark 1:1–10; Luke 3:1–22; John 1:6–12, 19–34; 3:24–36). Israel hadn't been visited by a prophet since Malachi, who had

trivial tidbit...

Orthodox churches celebrate the baptism of Jesus on the feast of the Epiphany and hold the Blessing of the Waters. The priest throws a crucifix into a body of water, and men dive in to search for it. The one who recovers the crucifix receives a special blessing.

lived about 450 years earlier. Clothed in a garment of camel's hair cinched with a leather belt, John began preaching in the region around the Jordan River. Sustained by a meager diet of locusts and honey, John exhorted people to turn from their evil ways and be baptized as a sign of their repentance. Warning them of imminent judgment and wrath, he advised them to share their possessions and treat others justly. John brought about a spiritual revival in the land.

When people wondered if John were the Messiah, he informed them that another was coming who was more powerful than he, someone whose sandal he was unworthy to untie. In other words, John didn't even deserve to perform the task of a slave for the Messiah. John explained, "He will baptize you with the Holy Spirit and fire," and foretold that the coming one would separate the wheat from the chaff, meaning the faithful people from the bad. Likewise, John warned the Pharisees and Sadducees that any tree that doesn't bear good fruit would be cut down and cast into the fire. John was a fire-and-brimstone preacher, unlike Jesus, who preached God's love and mercy. John, this prophet who had leaped in his mother's womb at the presence of the Lord in Mary's womb, fulfilled this prophecy: "I am sending my messenger ahead of you, who will prepare your way; the voice of one crying out in the wilderness: 'Prepare the way of the Lord, make his paths straight'" (Isaiah 40:3).

After leaving his home in Nazareth, Jesus joined the crowd that followed John. Some scholars think that John was his mentor. One day, as John is baptizing in the Jordan River, Jesus asks to be baptized too, a surprising request to us since we believe that Jesus was sinless. John protests, "I need to be baptized by you, and do you come to me?" This event has puzzled scholars as well. Some offer the explanation that in Jesus' case baptism signified not repentance for sins but an acceptance of his mission. Also, by being baptized Jesus demonstrates his solidarity with sinners. He assumes our burden of sinfulness in order to bring us new life. Going down into the water symbolizes Jesus' acceptance of death. This is the story that marks the beginning of Jesus' ministry. Some speculate that it is also the hour when he first realizes that he is, literally, the Son of God.

At Jesus' baptism a *theophany* occurs, a manifestation of the divine presence as Trinity. The Synoptics relate that after Jesus is baptized, the heavens are opened and the Spirit descends on Jesus like a dove, a vision that has led artists to portray the Third Person of the Trinity as this bird. A voice from heaven (the First Person of the Trinity) declares, "You are my Son, the Beloved; with you I am well pleased." Although John's Gospel omits the actual baptism, it does state that John the Baptist testifies to people that he saw the Holy Spirit descend on Jesus like a dove and remain with him. With his baptism, Jesus is anointed for his mission as king, prophet, and priest.

Later Jesus praises John: "He was a burning and shining lamp, and you were willing to rejoice for a while in his light" (John 5:35). Clearly, John's role was precursor—he led to Jesus. Scholars say that there might have been tension between the disciples of John and those of Jesus. Some people thought John was the Messiah. The evangelists, especially John, take pains to emphasize that Jesus was greater than John the Baptist.

Holy Land site...

Although most pilgrims visit the Jordan River in Israel as the place where Jesus was baptized, archaeological findings beginning in 1996 point to the Wadi-el-Kharra, a spring that feeds into the Jordan River on the eastern side in the country Jordan. Among the evidence are churches and baptismal pools dating back to just after Jesus' lifetime.

In Aramaic the word for lamb also means a male child, just as in English the word *kid* means either a baby goat or a child.

For example, in place of the baptism where Jesus joins sinners, John's Gospel relates that Jesus comes to John and John proclaims, "Here is the Lamb of God" and "This is the Son of God." Another time when both Jesus' disciples and John are baptizing, John's disciples remark to him that Jesus had more people being baptized than John. The Gospel shows John knows that competition is senseless. John compares himself to "the friend of the bridegroom who rejoices at the bridegroom's voice" and says, "He must increase, but I must decrease." When Jesus hears that people were comparing the popularity of the two, he leaves Judah and goes to Galilee. Ironically, after John dies and Jesus' reputation spreads, people—even Herod—deduce that Jesus is John raised from the dead.

Desert Ordeal

After his baptism, Jesus does not immediately plunge into his life's work (see Matthew 4:1–11; Mark 1:12–13; Luke 4:1–13). Instead the Spirit compels him to make a forty-day retreat in the wilderness, probably the Judean desert. This is reminiscent of three Old Testament periods: the Israelites' forty-year sojourn in the desert en route to the Promised Land, Moses' forty days on Mount Sinai before receiving the Law (Exodus 24:12–18), and the prophet Elisha's forty-day preparation for encountering God (1 Kings 19:8–13). No doubt these days were a form of "vision quest" for Jesus, during which he spent time listening to his Father, coming to a deeper realization of who he was and his vocation, and planning his strategy for carrying out his mission. Common belief at that time was that the wilderness was not only home to wild

John the Baptist, Prophet and Martyr

The Jews thought that the Old Testament prophet Elijah, who went to heaven in a chariot, would return before the end of the world. John was clothed in the same hairy garments Elijah wore, and he chastised King Herod just as Elijah had scolded kings. Naturally people concluded that John was Elijah. In fact, Jesus called him "Elijah who is to come" (Matthew 11:15) and praised him highly, saying, "Among those born of women no one has arisen greater than John the Baptist" (Matthew 11:11). And yet, John did not live to see Jesus' great acts of salvation as the followers of Jesus did. In this regard they were more blessed than John.

The Jewish historian Josephus recorded that Herod had John put to death to avoid an uprising. Mark and Matthew offer a different account (see Mark 6:17–29, Matthew 14:3–12). Herod had divorced his wife in order to marry Herodias, the wife of his brother Philip I, who was still alive. When John pointed out that this was unlawful, Herod imprisoned him. Although Herodias wanted John killed, Herod feared John and liked to hear him preach.

The woman outsmarts Herod. At Herod's birthday banquet, Herodias's daughter (named Salome in non-biblical sources) dances. Her performance is so pleasing that Herod, perhaps having had too much to drink, foolishly swears to give her whatever she asks, even if it is half his kingdom. Prompted by the vengeful Herodias, the daughter requests the head of John the Baptist on a platter. Herod keeps his oath before all his guests and John is beheaded. His disciples come and lay his body in a tomb. Then they tell Jesus what has happened. Matthew says that Jesus withdraws in a boat to a deserted place by himself. We can imagine Jesus' emotions: grief at losing a relative and a mentor, frustration at the circumstances of John's death, and dread at this foreshadowing of his own end. The Church commemorates the beheading of St. John on August 29.

Holy Land site...

Two miles west of Jericho is the Mountain of Temptation. Since the fifth century hermits lived on it in some thirty caves. Clinging precariously to the side of a cliff 200 yards above the ground is the hundred-foot-long Greek Orthodox Monastery of Temptation. As of 2005, only two monks remained there. A cable car takes visitors to the monastery, where they can view a stone where Jesus presumably sat.

beasts but to Satan. The Synoptic Gospels report that while Jesus was in the desert, the devil tempts him. Perhaps Satan wanted to size up his adversary.

In both Matthew and Luke the devil poses three temptations, but the last two are reversed. Jesus repels each temptation with a Scripture passage. First, when Jesus is starving from his forty-day fast, the devil tempts him to prove he is the Son of God by changing stones into loaves of bread. Jesus answers, "It is written, 'One does not live by bread alone but by every word that comes from the mouth of God.'" In the future Jesus would multiply loaves of bread and today provides us with living bread, but he refuses to work a miracle for himself just because he can.

Then, in Matthew, the devil takes Jesus to the pinnacle of the Temple. He urges Jesus to show he is the Son of God by throwing himself down and letting angels save him. The devil quotes Psalm 91, which says that God will send angels and "on their hands they will bear you up, so that you will not dash your foot against a stone." (Note that even the devil can quote Scripture!) Jesus counters with a Scripture verse of his own, "Do not put the Lord your God to the test."

Finally the devil takes Jesus up a high mountain and shows him all the kingdoms of the world. He, the Father of Lies, claims that he owns these and will give Jesus all of them if he will fall down and worship him. And Jesus responds by commanding Satan to depart, saying, "It is written, 'Worship the Lord your God, and serve only him.'" The devil leaves (Luke says "until an opportune time," meaning during the passion), and angels come and wait on Jesus. In clashing with Satan, Jesus emerges triumphant. Unlike the Israelites in the desert, Jesus is faithful to his call.

What are we to glean from this fantastic account? For one thing it shows that Jesus, like the rest of us human beings, was subject to temptation. More important, it presents Jesus as choosing the kind of Messiah he would be, one that corresponded to the will of the Father. Jesus would not be just a performer of flamboyant magic tricks. And to the chagrin of some of his followers, he would not be interested in political power, not even for the sake of restoring independence to Israel. Rather, he is a Messiah who conquers evil, whether it is personified in Satan or takes the form of sin, suffering, or death. For the rest of his life, Jesus would reject the false messiahship most Jews expected.

After this intensive training period, Jesus is ready to undertake his mission of launching the kingdom of God. He is not officially educated to be a Jewish teacher. His only credentials will be his miracles and the truth of his words. Jesus travels north to Galilee, where he begins to preach in synagogues, proclaiming the same message that John delivered: "Repent, for the kingdom of heaven has come near."

I came to bring fire to the earth and how I wish it were already kindled!

Jesus (Luke 12:49)

Unwelcome in Nazareth

Luke provides the most details about Jesus' first visit back home in Nazareth after the beginning of his public ministry (see Luke 4:16–30). On the Sabbath, Jesus goes to the synagogue for the service. Since any Jewish man over thirty can read Scripture and comment on it, Jesus stands up to be the lector, and someone hands him the scroll of the prophet Isaiah. Jesus unrolls the scroll until he finds and reads Isaiah 61:1:

Holy Land site...

South of Nazareth is Mount Precipice, where Jesus presumably was chased by his neighbors. Nearby on a hill stands the ruins of a church called Our Lady of Fright, where according to tradition Mary helplessly watched the attack on her son.

The Spirit of the Lord is upon me,
because he has anointed me
to bring good news to the poor.
He has sent me to proclaim release to the captives
and recovery of sight to the blind,
to let the oppressed go free,
to proclaim the year of the Lord's favor."

Jesus returns the scroll and sits down to teach about this passage. He begins with a mind-blowing statement: "Today this scripture has been fulfilled in your hearing." The passage from Isaiah that Jesus has chosen to read is his mission statement. He is the Christ, the anointed one sent to announce and bring about the kingdom of God, where the poor hear the good news and the captive, the blind, and the oppressed are freed from their afflictions. That is why he claims that the passage is being fulfilled that moment.

As Jesus preaches, everyone marvels at his words. After all, to them he is just Joseph's son. They know his family and the house where he grew up. They wonder why he hasn't worked miracles for them as he has in Capernaum. Perhaps they are already a little resentful of Jesus because, instead of remaining with his family and taking responsibility for them as a young Jewish man was expected to do, he had wandered off. Jesus remarks, "No prophet is accepted in the prophet's hometown." Then he gives examples of Old Testament prophets who helped foreigners rather than Israelites. This so enrages his neighbors that they rise up and chase him out of town to the edge of a cliff, intending to throw him off. But somehow he slips away from the mob. Imagine Jesus' hurt and frustration when the very people who should have been his most ardent fans try to kill him. These were the men with whom he went to school and for whom he made things in his carpenter's shop. Mark notes that Jesus is amazed at their lack of faith.

Unfortunately, the bad reception Jesus received in Nazareth is repeated in other towns. To his dismay, many people do not believe in him and his message. When Jesus' deeds of power do not result in repentance in the Jewish towns of Chorazin, Bethsaida, and Capernaum, he foretells that on judgment day pagan towns will be better off (see Matthew 11:22). Frustrated, Jesus laments over Jerusalem, using a touching, maternal image for God: "How often have I desired to gather your children together as a hen gathers her brood under her wings, and you were not willing" (Matthew 23:37). It is a case of unrequited love. In fact, when Jesus comes to Jerusalem and gazes at its Temple, its inhabitants, and its landscape—he cries. The Greek verb used here is not the one used for the silent crying Jesus did at Lazarus's death, but for sobbing. Jesus sadly predicts that enemies will crush that city to the ground and not leave one stone upon another because the people do not recognize their visitation from God (see Luke 19:41–44).

So, ironically and tragically, although Jesus' life's work was focused on Israel, most of his own people rejected him, their leaders arranged to eliminate him, and he died a failure in the eyes of the world. Only after Jesus rose from the dead and his message of love spread among the Gentiles would he be vindicated.

Holy Land site...

The Church of *Dominus Flevit* (The Lord Cries) on the Mount of Olives marks where Jesus wept over Jerusalem. In a chapel shaped like a tear, one window offers a wonderful view of the holy city.

trivial tidbit...

A Jewish legend is that the forty-day flood in the day of Noah was caused by God's tears on beholding the wickedness of human beings.

11 Master: The Disciples

Jesus was sometimes addressed as "Master." In ancient days a master was a teacher who had a following of students called *disciples*. It is clear from the beginning that Jesus wasn't an ordinary master. First, he spoke on his own authority. Second, the usual practice was that a disciple chose his or her master, but Jesus handpicked his closest disciples and summoned them. There's another difference. When disciples learn everything they can from a master, they move on to another master or become masters themselves. But being a disciple of Jesus was a lifelong engagement.

Twelve special male disciples of Jesus are called *apostles*, a word derived from the Greek word for "sent." An apostle is someone who has been called by God and sent to do God's work. Jesus himself is the apostle of the Father, for he explained, "I have not spoken on my own, but the Father who sent me has himself given me a commandment about what to say and what to speak" (John 12:49).

The Twelve

Jesus was a Jew, and as a Jew he would have been very aware of the symbolic importance of certain numbers. Most likely there were twelve apostles because there were twelve tribes of Israel, and the apostles were the foundation of the New Israel, the Church. Once Peter rather self-centeredly asks Jesus what they would receive for leaving everything and following him. Jesus replies that when the Son of Man is seated on his throne in glory they would also sit on twelve thrones and

quick quote...

G.K. Chesterton compared the call of the apostles to the call for jury duty. When a really important decision needs to be made in a trial, we choose not twelve geniuses but twelve ordinary people to make a jury.

judge the twelve tribes of Israel. He goes on to promise tremendous rewards to all who dedicate their lives to him: "Everyone who has left houses or brothers or sisters or father or mother or children or fields, for my name's sake will receive a hundredfold, and will inherit eternal life" (Matthew 19:29).

The apostles were the privileged ones who lived and worked with Jesus most closely during his public ministry. Day in and day out they walked with him from town to town, sharing meals and sleeping under the stars. They benefited from private instructions with Jesus, a kind of seminary experience, and were groomed to carry on his work after he died.

The Gospels, Mark in particular, present unpolished portraits of these quite ordinary men. For example, like children, the apostles actually argue over who is the greatest (see Mark 9:33–34). And the brothers James and John curry favor and have the gall to ask to be seated in places of honor in the kingdom, one on either side of Jesus (see Mark 10:35–37). Matthew's Gospel makes these two look much better by having their mother do the asking! Repeatedly, the apostles just don't get it. After the multiplication of loaves, the apostles forget to take bread for the next journey and misunderstand what Jesus has done. Like a teacher who explodes at having to explain something for the umpteenth time, Jesus shoots a barrage of nine questions at his men, all comparable to "Do you have eyes, and fail to see?" (Mark 8:18). The apostles are so obtuse that even at the Last Supper a frustrated Jesus chides, "Have I been with you all this time, Philip, and you still do not know me?" (John 14:9). When Jesus is captured, all the apostles except John abandon him. They flee for their lives and hide. Peter, the outspoken leader of the group, denies even knowing Jesus. Such unflattering pictures of the apostles indicate that the Gospels are authentic.

Jesus loved the apostles, as exasperating as they were. In the end the apostles become witnesses to Jesus' resurrection and are commissioned by him to carry on his teaching with the help of his Spirit. These envoys of his, except for Judas, were faithful to death. Tradition holds that all of the apostles were martyred for their faith but John, who died in exile. The pope and bishops of the Church today trace their authority to these apostles. And one of the four marks, or characteristics, of the Church is that it is "apostolic," which means that the Church and its beliefs stem from the apostles.

Lists of the apostles' names vary slightly in the Gospels. Traditionally the original apostles are Peter (Simon), James (the Greater), John, Andrew, Simon the Zealot, Philip, Nathanael (Bartholomew), Matthew (Levi), Thomas, James (the Lesser), Jude (Thaddeus), and Judas Iscariot. The Acts of the Apostles recounts that after the ascension Peter proposed to replace Judas with someone who had been with them from Jesus' baptism to his ascension, someone who could witness to Jesus' resurrection. Two men, Joseph (who was called Barsabbas and also known as Justus) and Matthias, were suggested. After praying for guidance, the apostles cast lots and Matthias was designated as the one to complete the twelve.

All of the apostles were from Galilee (and therefore spoke with the Galilean accent), except possibly Judas Iscariot. Most of them were fishermen; none

trivial tidbit...

The pope is said to save people by the "hook of the fisherman or the crook of the shepherd."

trivial tidbit...

James the Lesser might have been younger or shorter than James the Greater.

fyi...

In Rome, across the top of the façade of St. Peter's Basilica, stand nineteen-foot-tall statues of Christ the Redeemer, John the Baptist, and eleven apostles. Peter's statue is not there but on a pillar in front of the basilica, along with a matching giant statue of St. Paul. In 1968, Pope Paul VI announced that the Vatican feels that the bones found under the altar of St. Peter's Basilica thirty years earlier are actually those of Peter.

were scribes or Pharisees. The group includes at least two sets of brothers: Peter and Andrew, as well as James and John, whom Jesus nicknamed Sons of Thunder, perhaps because of their fiery temperaments. (Luke refers to Jude as "Jude of James," which suggests to some that Jude and James the Lesser were also brothers.) It's thought that all the apostles were married except John, the youngest. Three apostles formed an inner circle and were privy to certain key experiences: Peter, James, and John. This trio was with Jesus for the raising of the daughter of Jairus, the transfiguration, and the agony in the garden. The apostle who often spoke and acted for the others was Peter, now known as Prince of the Apostles. Jesus chose this spontaneous and impulsive man to lead in his place after he returned to heaven. So Simon the fisherman became Peter the first pope.

The Calling of the Twelve

The Gospels offer differing versions of Jesus calling the apostles (see John 1:35–51; Mark 1:16–20; Matthew 3:18–22; Luke 5:1–11). In John's Gospel, John the Baptist is with Andrew and another of his disciples (traditionally John) when Jesus passes by. John exclaims, "Look, here is the Lamb of God!" The two disciples walk behind Jesus until, sensing he is being followed, he turns and asks them, "What are you looking for?" Not knowing what else to say, they more or less blurt out, "Rabbi, where are you staying?" and he invites, "Come and see." They remain with him for the rest of the day, getting to know him. John the evangelist notes that it was four o'clock in the afternoon, a remembered detail that reveals how life-changing and precious the event was for the one who told the story.

Excited, Andrew wants to share the news of their discovery, first of all with his brother Simon. He tells Simon that they have found the Messiah, and he brings Simon to Jesus. Jesus looks at Simon, recognizes that he is to play a special role in his mission, and says, "You are Simon, son of John. You are to be called Cephas." This new name, which is *Peter* in Greek, means "rock," and therefore is fitting for a main foundation stone of Christ's Church.

The next day Jesus goes to Galilee where he comes across Philip and tells him, "Follow me." Then Philip finds Nathanael and declares that they have discovered the one Moses and the prophets wrote about, Jesus of Nazareth. Skeptical, Nathanael exclaims, "Can anything good come out of Nazareth?" And Philip invites, "Come and see." When Jesus notices Nathanael approaching, he remarks that he is an Israelite in whom there is no deceit. Surprised and puzzled, Nathanael inquires, "How do you know me?" Jesus replies that he saw him under the fig tree before Philip called him. We don't know what transpired under the fig tree, but Nathanael immediately professes that Jesus is the Son of God and King of Israel. Jesus promises that he will witness even greater things than Jesus seeing him under the tree, for Nathanael will see "the heavens opened and angels ascending and descending upon the Son of Man." This expression alludes to Jacob's dream in which he saw angels going up and down a ladder that connected earth to heaven. Jesus, our mediator, is like this ladder.

In Mark's and Matthew's Gospels, Jesus sees Peter

short prayer...

Jesus, for you I live.
Jesus, for you I die.
Jesus, I am yours in life and in death.

trivial tidbit...

Peter, Andrew, and Philip were all from Bethsaida, which means "house of fish."

and Andrew casting a net into the Sea of Galilee and calls out to them, "Follow me and I will make you fish for people." Immediately they leave their nets and follow him. The three walk along the shore and come to James and John, who are in their boat mending nets, and Jesus summons them too. They follow, leaving their father Zebedee and the hired men in the boat. No doubt these four apostles were already familiar with Jesus and decided that being his disciple was worth the sacrifice of family and what seems to have been a thriving business.

Luke combines this call of the fishermen with a miracle story. Jesus is at the Sea of Galilee, hemmed in by a crowd eager to hear him preach. Two boats float near the shore, and fishermen are by them, washing their nets after an unsuccessful night of fishing. Night fishing was best because then the fish were fresher for market. Jesus goes to Simon's boat, climbs into it, sits down, and asks Simon to take him a little from shore. When Simon does so, Jesus teaches the crowd from his boat, probably because sound carries better over water. This choice associates Jesus with Simon, the future head of his Church, which is often compared to an ark. After teaching, Jesus directs Simon to go out to deep water and lower his nets. Simon explains that they have fished all night in vain. Yet he obeys. They catch so many fish that the nets tear, and Simon and his crew must signal their partners in the other boat, James and John, for help. Soon both boats are so loaded with fish that they begin to sink. All are amazed. Simon, recognizing his unworthiness in the presence of divinity, falls to his knees before Jesus and says, "Go away from me, Lord, for I am a sinful man!"

Jesus replies, "Do not be afraid; from now on you will be catching people." The Greek word for *catch* used here implies "keeping people alive." In other words, bringing them into eternal life. When they land on shore, Simon, James, and John abandon everything—boats, nets, fish, and families—and follow Jesus.

The Synoptics all include the call of a tax collector, but Mark and Luke name him Levi, while Matthew dubs him Matthew. As Jesus is walking, he spots Levi sitting at the tax booth, where he is probably collecting taxes on goods passing through Capernaum. Jesus commands, "Follow me." Without hesitating, Levi makes the most drastic decision of his life and obeys Jesus. He immediately gets up and leaves his post behind. In his joy, Levi celebrates by throwing a party. He invites Jesus and his disciples to his house for a banquet, along with a large crowd of his own friends, who are fellow tax collectors and other people who would be considered sinners. In Jewish culture to dine with someone is a sign of friendship and bonding. Jesus overhears the Pharisees asking his disciples why he eats with tax collectors and sinners and chimes in. He, the divine physician, states that the sick, not the healthy need a physician and explains that he has come to call not the righteous but sinners (see Luke 5:30–32).

Tax collectors were despised by the Jews because they worked for the pagan Roman oppressors. They were excommunicated and not permitted in the synagogues or the Temple. Tax collectors were also held in contempt because they often charged exorbitant taxes and then pocketed a portion for themselves. Law-abiding Jews would not come into contact with tax collectors, much less dine with them.

The Primacy of Peter

One day, Jesus takes an opinion poll (see Matthew 16:13–19). He asks his disciples, "Who do people say that the Son of Man is?" They answer, "John the Baptist, Elijah, Jeremiah or one of the prophets." Then Jesus makes the question personal and asks, "Who

trivial tidbit...

Of all the apostles, perhaps St. Jude is invoked most often, for he is the patron of impossible cases. For example, entertainer Danny Thomas once promised St. Jude that if his prayers were answered he would build a shrine to him. As a result, Thomas founded the St. Jude's Children's Research Hospital in Memphis, Tennessee.

do you say that I am?" Simon declares, "You are the Messiah, the Son of the living God." Delighted, Jesus exclaims, "Blessed are you, Simon, son of Jonah!" He states that the Father has revealed this to Simon. Then Jesus renames Simon "Peter" (Rock) and says that he will build his Church on Peter, the rock, and that "the Gates of Hades" will not prevail against it. In other words, death will not overwhelm it. Jesus further promises to give Peter the keys of the kingdom of heaven. Whatever Peter binds on earth will be bound in heaven, and whatever he looses on earth will be loosed in heaven. In this way Jesus singles out and empowers Peter to lead his community of believers. Peter will guide and govern the Church as Jesus' representative.

The Other Disciples

Besides the Twelve, many other people followed Jesus. Jesus sends seventy of them ahead of him in pairs with the message, "The kingdom of God has come near you" (Luke 10:9). Seventy was the number of Moses' assistants. Also it was thought at the time that there were seventy nations in the world, so the number stands for universal outreach. Jesus viewed these seventy disciples as an advance guard to prepare the way for him by proclaiming the kingdom and curing the sick. The disciples find that they are able to replicate the marvels Jesus does. When the disciples return, they are elated at their success and their power even over Satan. Jesus tells them that he has given them this authority but they ought to rejoice instead that their names are written in heaven (see Luke 10:17–20). Jesus also points out to the disciples that they are blessed in seeing and hearing what prophets and kings desired to see and hear (Luke 10:24).

The Women

Luke informs us that along with the twelve who journeyed with Jesus were many women whom Jesus had cured and others (see Luke 8:1–3). Among them were Mary from Magdala; Joanna, who was the wife of Herod's steward and therefore well-to-do; and Susanna. These women supported Jesus and the apostles financially, so they must have had substantial means. This implies also that Jesus didn't have much personal money. The women probably also helped prepare the meals for Jesus and the apostles, as was the custom of the time.

Jesus showed great respect for women in an era when cultures viewed them as second-class citizens. For a man to speak to a woman in public was taboo, and being in contact with a woman during her period made a man ritually unclean. Jesus, as part of his new world vision, ignores these manmade customs and raises the status of women. He speaks openly with a Samaritan woman at a well and with a Canaanite woman. At a dinner party, he lets a sinful woman wipe her tears from his feet with her hair, and he mercifully spares a woman accused of adultery. When a woman with an issue of blood touches him, he doesn't rebuke her. He enjoys the friendship of the sisters Mary and Martha, and praises Mary for sitting at his feet like a disciple when in his culture only men were disciples. And, according to John's Gospel, Jesus favors Mary from Magdala by appearing to her before anyone else after his resurrection.

trivial tidbit...

After helping to organize the Church in Antioch, St. Peter founded the Church in Rome and became the leader there and was eventually martyred. Tradition says that he was crucified upside down at his request because he was not worthy to die as his Master had done. This connection with Peter is why Rome is at the heart of the Roman Church today.

During a drought in 1986, two brothers discovered a first-century boat sunk in the mud of the Sea of Galilee. Twenty-seven feet long and seven feet wide, the boat is made of fourteen kinds of wood pieced together from other boats. It is probably similar to the boats Jesus sailed in. After nine years of a chemical bath as a conservation treatment, the boat is now displayed in Israel along with artifacts found in it.

In a time when women were invisible, Jesus involves them in his ministry. Whereas his male disciples, except for John, desert and disown him at the crucifixion, some of the women disciples are faithful to the end. In the early Church, women held roles recognized as special vocations: widows, deaconesses, and consecrated virgins.

The Much Maligned Mary Magdalene

The only information the Gospels provide about Mary of Magdala's background is that Jesus cast seven devils from her. This was probably an expression for being healed from illness. However, people jumped to the conclusion that it meant Mary was a prostitute. In time, Mary Magdalene became confused with both Mary of Bethany and the woman who washed Jesus' feet with her tears and sometimes even with the woman caught in adultery. She was none of those. Instead, she was a faithful and strong disciple and a friend and financial supporter of Jesus.

Some Scripture scholars theorize that some in the early Church, who were threatened by Mary's close relationship with Jesus and probably of women in general, sullied her reputation. The Gospel of Mary, which was attributed to her, never made it into the canon of the Bible. However, the Church calls her a saint and celebrates her feast day on July 22.

Secret Followers

Many people, even leaders, believed in Jesus, but for fear of being put out of the synagogue they kept quiet about it (see John 12:42–43). Nicodemus, a Pharisee, stealthily comes to Jesus under cover of night and is treated to a private lesson. It includes the oft-quoted centerpiece of Christian faith: "For God so loved the world that he gave his only Son, so that everyone who believes in him may not perish but may have eternal life" (John 3:16). After Jesus dies, Nicodemus, together with Joseph of Arimathea, another secret disciple, buries his body.

Salt and Light

Jesus gave many motivational talks to his followers (see Matthew 5:13–16): "You are the salt of the earth; if salt has lost its taste, it is no longer good for anything. It is thrown out and trampled underfoot." Salt is an apt metaphor for a disciple because it is a spice as well as a preservative. Jesus goes on to say: "You are the light of the world. A city on a hill can't be hid. No one after lighting a lamp puts it under a bushel basket, but on the lampstand and it gives light to all in the house. In the same way, let your light shine before others, so that they may see your good works and give glory to your Father in heaven." In Mark and Luke, Jesus warns not to put your lamp under a jar (where the fire would go out) or a bed (which would catch fire from the oil lamp's flame)—ridiculous images that probably drew laughter. Relating salt and light to the disciples' mission stresses its importance, for as Pliny, a Roman writer, noted, "Nothing is more useful than salt or sunshine."

for your spiritual health...

Catholics pray the rosary, a circle of prayer beads. It is called "the Gospel on the beads" because while praying the Our Father, Hail Mary, and Glory Be, we meditate on events in Jesus' life. These mysteries are in groups of five called Joyful, Luminous, Sorrowful, and Glorious. You might become a stronger disciple by giving the rosary a larger role in your life. For details go to www.holyrosary.org.

quick quote...

The harvest is plentiful, but the laborers are few; therefore ask the Lord of the harvest to send out laborers into his harvest.

Jesus of Nazareth
(Matthew 9:37–38)

The Radical Character of Discipleship

Several people express the desire to follow Jesus, and he points out how complete their dedication needs to be and how urgent their mission is (see Matthew 10:16–39; Luke 9:57–62, 14:25–33). To one he warns, "Foxes have holes, and birds of the air have nests; but the Son of Man has nowhere to lay his head." To someone who wants to first bury his father, Jesus says, "Let the dead bury their dead; but as for you, go and proclaim the kingdom of God." This was a startling statement because for Jews burying the dead was a sacred duty, especially burying one's father. Jesus again uses exaggeration and shock value to make a point. To someone who first wants to say good-bye to his family, Jesus cautions, "No one who puts a hand to the plow and looks back is fit for the kingdom of God." Plowing fields in Palestine took concentration. If the farmer looked back, the furrows would not be straight.

Later Jesus says that being his disciple requires hating father, mother, wife, children, siblings, and even life. Matthew softens this harsh saying to loving Jesus more than family. But this too was an outrageous statement, for the Jews highly prized the family. All of these hyperboles are meant to illustrate the total commitment demanded of a disciple. Being a disciple is all-consuming. It requires prizing Jesus above everyone and everything else. The kingdom is an absolute priority.

Jesus' disciples are also expected to share his cup of suffering. He reveals that discipleship entails taking up the cross and following him. To the Jews *cross* was a metaphor for suffering even prior to Jesus' death.

Jesus warns his disciples, "If they have called the master of the house Beelzebul, how much more will they malign those of his household!" (Matthew 10:25). Christians are to die to self and die to the world in order to live forever. Clearly, Christianity is not for the fainthearted.

Disciples of Jesus are also to serve others. When James and John finagle for the places of honor, Jesus teaches his disciples that the greatest ruler is the one who is a servant or a slave (see Matthew 20:25–27). By serving others they imitate him, for Jesus says, "The Son of Man came not to be served but to serve, and to give his life a ransom for many" (see Mark 10:45). When Jesus proposes a child as a model, he repeats that the disciples must be servants. At the Last Supper he reinforces this lesson visually by washing their feet.

Jesus advises discerning carefully the decision to follow him. He compares weighing the demands of discipleship to two situations. He points out that someone building a tower first estimates the cost. This will prevent being mocked for having an incomplete building. Then Jesus uses the example of a king going out to wage war who in advance prudently considers whether he can win with ten thousand troops if the enemy has twenty thousand. If his troops are outnumbered two to one, they had better be skilled warriors with superior weapons and loads of courage.

In Mark's Gospel, a rich young man asks Jesus what he must do to inherit eternal life (see Mark 10:17–22). He tells Jesus that he already keeps the commandments. Jesus, who loves the young man, counsels, "Sell what you own, and give the money

trivial tidbit...

In Matthew's Gospel, the apostles and those on their way to faith address Jesus as "Lord," while outsiders and Judas address him as "teacher" ("rabbi").

quick quote...

The thought that at any moment I may lose Jesus distresses me in a way that I cannot explain; only a soul that loves Jesus sincerely can understand what this means.

St. Pio of Pietrelcino
(Padre Pio)

to the poor…then come, follow me" (Mark 10:21). The man, unable to part with all his possessions, leaves dejected. No doubt Jesus too was sad. There is a heartening tradition that the young man had second thoughts, returned, and became a follower of Jesus.

Despite the challenges of believing in him, Jesus has attracted millions of followers, many of whom have given their lives for him. They all rely on Jesus' promise, "Those who find their life will lose it, and those who lose their life for my sake will find it" (Matthew 10:39). Echoing St. Paul, they exclaim, "To me, living is Christ and dying is gain" (Philippians 1:22).

12 Healer: Power and Signs

Every once in a while an event occurs that science cannot explain. For instance, a life-threatening tumor suddenly vanishes, baffling doctors. We exclaim, "It's a miracle!" In the Synoptic Gospels miracles by Jesus are deeds that show his power, whereas in John's Gospel, which relates only seven miracles, they are aptly called "signs." When Jesus works miracles, they are signs of God's kingdom breaking into our world. Jesus explodes the parameters of the present reality.

Thomas Jefferson, who did not believe in miracles, created his own gospel by cutting and pasting together mainly the ethical passages in the Gospels. In his book, which is preserved in the Smithsonian, Jefferson eliminated the miracles, including the resurrection. But you can't separate Jesus from his miracles. He was known as a wonderworker, but during his time other wonderworkers roamed Israel. For example, Honi the Circle-Drawer, who lived in the first century B.C., controlled rain. Hanina ben Dosa, who was born about 20 A.D. and therefore was younger than Jesus, healed at a distance and expelled demons. In addition, magicians of the time apparently could do fantastic things, and some people even practiced "black" magic, working through Satan's power. But no one performed as many or as many different kinds of miracles as Jesus. For him the extraordinary was ordinary, the impossible was possible. He worked a burst of miracles. Moreover, his miracles were not wrought by prayer but at his own command.

trivial tidbit...

Jewish literature tells about Honi the Circle-Drawer. It's said that when Israel needed rain, Honi drew a circle in the dust, stood in it, and told God that he wouldn't move until rain was sent. Then it rained—harder or softer according to Honi's requests.

The kind of miracles Jesus worked meshed with his mission on earth, namely, to break evil's stranglehold on the human race. His miracles show him conquering all forms of evil and the effects of sin: disease, possession, and, yes, even death. No doubt at each miracle Jesus was as jubilant as the person who benefited from it. The supernatural works of Jesus can be classified as miracles of healing, of exorcism, over death, and over nature.

Miracle Motives

Jesus also stands head and shoulders above other miracle workers because of his motives. He did not work wonders to punish people or to gain popularity or profit. Nor did he work them to cause a sensation. Jesus didn't perform miracles to satisfy curiosity. When Herod asked Jesus to entertain him with tricks, he didn't comply. And when the Pharisees asked him for a sign, Jesus "sighed deeply in his spirit" and walked away (see Mark 8:12). Although he could have, Jesus didn't work miracles for himself, for example to provide food or even to save his life. No, Jesus worked miracles primarily to make it clear that the kingdom of God had come. His miracles were protests against the misery that sin had brought to the human race.

Miracles are the hallmark of the promised Messiah. As far as we know, John the Baptist worked no miracles. When two of his disciples ask Jesus, "Are you the one who is to come, or are we to wait for another?" (Luke 7:20), Jesus, having just wrapped up a session of cures, answers, "Go and tell John what you have seen and heard: the blind receive their sight, the lame walk, the lepers are cleansed, the deaf hear, the dead are raised, the poor have good news brought to them" (Luke 7:22). Such works were listed by the prophet Isaiah foretelling how God would come to save (see Isaiah 35:5–6).

In addition, most of Jesus' miracles were done out of compassion. The Revised English Bible translates *compassion* as, "His heart went out to them." Usually Jesus used his remarkable power in response to someone's plea: "Have pity;" "Lord, if you wish, you can make me clean;" "Lord, save us;" and "Lord, that I may see." Jesus' miracles reveal that our God is a loving and saving God. Often a miracle was the result of a person's faith in Jesus, and he called attention to this. In Nazareth where he is amazed at their unbelief, "he could do no deed of power there" (Mark 6:5–6). Jesus also used miracles as a teaching device, as when he worked them on the Sabbath to illustrate that love of neighbor supersedes the keeping of the law. In John's Gospel, Jesus' miracles are recounted in order to manifest his divinity.

Jesus' first miracle according to John was providing wine at a wedding. His last miracle, which occurred at his arrest, was healing the severed ear of Malchus, the servant of the high priest.

Miracles of Healing

In Jesus' time the practice of medicine was primitive. Healers used words and saliva to cure diseases. Sometimes Jesus used the same methods, but his cures were instantaneous. What's more amazing, people were cured merely by touching his clothes. Jesus' healings attracted people from other lands. His power resulted in hordes of sick people around him. Once "he told his disciples to have a boat ready for him because of the crowd, so that they would not crush him; for he had cured many, so that all who had diseases pressed upon him to touch him" (Mark 3:9–10). In those

trivial tidbit...

Peter's wife must have joined him later in his missionary work, for Paul wrote, "Do we not have the right to be accompanied by a believing wife, as do the rest of the apostles, and the brothers of the Lord, and Cephas [Peter]?" (1 Corinthians 9:5)

days there were no doctors or hospitals. Consequently there were many sick, and they mingled with society. The exceptions were the victims of leprosy, who could not come within six feet of others by law. Here are some of the miracles of healing:

✦ *Peter's Mother-in-Law* (see Matthew 8:14–15; Mark 1:29–31; Luke 4:38–39). In Mark and Luke the first person Jesus heals of a disease is a woman and the relative of a friend. One Sabbath after teaching and performing an exorcism in the synagogue at Capernaum, Jesus goes to Peter's house, perhaps to eat and relax. Peter's mother-in-law is in bed with a high fever. Jesus simply takes the woman's hand and, like the personal touch of a caring doctor, helps her up. The fever leaves. In Luke, Jesus "rebukes" the fever, as though speaking to a demon. The woman gets up and waits on the group. (Matthew says she "serves Jesus," using an expression that implies she became a disciple.) The woman's action proves that her healing is immediate and complete. It also makes her a model of service for Christians everywhere who have been healed by Christ.

✦ *One Leper* (see Matthew 8:1–4; Mark 1:40–45; Luke 5:12–15). One day a leper shows great faith. Ignoring the law that he must keep his distance, he kneels in homage before Jesus and states with absolute faith, "Lord, if you choose, you can make me clean." Jesus actually stretches out his hand and touches the leper, without fear of contagion and disregarding the fact that his action makes him unclean, that is, unfit to enter the Temple. Jesus replies, "I do choose. Be clean." (In one translation Jesus answers, "Of course,

Leprosy, Symbol of Sin

In the Bible the word *leprosy* encompasses not only the dread skin disease we know today as Hanson's disease but other skin diseases too. According to Jewish law, lepers had to live outside of town, wear torn clothes, have disheveled hair, and cry, "Unclean! Unclean" to warn people of their approach. Lepers were isolated and shunned not only for fear of contagion, but because their sickness was viewed as the result of sin. Deprived of family, friends, and work, a leper suffered both the psychological pain and the horror of the condition. This often involved deformity and decay of body parts, making leprosy a picture of sin.

Mosaic law required that if cured, lepers had to be approved by the priests and pay something before they were reinstated. Jesus often reaches out to these social outcasts and heals them, just as in the sacrament of Penance he heals us from the sin that disfigures us and cuts us off from God and others.

Leprosy is now called Hansen's disease, after the man who in 1873 discovered the bacterium that causes it. This disease affects the peripheral nerves and upper respiratory tract. Its symptom is skin lesions. Today drugs and the World Health Organization are working to eliminate leprosy, but it's on the rise in the United States.

quick quote...

If we Christians lived as we should, nonbelievers would be more astonished at our lives than at miracles.

St. John Chrysostom

trivial tidbit...

Mark says that Jesus is "moved with pity," on seeing the leper, but early manuscripts have "moved with anger." It's possible that Jesus was angry on coming face-to-face with sickness, one of the ugly effects sin has on the human race.

I want to!") The leper is immediately cured. His sores disappear, and feeling returns to his hands and feet. He will no longer be a pariah. Jesus orders the cured man not to tell anyone, possibly because miracles can hinder his main mission. Jesus also directs the man to show himself to a priest and offer the prescribed gift. Notice that Jesus complies with Jewish rules and respects the priests. The cured leper, deliriously happy now, can't keep quiet about his marvelous experience. He disobeys Jesus, and word of the cure spreads. What Jesus had hoped to avoid happens. So many people search him out that he can no longer walk about freely.

✥ *Ten Lepers* (see Luke 17:11–19). One day as Jesus enters a village, he is approached by ten lepers, maybe men, women, and children. They stay at a distance and call to him, "Jesus, Master! Have mercy on us." Jesus doesn't do anything outwardly to cure them. He merely tells them to show themselves to the priests. The lepers obey and depart from Jesus, perhaps wondering why he didn't cure them. Only as they walk along do they realize that they are healed. Their dignity has been restored. One cured leper, a Samaritan (an enemy of the Jews), stops, turns around, and hurries back to Jesus, loudly praising God. He falls at Jesus' feet and thanks him. But Jesus focuses on the missing nine and asks plaintively: "Were not ten made clean? Where are the other nine? Has no one but this foreigner returned to give praise to God?" Jesus has done a tremendous favor for these people, something better than handing them a million dollars. Yet they don't even say thank you. Then Jesus tells the former leper, "Get up and go on your way. Your faith has made you well." The story illustrates that Jesus, like the rest of us, appreciates gratitude. The excitement of the cured nine lepers or their eagerness to be declared clean is no excuse for their bad manners.

for your spiritual health...

List three things that God has done for you recently. Thank God for each one.

◆ *The Deaf Hear* (see Mark 7:31). Once Jesus makes a foray into Decapolis (a region of ten cities), and people bring him a deaf man who has a speech impediment. They beg Jesus to lay a hand on him. Jesus considerately draws the man away from the crowd. In the manner of healers of the time, Jesus puts his fingers into the man's ears. Then he spits and touches the man's tongue. Jesus looks to the sky, sighs, and utters, *"Ephphatha"* ("be opened"). Instantly the man can hear and speaks clearly. Jesus orders everyone not to tell about it, but the astounded people enthusiastically spread the word and sing the praises of Jesus. Today the *"Ephphatha"* is an optional part of our baptismal rite, during which the celebrant prays that Jesus may open the elect's ears to receive his word.

◆ *Long-distance Cures for Gentiles* (see Matthew 8:5–13; Luke 7:1–10; John 4:46–54). One day in Capernaum a Roman centurion comes personally to Jesus (in Luke he sends messengers). A centurion is an army official who oversees a hundred men. This centurion states that his servant boy, who is dear to him, is paralyzed and in great pain. Jews speak on the soldier's behalf, explaining to Jesus that this Roman is a worthy pagan who has been good to them, even building a synagogue. Jesus is impressed with the man's faith and goodness and agrees to come and cure the boy. The centurion, aware that entering his Gentile house would render Jesus ritually unclean, responds with the

big book search...

There is a hypothesis that the four friends who carried the paralyzed man were Peter, Andrew, James, and John.

act of faith that has been incorporated into the Mass as a prayer before Communion: "I am not worthy to have you enter under my roof. Only say the word and my servant will be healed." The centurion believes that Jesus has boundless power that doesn't depend on his even being present. Respectfully the centurion then elaborates that he understands authority, for soldiers and servants under him do his bidding. At this, Jesus exclaims that he has not found such faith in Israel. He says that Gentiles will enter the kingdom but that those who were first called will be left out in the dark. Jesus sends the centurion home saying, "You have believed, so let this be done for you." The servant is healed. John tells a similar story that takes place in Cana. A royal official implores Jesus to heal his sick son, who is at death's door. (The Greek word for "servant" can also be translated "boy" or "son.") Jesus instructs him to go and his son will live. The man trusts Jesus and leaves. On the way home the anxious father is met by his servants. They give him the news that the fever left the boy at 1:00 p.m., exactly the time Jesus declared that the boy would live.

◆ *A Little Help from Friends* (see Matthew 9:1–8; Mark 2:1–12; Luke 5:17–26). While Jesus is teaching at home in Capernaum, a paralyzed man on a mat is carried to him by four friends hoping for a cure. Because of the crowd blocking the door, the determined friends carry the man up the stairs to the roof. They break through it, making a good-sized opening, and lower the man to Jesus (a colorful detail omitted by Matthew). Imagine the noise and the dirt and thatch falling on the crowd in the house—and the dismay of the house's owner, possibly Peter! Naturally Jesus stops talking and watches, probably with an amused expression on his face. When the man is safely settled on the floor, Jesus, impressed by his faith and that of his friends, says to him, "Courage, child, your sins are forgiven." The Jewish teachers are aghast. To them this is blasphemy because only God can forgive sins. But Jesus, who is a mind reader, turns to them and asks, "Why do you think such things in your heart? Which is easier to say, 'Your sins are forgiven' or to say 'Pick up your mat and walk'? To show that I have authority on earth to forgive sins…" Jesus turns back to the man and says, "Rise, pick up your mat and walk." To everyone's astonishment the paralyzed man stands, lifts up the mat, makes his way through the crowd, and walks home. Jesus, the divine physician, validates his power to heal invisible wounds by a visible healing.

for your spiritual health…

Call to mind your sick friends and relatives. Ask Jesus to cure them now, in your daily prayers and in your prayer at Mass.

❖ *A Poolside Healing* (see John 5:1–18). John tells a similar story. In Jerusalem near the Sheep Gate, through which sheep for the Temple sacrifices were driven, there was a pool much like the healing waters of Lourdes. It was called Bethesda, which means House of Mercy. On its five porches people with various disabilities—the blind, the lame, and the paralyzed—waited for the water to move, or bubble up like a healing spring. (A later addition to the Gospel says that the water was stirred by an angel.) After the movement, the first one to enter the water was cured. One man there had been paralyzed for thirty-eight years—since before Jesus was born. Jesus knows this and asks the man if he really wants to be cured,

trivial tidbit...

Some scholars have questioned the historicity of the cure of the paralytic by the Temple, because no pool with five porches had been found in Jerusalem. But in 1871, archaeologists uncovered just such a pool, and it was verified as authentic in 1956.

a question with an obvious answer. Perhaps Jesus is wondering if the man is doing enough to help himself. The paralytic explains that when the water is stirred, there's no one to help him get to the pool. As he is slowly making his way to the pool, maybe dragging himself along with his arms, someone always beats him into the water. At best, the man is hoping that Jesus will carry him to the pool. However, Jesus commands the paralytic, "Rise, take up your mat and walk." The man obeys Jesus, even though Jesus is a stranger to him. To his amazement and great joy, the paralyzed man discovers he is healed, but he apparently isn't even curious enough to find out who his benefactor is. As he walks along, the man is stopped by Pharisees who admonish him for carrying the mat on the Sabbath. In defense, the cured man says that his healer told him to. When the Pharisees ask who the healer was, the man can't identify him. Neither can the cured man point out Jesus, who has slipped away because a crowd has gathered. Later Jesus goes to the healed man at the Temple and warns him, "See, you have been made well. Do not sin any more so that nothing worse may happen to you." The man asks his name and reports back to the Pharisees. They begin to persecute Jesus for healing on the Sabbath. Jesus explains, "My Father is at work...so I am at work." This statement in which Jesus claims equality with God only makes the Pharisees more intent on killing him.

◆ *Man with a Withered Hand* (Matthew 12:9–14; Mark 3:1–6; Luke 6:6–11). Jesus worked several healing miracles on the Sabbath, at least the seven that are recorded in the Gospels. Because Jewish prescriptions forbade many kinds of work on the Sabbath, Jesus' Sabbath cures irked the Jewish leaders. Jesus tried to get them to see that love of neighbor takes precedence over their manmade laws. One Sabbath, when Jesus is teaching in a synagogue, the Jewish leaders watch closely to see if they can accuse him of anything. Jesus doesn't disappoint them. A man there has a withered right hand, a condition that prevents him from earning a living. Jesus calls the man forth. He challenges the leaders, "Is it lawful to do good or to do harm on the Sabbath, to save life or to kill?" The Jewish leaders know the answer, but they are obstinately silent. In Matthew's account Jesus asks, "Suppose one of you has only one sheep and it falls into a pit on the Sabbath; will you not lay hold of it and lift it out? How much more valuable is a human being than a sheep!" Mark notes that Jesus looks all around at the Jews with anger and is deeply saddened at their hard hearts, their lack of compassion. Jesus then directs the man to stretch out his hand. When the man obeys, his hand instantly fills out and becomes normal again. Ironically, Jesus hasn't done any work to effect this cure. He has only spoken. Regardless, this marvelous kind deed of Jesus causes the Pharisees to discuss putting him to death.

quick quote...

I have a great need for Christ; I have a great Christ for my need.

Charles Spurgeon

◆ *The Stooped Woman* (see Luke 13:10–17). Another time when Jesus is teaching in the synagogue, a woman is present who for eighteen years has been so sick that she is bent over. Jesus notices her and calls her to him. She hobbles over and he says, "Woman, you are free of your infirmity." He lays his hands on her, a gesture of healing and blessing, and she straightens

trivial tidbit...

Originally the word *hypocrite* was a technical term for a Greek actor, someone who play acts.

up. Unlike the men who have been cured on the Sabbath, the woman responds by praising God. The chief of the synagogue overlooks Jesus' "crime" of touching a woman but orders the crowd not to come for cures on the Sabbath. Jesus retorts, "You hypocrites!" He proceeds to point out to the Jewish leaders that they don't hesitate to untie their ox or donkey and lead it to water on the Sabbath. He asks why then this woman, a daughter of Abraham, should not be set free from her bondage. At that, his opponents are still upset, but everyone else rejoices in his wonderful acts. Jesus has made the woman stand tall and straight not only by healing her, but by referring to her relationship with the patriarch Abraham. The leaders, on the other hand, are now bowed down in shame.

◆ *Man with Dropsy* (see Luke 14:1–6). Another time on a Sabbath Jesus goes to dine at the house of a leading Pharisee. As usual his opponents watch him like a hawk, ready to pounce on the least infraction of the law. Suddenly in front of Jesus stands a man who has dropsy, or edema, a condition in which excess fluid makes the arms and legs swell. We don't know if the man was a Pharisee, a guest, or an onlooker. Some commentators think that the man was planted there as a trap. Jesus quizzes the scribes and Pharisees, "Is it lawful to cure people on the Sabbath, or not?" No one answers. If the opponents say yes, they will have no case against Jesus. If they say no, they will appear to have no heart. So Jesus heals the man and sends him away, which suggests he hadn't been a guest. Then Jesus questions the Pharisees, "If one of you has a child or an ox that has fallen into a well, will you not immediately pull it out on a Sabbath day?" Again there is silence. The Jewish leaders, swelled up with self-importance, know that Jesus' reasoning is logical and right, but stubbornly they won't admit it.

for your spiritual health...

On the Sabbath Jesus made people whole. Sanctify your Sundays by reaching out to help others in a special way on this day.

◆ *The Blind Beggar* (see Matthew 20:29–34; Mark 10:46–52; Luke 18:35–43). As Jesus leaves Jericho, a crowd follows. Bartimaeus, a blind beggar sitting at the roadside, hears the commotion and asks what's happening. When he finds out that Jesus of Nazareth is passing by, he has hope for being saved from his world of darkness. He has heard stories of what Jesus has done for others and believes. Seizing the moment before it disappears, the blind man boldly shouts, "Jesus, Son of David, have pity on me." People order the man to be quiet. This could be because his yelling is aggravating or because it is dangerous: *Son of David* is a messianic title that could invite trouble. But the bystanders' efforts to muzzle Bartimaeus are in vain. He cries out even louder. Over the rumble of the crowd Jesus hears the voice of the needy one who calls to him. He stops in his tracks and tells people to bring the beggar to him. Bartimaeus throws off his cloak so that nothing will drag him down, even though this is one of his few possessions. And he jumps up, something blind people don't usually do. Then, no doubt with others guiding him, Bartimaeus staggers over to Jesus, who asks him, "What do you want me to do for you?" It's obvious what Bartimaeus needs, but Jesus wants him to articulate it, perhaps so he can take some responsibility for his own healing. "Master, I want to see," Bartimaeus replies. Jesus simply says, "Go your way; your faith has saved you." Instantly

trivial tidbit...

Siloam means "Sent," which is also a name for Jesus. The blind man washing in "Sent" prefigures our baptismal washing in Jesus. We are all "sent forth" from Mass at the Dismissal to be Christ to the world.

Bartimaeus can see, and he beholds the face of Jesus. Someone has remarked that it was love at first sight. For Bartimaeus disobeys. Instead of going his way, he follows Jesus, the Way, down the road. This blind man is the only cured person named in the Gospels. He is also the only one who calls Jesus by his given name. In Matthew's account of this story, by the way, there are two blind men.

◆ *Another Blind Man* (see Mark 8:22–26). Mark tells of a blind man brought to Jesus in Bethsaida. People who have faith in Jesus earnestly beg him to touch the blind man. Jesus does. He takes the man by the hand and carefully leads him out of the village to where the cure will be more private. He puts saliva on the man's eyes and lays his hands on him, both customary healing practices at that time. Then Jesus asks, "Do you see anything?" The man answers, "I see people looking like trees and walking." Jesus lays hands on his eyes again, and this time the man opens his eyes to twenty-twenty vision. Jesus tells him to go straight home without going to the village. This two-stage cure is peculiar. It is said to be a metaphor for peoples' gradual realization of Christ as Messiah. The fact that it takes two tries for Jesus to work this miracle attests to the story's authenticity. The evangelist wouldn't make up a story where Jesus' power isn't immediately effective: This must be the way this miracle happened.

◆ *The Man Born Blind* (see John 9:1–41). Right after Jesus escapes being stoned in the Temple, he is walking along and passes another blind man. The disciples ask whose sin caused the blindness, the blind man's or his parents'. (It doesn't cross their minds that the man couldn't have sinned before he was born!) Their question springs from the common belief that sickness is a punishment for sin. Jesus replies that the man is blind not because of sin but "so that God's works may be revealed in him." Then he proclaims, "As long as I am in the world, I am the light of the world," and proceeds to bring light to the blind man, even though the man hasn't asked for his help. Jesus spits on the ground and makes clay, which he smears on the blind man's eyes. He instructs the man to wash in the Pool of Siloam. St. Irenaeus taught that by using saliva and clay here, Jesus was making it clear that this was the same hand of God through which Adam was formed from clay.

When the man returns, he can see for the first time in his life. This is the only Gospel story about the cure of someone with a congenital sickness or disability. On seeing the man walking about, his neighbors and others debate whether or not he is the blind beggar, and he insists he is. When they ask how he was cured, the former blind man relates how Jesus gave him sight. The people take the man to the Pharisees. On hearing about the miracle, the Pharisees are not too pleased because although it is the Sabbath, Jesus has not only worked by making clay but has "worked" a cure. Some Pharisees deduce that Jesus is not from God because he did not observe the Sabbath. Others argue that a sinful man couldn't work such signs. When the Pharisees ask the once-blind man for his opinion, he claims that Jesus is a prophet. The Pharisees summon the man's parents to verify that their son had been blind. The parents do so, but when asked

Holy Land site...

In 2005, it was announced that what seems to be the original Pool of Siloam had been uncovered. It is 225 feet long, a trapezoid and has three sets of steps going into it. It is near to and lower than the pool that has previously been accepted as the biblical one, a pool which the Byzantines rebuilt in the fifth century.

Miracles are not tall stories but deep stories.

William Barclay

how he came to see, they sidestep the question and merely say, "Ask him." They do this because the Pharisees had decreed that anyone who claimed that Jesus was the Messiah would be put out of the synagogue. This was dire punishment because the cast out person would also be shunned socially. The Pharisees again call for the cured blind man and categorically state that they know Jesus is a sinner. The man shoots back that he doesn't know that, but he does know that he was blind and now he can see. When asked to repeat his story, he sarcastically taunts, "Why? Do you want to become his disciples too?" The man vehemently insists that Jesus had to be from God to do such an unheard of thing. Clearly the man, in addition to physical sight, has gained spiritual sight. The haughty Pharisees retort, "You were born entirely in sins, and are you trying to teach us?" And they drive him out.

Hearing what happened, Jesus considerately seeks out the cured man, who is now banished from the synagogue. On finding the man, Jesus evokes an act of faith from him, and the man worships Jesus. Then Jesus declares that he came into the world that the blind may see, and that those who see might become blind. Overhearing this, the Pharisees take these words personally, as they were meant to be taken, and inquire, "Surely we're not blind, are we?" Jesus answers, "If you were blind, you would not have sinned. But now that you say, 'We see,' your sin remains." The Pharisees refuse to see what is right before their eyes.

◆ *A Canaanite Woman Matching Wits with Jesus* (see Matthew 15:21–28; Mark 7:24–30). Jesus never denied a healing to anyone, even when he was exhausted. In one case though, a woman had to become a nuisance and wheedle it out of him. In the Gentile district of Tyre, a Canaanite (Greek) woman accosts Jesus and pleads, "Have pity on me, Lord, Son of David! My daughter is tormented by a demon." The mother kneels at Jesus' feet in homage and supplication, but he doesn't answer her. The disciples, annoyed because she keeps calling out, ask Jesus to get rid of her. Jesus tells the Gentile woman that he has been sent only to the lost sheep of Israel. He says to her, "Let the children be fed first, for it is not fair to take the children's food and throw it to the dogs." Undaunted, the Greek woman retorts, "Sir, even the dogs under the table eat the children's crumbs." Jesus, impressed by the woman's spunk and her staunch faith in him, exclaims, "O woman, great is your faith! Let it be done for you as you wish." The mother returns home to find her child lying in bed, free from the demon from the hour Jesus spoke with her. Jesus has given this "beggar" more than crumbs. Referring to the woman as a dog doesn't sound very Christian. The Jews had a habit of referring to Gentiles as dogs. It was a derogatory term. For example, Jesus warns his followers not to give what is holy to dogs or throw their pearls before swine (see Matthew 7:6). Some scholars have softened Jesus' word to the woman by explaining that it is more accurately translated as "puppies." The most important thing about this particular miracle is that it taught *Jesus* something. Apparently at the time he encounters this woman, Jesus

Christ the Redeemer of the Andes is a monument 12,572 feet above sea level between Argentina and Chile. A bishop had it built as a reminder of peace when the two countries were disputing boundaries. A woman proposed moving the statue to the Andes as a symbol of unity if peace were attained. In 1902, the two countries resolved their problems. The statue was moved in pieces by train and then mule. It was unveiled in 1904 amid gun salutes by both armies. Christ, standing on a globe, faces the border. He holds a large cross, and his hand is raised in blessing.

One storytelling technique that Mark uses is "the sandwich." He inserts a related or contrasting story within another one. The raising of Jairus' daughter (the two slices of bread) with the healing of the woman who is bleeding (the meat) is an example. The girl has lived as long as the woman has suffered, twelve years. Jesus brings them both back to life.

understands his mission to be limited to the Jews. The faith of the Canaanite woman helps him to change his mind. Through his interactions with Gentiles like her, Jesus allows his vision of this mission to be stretched. In doing so, he lays the foundation for the spread of his Gospel throughout the entire world.

❖ *A Stolen Cure* (see Matthew 9:20–22; Mark 5:25–34; Luke 8:43–48). As Jesus is on his way to heal Jairus' twelve-year-old daughter, one woman in the crowd around him has suffered from constant menstrual bleeding for twelve years. Because women were considered unclean during their periods, this woman had been isolated all this time. No one, not even her family, could touch her, and she wasn't allowed to enter the synagogue or Temple. (Mark says that she has suffered greatly under the hands of many physicians, but the doctor Luke omits that comment!) Despite spending all her money on physicians, the woman has only grown worse. The desperate woman sneaks up behind Jesus and touches the fringe of his cloak, thinking that this contact alone will heal her. She's right. Immediately her bleeding stops (except in Matthew where she is healed only after Jesus speaks to her). Jesus asks, "Who touched me?" Everyone denies doing it, and Peter, probably rolling his eyes, points out that Jesus is surrounded by people all pressing on him. Looking about, Jesus insists that someone has touched him. He declares, "I noticed that power had gone out from me." Finally the woman emerges and falls down before Jesus. She is trembling with a mix of joy and fear: joy at being healed and fear because by touching Jesus she has made him unclean. The woman explains why she has touched him and how she has been healed. Jesus lovingly acknowledges her faith. He says, "Take heart, daughter; your faith has made you well. Go in peace." Jesus' clothes were not magic. It was the woman's faith that gave her back her life.

trivial tidbit...

In the apocryphal *Acts of Pilate*, the cured woman is named Bernice. Another ancient writing says she is a Gentile from Caesarea Philippi.

13 Wonderworker: Power over Satan, Nature, and Death

Mel Gibson's movie, *The Passion of the Christ*, presents two striking images that show Jesus' power over the forces of evil. In the beginning, a sandaled foot dramatically trounces on the head of a serpent. This image stems from the book of Genesis, where God promises that a woman's offspring, namely Jesus, will crush Satan's head with his heel (see Genesis 3:15). After the crucifixion, the film has another memorable image that depicts Satan screaming like a maniac in rage and torment at being conquered by Jesus. The Gospels too show Jesus' power over Satan, someone who literally casts the devil out of people.

At the time of Jesus, demon possession was widespread over various cultures. Exorcists routinely cast out demons, who were thought to cause diseases in people. Undoubtedly because of this mindset, some miracles Jesus worked that were considered exorcisms were actually cures of sicknesses and conditions that have since been identified, such as epilepsy and psychosomatic diseases. However, the fact remains that evil exists, and some of Jesus' "exorcisms" were really just that—the casting out of the personification of evil we call Satan or the devil. These miracles are signs that Jesus has power to break the hold of evil over the human

trivial tidbit...

In the Catholic Church, exorcisms may still be performed by a priest appointed for this ministry. In 1999, the ritual for exorcisms was revised. Most people referred for exorcisms turn out to have psychiatric problems. The rite of Baptism includes a form of exorcism in which the person being baptized rejects Satan and sin.

for your spiritual health...

In time of temptation call on Jesus, the consummate exorcist, for help in overcoming evil.

race. Through his cross and resurrection, Jesus has in effect exorcized the whole world. Here are a few of the exorcisms Jesus performed:

◆ *The First Exorcism* (see Mark 1:21–27; Luke 4:31–36). Not by chance is an exorcism the first miracle related in Mark and Luke. Jesus has come to free the world from the sin and the dark forces that have enslaved human beings from the first days of their existence. He will put to end the demon's power and restore God's order. Jesus is teaching in the synagogue in Capernaum on the Sabbath when suddenly a possessed man cries out, "What have you to do with us, Jesus of Nazareth? Have you come to destroy us? I know who you are, the Holy One of God." Unlike the Jewish leaders, Satan apparently knows Jesus' identity and fears him. Jesus rebukes the demon, "Be silent and come out of him!" The demon convulses the man, gives a loud cry, and departs. No rituals or magic formulas are needed; Jesus' word is sufficient. The people are amazed that unclean spirits obey Jesus.

◆ *The Possessed Boy: A Lesson in Faith* (see Matthew 17:14–20; Mark 9:14–29; Luke 9:37–43). One miracle presented as an exorcism sounds very much like a cure of epilepsy. After the disciples fail to heal a boy, his father tells Jesus that his son is possessed by a spirit that casts him down so that he falls into fire and water. The boy foams at the mouth, grinds his teeth, and becomes rigid. He is deaf and mute also, so he can't call for help when he is in distress. Jesus laments, "O faithless generation. How long will I be with you?" and has the boy brought to him. In Mark, the boy has a convulsion and Jesus asks how long this has been going on. The desperate father replies, "Since childhood," and pleads, "If you can do anything, have compassion on us and help us." Jesus answers, "If you can! Everything is possible to the one who has faith." The man then voices a prayer that is worth our repeating: "I do believe, help my unbelief." Jesus commands the demon to leave and never return, and just like that the boy is cured. In Matthew, when the disciples ask why they couldn't expel the demon, Jesus answers, "Because of your little faith." In Mark, Jesus replies, "This kind is only cast out through prayer." Some versions add "and fasting."

◆ *From Possessed Man to Evangelizer* (see Matthew 8:28–34; Mark 5:1–20; Luke 8:26–39). One miracle story resembles a colorful folktale. Jesus and the disciples cross the Sea of Galilee and disembark on the land of the pagan Gadarenes. A naked man possessed by demons for a long time approaches them. (Typically, Matthew says two men.) The demoniac has lived in burial caves, where the Jews believed evil spirits dwelt. This contact with the dead has made the man ritually unclean. His life is a nightmare. Day and night he howls and gashes himself with stones. When people restrain him with chains, he bursts out of them. As soon as Jesus gets out of the boat, the man appears and addresses him saying, "Jesus, Son of the Most High God, what do you want of me?" Calling someone by name was a strategy for having power over them. Jesus demands, "Come out of the man, evil spirit!" The man responds, "I beg you, don't punish me." Then Jesus, turning the tables, asks the demon's name, and the answer is "Legion," which means

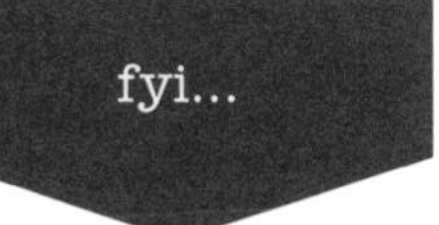

Demons apparently sensed that Jesus was somehow related to God. They feared him and left at his first command. Jesus didn't use the paraphernalia and long, complex rites that other exorcists do. His apostles too had success over demons in his name. When they joyfully report this, Jesus says, "I saw Satan fall from heaven like a flash of lightning" (Luke 10:17–20).

quick quote...

If you had faith the size of a mustard seed, you could say to this mulberry tree, "Be uprooted and planted in the sea," and it would obey you.

Jesus of Nazareth
(Luke 17:6)

6,000 Roman troops. This is either the storyteller's jab at the Romans or a way to convey that there are many demons. The spirit asks to be sent not back into the abyss but into the herd of 2,000 some pigs nearby. Jews regarded pigs as unclean and also called the Romans pigs, so surely they told this story with great delight. "Go," Jesus orders, and the demons go out of the man and enter the pigs. The herd, crazed and squealing, stampedes, falls down the cliff into the lake and is drowned, which would have been quite a spectacle! The swineherds, having witnessed the destruction of the pigs they were guarding, frantically run to town and relay the amazing occurrence. The villagers come and see the man clothed and sitting at the feet of Jesus like a disciple and in his right mind. They are frightened by Jesus' power and no doubt upset at the loss of their livestock. So they ask Jesus to leave! He obliges. As Jesus and the apostles get into the boat, the cured man begs to go with him, but Jesus sends him home as a missionary to tell his Gentile friends what God has done for him. In Decapolis (the Ten Cities) the man recounts the story of his healing, a story that some wit quipped was history's first record of devilled ham!

Power over Nature

Because we Catholics believe that Jesus is God, it is no surprise to us that nature bows to his commands. In the Gospels we see Jesus suspending the physical laws that ordinarily govern the universe—specifically wind, water, bread, and fish. These miracles over nature serve as a sign of a kingdom in which God overturns the present reality. They attest to Jesus' divinity, but like his other miracles they are called forth not by Jesus' desire to flaunt his powers but by people's need:

◆ *Water into Wine* (see John 2:1–11). According to John's Gospel, the first miracle that Jesus performed occurred at a wedding feast, and it was his mother, Mary, who catapulted him into his public ministry. John notes that it is the "third day," a symbolic time that signals a *theophany* (revelation of God). Mary is at the wedding in Cana of Galilee, perhaps assisting with the festivities. Jesus and his disciples are guests too, singing and dancing with everyone else. Their presence shows that Jesus enjoyed celebrations and mingling with people. In fact, on this occasion he proves to be literally the life of the party. Mary notices that the wine has run out, a humiliating gaffe that could spoil memories of the wedding for the family from then on. Turning to her son, Mary simply states, "They have no wine," counting on him to do something. Apparently Jesus is not expecting to go public yet. Taken by surprise, he responds somewhat coldly, "Woman, what concern is that to you or to me? My hour has not yet come." But being a good son, Jesus changes his plans and accedes to his mother's wishes. He would again address Mary as "Woman" at the crucifixion, the prelude to his actual hour of glorification. (This is a formal title of respect, not a put-down as it might sound today.) Mary knows her son well. Despite his reluctance, she orders the servants, "Do whatever he tells you," something she still says to us today. In the house near the door stand six stone 20- or 30-gallon jars used for ceremonial washings before

quick quote...

All wonder to see water turned into wine. Every day the earth's moisture, being drawn into the root of a vine, is turned by the grape into wine, and no one wonders.

St. Gregory the Great

trivial tidbit...

Dionysius, the Greek god of wine, also changed water into wine. His feast was January 6. On this day, the early Eastern Church chose to celebrate the Epiphany, focusing on the manifestation of the miracle at Cana.

Holy Land site...

In Cana there is a "wedding" church that Franciscans built over Byzantine ruins in 1881. People propose marriage and renew wedding vows there. On its floor is a fourth-century mosaic, and a replica of the water jar is displayed in a crypt. Across the street there is a Greek Orthodox "wedding" church.

and after meals. Jesus tells the servants to fill the jars with water, and they pour water into them up to the brim. Then Jesus orders the servants to take some to the chief steward. They are dumbfounded as they pour some of the water that is now wine into a cup and offer it to the chief steward. On tasting it, the steward calls the bridegroom over and declares, "Everyone serves the good wine first, and the inferior wine after the guests have become drunk. But you have kept the good wine until now." The bridegroom, of course, doesn't know what he is talking about or that he himself has been spared a great embarrassment. The bliss of his wedding celebration is unspoiled, thanks to Jesus and Mary. Notice that not only has Jesus supplied excellent wine, but wine in abundance—160 to 180 gallons, the largest six-pack in history! Isn't that typical of God's lavish love? John notes that this feat revealed Jesus' glory (a synonym for God) and led his disciples to believe in him.

❖ *Calming the Storm* (see Matthew 8:23–27; Mark 4:35–41; Luke 8:22–25). To the Jews, the sea was a hostile place of chaos where evil creatures and monsters lurked. In the psalms, God controls the seas. By mastering the sea, Jesus manifests that he possesses divine power that is able to conquer evil. One evening Jesus has his disciples cross the Sea of Galilee. It's a temperamental sea, subject to sudden gales and storms because of its lowness and location between mountains. Jesus, bone-tired from a full day's work, is asleep on a cushion in the back of the boat when without warning a storm arises. Soon in the dark, waves toss the boat like a toy and begin to swamp

The Meaning of the Cana Miracle

The miracle of transformation that occurred at the wedding feast at Cana teaches us that Jesus is changing the old ritual-bound religion, symbolized by the plain water used for purification. He is inaugurating a new era symbolized by plentiful, exceptional wine, a drink that is intoxicating and therefore a fitting sign of ecstasy and fullness of life. The changing of water into wine also paves the way for the greater miracle that Jesus works today: changing wine into his sacred blood. And, it foreshadows the greatest miracle: Through his death and resurrection Jesus changes hell into heaven for us.

The Cana miracle signals the kingdom of heaven for several reasons. First, a prophecy linked abundant wine to the restoration of David's kingdom: "The mountains shall drip sweet wine, and all the hills shall flow with it" (Amos 9:13). Second, in his parables Jesus often speaks of God's kingdom of heaven in terms of a wedding feast. Similarly, in the Book of Revelation those in heaven cry out, "The marriage of the Lamb has come, and his bride has made herself ready" (Revelation 19:7). Third, John introduces the miracle with "on the third day," a hint of the greatest miracle, the resurrection of Jesus, that also took place on the third day. Scholars reflecting on the six jars of wine point out that six is less than the perfect number seven, suggesting that the fullness of the kingdom has not yet arrived.

The Church identifies the wedding at Cana as the basis for the sacrament of Matrimony in which God unites and blesses a couple. She also views the miracle as confirming Mary's role as our intercessor with God. We ask Mary to pray for us, confident that her son still will not refuse her.

short prayer...

Most Sacred Heart of Jesus, I place my trust in you!

it. The disciples panic. They wake Jesus and shout, "Lord, save us. We are perishing!" (Mark bluntly puts, "Don't you care that we're perishing?") Jesus rebukes the wind, just as evil spirits are "rebuked," and says, "Peace, be still" to the raging sea. There's dead calm. The miracle is a complete one. Jesus chides the disciples for being afraid and having little faith. They should know that he cares for them even when he seems to be asleep. Awed by the power of Jesus, the disciples ask, "Who then is this, that even the wind and the sea obey him?" This miracle shows Jesus' humanity in being so exhausted that he can sleep in the midst of a terrific storm. It also hints at the day when in the sleep of death Jesus will be raised in the ultimate triumph over evil.

❖ *Walking on Water* (see Matthew 14:22–33; Mark 6:45–52; John 6:16–21). Jesus again shows divine power over water by walking on the Sea of Galilee. For the Jewish people, this miracle calls to mind the Exodus, when God saved them by leading them safely through the parted Reed Sea. It also echoes a psalm: "When the waters saw you, they were afraid; the very deep trembled.... Your way was through the sea, your path through the mighty waters; yet your footprints were unseen" (Psalm 77:16, 19). This time Jesus is not with the disciples as they cross the sea at night. A strong wind creates huge waves, and for three or four miles the disciples are straining at the oars. Early in the morning, however, they see Jesus walking on the sea towards them. John says that he meant to pass them. However, thinking that they're seeing a ghost, the apostles cry out in terror. At once Jesus calms their fears by saying, "Take heart, it is I; do not be afraid." Then he boards the boat and the winds die down. In John's version, the disciples intend to take Jesus into the boat with them, but in a flash they find themselves at the shore, another eerie experience. Matthew alone adds an event that highlights Peter, the future leader of the Church. On hearing the "ghost" identifying himself as Jesus, Peter impulsively responds with a creative and daring request: "If it is you, command me to come to you on the water." Jesus humors Peter and invites, "Come." So Peter clambers out of the boat and starts walking on top of the turbulent water toward Jesus, as though the sea were solid. The water supports Peter until he loses his nerve. He starts to sink into the sea and cries out, "Lord, save me!" Jesus catches hold of Peter and scolds, "O you of little faith; why did you doubt?" The two walk over the water to the boat, climb into it, and the wind stops. Awed by what they've just witnessed, the disciples worship Jesus saying, "Truly you are the Son of God." Over and over Jesus expresses his wish that his followers would trust his care for them. This is a good reminder to us, especially in times of crisis when we are called to "walk on water."

trivial tidbit...

In the feeding of the 4,000 there are seven baskets of leftovers. It's thought that these represent the Gentiles, because there were seven nations in Canaan according to Acts 13:19. This theory is supported by the story of the Canaanite woman, when she tells Jesus that even the dogs, the Jewish image for Gentiles, eat the crumbs from their master's table. Also, Mark's multiplication miracle takes place in Decapolis, Gentile territory.

❖ *Bread Mass-Produced* (see Matthew 14:13–21; Mark 6:30–44; Luke 9:10–17; John 6:1–15). Throngs follow Jesus, drawn by his miracles. At least once, when the people were tired and Jesus was concerned that they might collapse on the way home, he provides a meal for all of them. This miracle, with variations, is the only one found in all four Gospels. In fact, there are six accounts of the multiplication of bread

Holy Land site...

In the town of Tagbha, two miles west of Capernaum, is a church that supposedly marks the site of the multiplication of loaves and fishes. In the floor under the altar there is a rock on which, according to legend, Jesus set the five loaves and two fish. In front of the rock, a fourth-century mosaic depicts a basket of loaves with a fish on either side.

and fish. All the Gospels contain stories of the feeding of five thousand, and Matthew and Mark have an additional story of the feeding of four thousand (see Matthew 15:32–39, Mark 8:1–10). These large totals don't even take into account the women and children present. In some versions of the story, Jesus distributes the meal, while in others the apostles carry out this task. Mark includes the detail that the people were neatly seated in rows on the green grass in groups of fifty or a hundred. He also notes that Jesus is motivated by compassion to perform this miracle because in his eyes the people were like sheep without a shepherd. The following is John's description of the grand picnic. After teaching a crowd of five thousand, Jesus asks Philip, "Where are we to get bread for all of them?" Philip, probably wondering if Jesus is out of his mind, states the obvious: Not even six months' wages would buy enough to give each person a little. Then Andrew, trying to be helpful, points out that a boy has five barley loaves and two fish, but he realizes that this is nothing for so many people. Jesus has the disciples make the crowd sit on the grass. Then Jesus takes the loaves from the boy, says the Jewish prayer of thanks, and distributes the bread. He does the same for the fish. People are able to help themselves to as much as they want. After all the people have eaten, Jesus directs the disciples to gather the leftover bread so nothing is wasted. When they do so, the remnants of the meal fill twelve baskets, presumably the wicker baskets the apostles each carried as they accompanied Jesus. Just as Jesus provided abundant wine at the wedding, here he multiplied food in an extravagant way—so like God with all of creation!

The Bread of Life

The multiplication of bread recalls the Exodus when God fed his people with manna in the desert (Exodus 16:4–18), as well as the time the prophet Elisha multiplied bread for a hundred people (2 Kings 4:42). On the other hand, it foreshadows the Eucharist, the bread in which Jesus nourishes millions of people all over the world. In describing both of Jesus' miraculous meals, the evangelists use the same four words: *took, blessed, broke,* and *gave*.

In John's Gospel the miracle of the loaves and fishes is followed up the next day by a lengthy discourse in which Jesus drops a bombshell. He claims, "I am the living bread that came down from heaven. Whoever eats of this bread will live forever; and the bread that I will give for the life of the world is my flesh.... Those who eat my flesh and drink my blood have eternal life, and I will raise them up on the last day" (John 6:51–54). For Jews, blood was taboo; they drained their meat of blood. To them this saying of Jesus sounds like cannibalism and is repulsive. Many of Jesus' followers could not accept this difficult teaching, the mystery of the Eucharist, and left Jesus at that point. This desertion doesn't make him retract or alter his message. Discouraged, Jesus asks the twelve apostles if they too will abandon him. His spirits are lifted when Peter answers with a beautiful act of faith: "Lord, to whom can we go? You have the words of eternal life. We have come to believe and know that you are the Holy One of God" (John 6:68–69). For Catholics, of course, we believe in the "real presence" of Jesus in the consecrated bread and wine. For us, this is not a symbol or a metaphor but a reality based on faith in the promise of Jesus.

big book search...

Read the six accounts of the multiplication of loaves, noting the differences. See Matthew 14:13–21, 15:32–39; Mark 6:30–44, 8:1–10; Luke 9:10–17; John 6:1–15.

The people conclude that Jesus is a prophet and are about to make him king, but Jesus, realizing this, goes off alone up the mountain. Palaces and armies are not part of his agenda.

◆ *Peter's Fish* (see Matthew 17:24–27). An intriguing miracle is linked to the Temple tax of one-half shekel (two-days' wages) that every Jew had to pay. Tax collectors approach Peter and ask, "Does your master not pay the Temple tax?" Peter replies, "Yes, he does." He goes to their home in Capernaum, presumably to get money. But before Peter can report what happened, Jesus asks whether kings collect taxes from their children or from others. The answer is obvious, because Rome didn't tax its own citizens. When Peter says, "From others," Jesus agrees that children are free, implying that he, the Son of the Father, as well as the disciples, who are citizens of God's kingdom, are not obliged to pay the Temple tax. But so as not to give scandal, Jesus, no doubt with a twinkle in his eye, sends Peter, the fisherman, to the sea to fish and take the first fish he hooks. In its mouth, he will find a coin to pay the tax for both of them. This coin could have been a Greek stater, which was worth a shekel. The Gospel doesn't go on to describe Peter catching this money-bearing fish, so strictly speaking this isn't a miracle story. Some scholars conjecture that this pericope is a "fish tale" that Matthew told his Jewish Christian readers to teach that, despite the conflict between Jewish leaders and Christians, they ought to pay the Temple tax. Those who take this story literally see it as a lesson on avoiding scandal, another demonstration of Jesus' power, and a glimpse of the playful side of Jesus.

◆ *A Cursed Fig Tree* (see Matthew 21:18–22; Mark 11:12–14, 20–21). One day when Jesus is hungry, he searches a fig tree for fruit. Because it is not the season for figs, he doesn't find any among the leaves. Jesus says to the tree, "May no one ever eat fruit from you again!" The next day as Jesus and the disciples are walking along, they see that the fig tree is withered to its roots. Peter exclaims, "Rabbi, look! The fig tree that you cursed has withered." This strange incident can be interpreted as prophetic action. The point made is that Israel is like a fruitless tree for not believing in Jesus. Its fate will be the destruction of Jerusalem. Some commentators, however, think that the story is not an actual occurrence but a transformation of the parable about the fig tree, especially because it shows Jesus acting irrationally in expecting figs out of season and because it depicts him destroying something. In Matthew's Gospel, the fig tree withers immediately, not the next day, and Jesus uses the incident to teach that with faith people can even make mountains throw themselves into the sea.

trivial tidbit...

Today in some restaurants in Israel you'll find Peter's fish on the menu. Tradition holds that both the fish bearing the coin and the fish that were multiplied by Jesus were tilapia.

Power over Death

The most horrible consequence of sin is death, the end of life. Yet Jesus was willing to subjugate himself to death in order to conquer it for us. Because through his death and resurrection he won eternal life for us, now our death is merely a door to a fuller life. The Gospels offer three accounts where Jesus demonstrates his power over death by bringing people back to life. In each case, the death is premature and Jesus shows compassion for the survivors. These resuscitations foreshadow his resurrection in which Jesus is not

quick quote...

The mystery of Christ runs the risk of being disbelieved precisely because it is so incredibly wonderful.

St. Cyril of Alexander

merely resuscitated but rises to a new, glorified life:

◆ *A Widow's Only Son* (see Luke 7:11–17). As Jesus and a crowd approach the gates of Nain, they encounter a large funeral procession leaving the city. It's likely that this procession included friends and relatives as well as hired mourners and musicians. A young man, the only son of a widow, is being buried. Without a man to support her, this woman is left in dire straits. Perhaps seeing her makes Jesus think of how his own mother will soon be enduring his death and grieving for him. Full of pity, Jesus tells the woman, "Do not weep." But the words are not just customary words of sympathy to comfort her. He has a grand surprise in store. Jesus walks up to the bier, a board on which the corpse lies. He puts his hand on the bier, which automatically makes him unclean in the eyes of Jewish law. The bearers stop in their tracks. Addressing the corpse, Jesus commands, "Young man, I say to you, rise." The man wrapped in burial strips sits up and begins talking. What he says is left to our imagination. Jesus hands him to his mother. Jesus has restored her son and her life to her. The witnesses are understandably frightened to see a dead man suddenly come to life. They praise God and exclaim, "A great prophet is risen among us!" Naturally, news of this miracle spreads rapidly. No one asked Jesus to work this miracle. Neither did he demand faith of the grieving mother. The resuscitation was the result of sheer compassion.

◆ *The Daughter of Jairus* (see Matthew 9:18–26; Mark 5:21–43; Luke 8:40–56). One day while Jesus is teaching a crowd, Jairus, a synagogue official, falls at his feet and pleads with him to come to his house, for his twelve-year-old daughter is dying. (In Matthew and Luke she is already dead.) Jairus begs Jesus to lay his hands on her. Jesus stops what he's doing and goes, followed by many people. The procession halts briefly when a sick woman touches his clothes and is healed. During this delay, Jairus must have been panicking. Sure enough, his worst fear is realized. Messengers arrive and report to Jairus that his little girl has died. There's no need to trouble Jesus. But Jesus encourages the distraught father, "Do not fear. Only believe," and so they walk on. At Jairus' home, the funeral is already in full swing. The flute players are playing their high-pitched sad tunes, and the mourners are wailing loudly to express the family's sorrow. Jesus lets only Peter, James, John, and the girl's parents enter the house with him. He tells the professional mourners that the child is not dead but sleeping. They laugh at him, for they're positive that she is dead, and he puts them out of the house. Then Jesus goes to the mat on the ground where the girl lies, pale and still. Jesus holds the dead girl's hand, an act that makes him unclean, and commands in Aramaic, "*Talitha cum*" ("Little girl, get up"). Immediately she begins breathing and color returns to her cheeks. She opens her eyes to behold the face of Jesus, gets up, and walks around the room. Jesus tells the parents to give their daughter something to eat. Possibly this is because of the common notion that ghosts don't eat, and Jesus wanted to prove that the girl was alive. It could also be that Jesus merely was concerned that after her illness she was hungry. As for the mocking mourners—Jesus has the last laugh.

trivial tidbit...

The Aramaic words preserved in the story of Jairus' daughter do not agree grammatically. *Talitha* is feminine while *cum* is masculine. This suggests that Jesus spoke the language of the street rather than scholarly language.

Holy Land site...

In Bethany there is an opening on the street that leads to what purportedly is Lazarus's tomb. One can enter, carefully go down twenty-two winding stone steps, and then stoop and waddle through a small entrance to the inner chamber. A church nearby commemorates Jesus bringing Lazarus back to life. On the wall behind the altar, where the bread of life is broken, are inscribed the words, "I am the resurrection and the life."

❖ *Lazarus, Called Forth* (see John 11:1–44). Jesus loved Mary, Martha, and their brother Lazarus, who lived in Bethany. He often stayed with them. One day Jesus receives a message from the sisters, who obviously were aware of his travel plans. The message was, "Lord, he whom you love is ill." The friends don't ask him for help but simply state the fact, trusting Jesus to do something. Jesus explains that the illness doesn't lead to death but is for the glory of God and the Son of God. Curiously, he waits two days before he says to his disciples, "Let's go to Judea." They resist because some people there had just tried to stone Jesus, but in the end Thomas loyally says, "Let us go that we may die with him." Why did Jesus delay? It could be so that Lazarus is unquestionably dead, making the miracle more significant. Imagine, however, the anxiety, disappointment, and hurt of Mary, Martha, and Lazarus himself when Jesus didn't come at once. When Jesus finally arrives at Bethany, Lazarus has died and has already been in the tomb four days. Martha goes out to meet Jesus and gently chides, "If you had been here, my brother would not have died." Then she voices hope in Jesus by saying, "But even now I know that God will give you whatever you ask." Jesus replies, "Your brother will rise." Misconstruing Jesus' incredible meaning, Martha says, "I know he will rise on the last day." Then Jesus makes the consoling promise, "I am the resurrection and the life. Those who believe in me, even if they die, will live." Martha boldly professes, "I believe you are the Messiah, the Son of God, the one coming into the world." Martha returns home to Mary and tells her that Jesus is calling for her. Mary springs up and goes to

Jesus, followed by mourners. Kneeling before Jesus, she too remarks, "If you had been here, my brother would not have died." Mary and the others are weeping, probably audibly in the oriental fashion. Jesus is distressed and, according to one translation, shudders with sacred horror. He asks, "Where have you laid him?" When they answer, "Come and see," Jesus too bursts into tears, so that some people comment, "See how he loved him!" Others wonder why Jesus, who cured the blind, didn't help his friend. And we might ask why Jesus would cry if he knew he was going to bring Lazarus back to life. Perhaps he was weeping in sympathy with Martha and Mary and all of us who grieve because of death, or maybe he realized that even though his friend Lazarus would come back from the end, he would die again later, because that is the human condition. At the cave where Lazarus was buried, Jesus is again greatly disturbed. He orders, "Take away the stone," but practical Martha points out that there will be a stench. Jesus explains to her that belief will lead to God's glory. Therefore, the stone over the entrance is removed, and Jesus looks skyward and prays a prayer of confidence: "Father, I thank you for having heard me. I know that you always hear me, but I have said this for the sake of the crowd that they may believe that you have sent me." Then in a great voice loud enough to awaken the dead, Jesus commands, "Lazarus, come out!" Lazarus walks out of the tomb, wrapped in the linen burial cloths. Jesus orders, "Unbind him and let him go." The Gospel doesn't record people's reaction to this astounding event, but we can imagine the looks on their faces, as well as the joy in the hearts of Mary, Martha, and Lazarus.

trivial tidbit...

It's been said with humor that Jesus had to call Lazarus by name when he said, "Come out," or else all the dead buried there would have come out at his command!

quick quote...

In Jesus all broken lines unite; in him all scattered sounds are gathered into harmony.

Phillip Brooks

Belief in Miracles

It is undoubtedly true that some miracle accounts have been embroidered by the Gospel tellers and modified by the use of literary devices, but the sheer number of them testifies to the fact that Jesus did superhuman things. Mark's Gospel is 40% miracle stories. In addition to some thirty-seven stories of individual miracles, the Gospels, especially Matthew, also contain sweeping statements such as, "And all who came to him were healed" (Matthew 5:24). This suggests that Jesus worked hundreds of miracles that were not recorded. To those who wonder if Jesus really did work miracles and continues to work them today, John LaFarge answers, "For those who believe in God, no explanation is necessary. For those who do not, no explanation is possible."

14 Wisdom: Teachings of Jesus

In Hebrew Scriptures, wisdom—which is the activity of God—is personified. Her qualities, which are catalogued in the Wisdom of Solomon 7:23, are the characteristics of God. Wisdom, *Sophia* in Greek, existed before the beginning of the earth and was present at creation. She is a street preacher crying out to people to live rightly (see Proverbs 8:1–7). She beckons to us, "Come, eat of my bread and drink of the wine I have mixed" (Proverbs 9:5). It's easy to see how Christians quickly identified Jesus with this Wisdom because his sound, beautiful teachings reveal God completely and perfectly, reflecting the best in human knowledge and understanding of the human heart. People marvel at Jesus' wisdom. The Pharisees ask, "Where did he get his knowledge? He is not educated." To draw the crowds and the disciples that Jesus did, his words and his teaching style had to be electrifying. Jewish historian Joseph Kleusner wrote, "In his ethical code here is a sublimity, distinctiveness with originality in form unparalleled in any other Hebrew ethical code: nor is there any parallel in the remarkable art of his parables."

How Jesus Taught

Today we thrive on competition, as shown by the popularity of sports events and contests like spelling bees and "American Idol." In Jesus' day, people were

big book search...

Read Proverbs 8:22–36 and compare it to John 1:1–5. Which do you like better? Why?

entertained by verbal contests. Consequently, Jesus and the religious leaders often engage in sometimes heated dialogues, sparring with words. Not only does Jesus prove himself the champion in debates and awe bystanders, but through this process of argumentation he makes known some of his central teachings. To make his lessons understandable and memorable, Jesus draws lessons from nature and objects familiar to his audience, moving them from the known to the unknown. He teaches with sayings, proverbs, parables, and stories.

Besides teaching by words, Jesus teaches by example. Looking at him, we see what it means to love God and others, to do the Father's will, to forgive, to have a heart for the poor and marginalized, and to sacrifice self for others. He is the Law of God in the form of flesh and blood.

The Authority of Jesus

After the resurrection, on the day Jesus was to ascend to heaven, he spoke to his apostles and claimed, "All authority in heaven and on earth has been given to me" (Matthew 28:18). During his ministry, Jesus spoke with real authority. Historically, Jewish prophets introduced their statements with "Thus saith the Lord." And teachers usually cited Hebrew Scriptures or other teachers to back up what they were saying. Not Jesus. He spoke on his own authority, declaring often, "I say to you." In addition, some seventy-five times in the Gospels Jesus prefaces a statement with "Amen." This is unusual, because other teachers at the time concluded their statements with "Amen," much as we do prayers today. Moreover, in John, Jesus doubles the word and says, "Amen. Amen." This was a signal that an especially authoritative pronouncement would follow. It can be translated "Let me firmly assure you."

In the Synoptic Gospels, when the Pharisees ask Jesus the source of his authority, he shrewdly makes a deal with them: If they answer his question, he will answer theirs. Then he asks, "On whose authority did John the Baptist speak?" His opponents are stymied. If they say, "God's," Jesus will ask why then didn't they accept John's teaching. But if they don't say, "God's," the people, who regarded John as a prophet, will turn on them. When the Pharisees lamely respond, "We don't know," Jesus states that then he will not tell them by what authority he taught.

In John's Gospel, the source of Jesus' authority is his oneness with the Father. Jesus explains, "Whatever the Father does, the Son does likewise. The Father loves the Son and shows him all that he himself is doing.... The Father judges no one but has given all judgment to the Son.... Anyone who does not honor the Son does not honor the Father who sent him" (John 5:19–23). Later, Jesus says, "My teaching is not mine but his who sent me" (John 7:16). The following are a few of Jesus' main teachings:

Men need only trust in Christ's teaching and obey it, and there will be peace on earth.

Leo Tolstoy

❖ *Radical Trust in Providence* (see Matthew 6:25–33; Luke 12:22–31). In one of the most beautiful passages of Scripture, Jesus turns to creation to teach about God's loving care for us. He assigns God two roles ordinarily associated with mothers—feeding and clothing—in order to show us we need not worry or be preoccupied about what to eat or drink or wear. We

The *Didache* reveals that the early Christians prayed the Our Father three times a day. Today we pray it during the Eucharist, in the Divine Office, in the Rosary, and at other public and private prayer times. In the *Catechism of the Catholic Church*, the fourth and last part, which is on prayer, has an extensive analysis of the Our Father.

can picture Jesus walking along with his disciples and gesturing to the birds and the wildflowers. He says, "Look at the birds. They neither sow nor reap nor gather into barns, and yet your heavenly Father feeds them. Are you not of more value than they? Can any of you by worrying add a single hour to your life?" Then he offers a second example: "And why do you worry about clothing? Consider the lilies of the field. They neither toil nor spin, yet even Solomon in all his glory was not clothed like one of these." Jesus then points out that our heavenly Father knows what we need. Our "social security" plan is to strive for God's kingdom and his righteousness. Then all things will be given us as well. At another time Jesus, no doubt with a smile lighting his face, says, "Are not five sparrows sold for two pennies? Yet not one of them is forgotten in God's sight. But even the hairs of your head are all counted. Do not be afraid; you are of more value than many sparrows" (Luke 12:6–7). What an unusual and touching image of God Jesus presents: someone who knows us so well and loves us so much that he counts the hairs on our head! Faith and worry are incompatible.

✦ *Lessons on How to Pray* (see Matthew 6:5–8, 7:7–11; Luke 11:9–13). Because Jesus was the Son of God, prayer was his native language. He teaches us this language. Jesus reasons with the crowd of parents, "If your child asks for a fish will you give a snake, or if your child asks for an egg, will you give a scorpion?" Of course not. Jesus then says that if we who are evil, in other words marked by sin, give our children good gifts, how much more will the heavenly Father give us good things. In Luke instead of "good things" Jesus says, "the Holy Spirit." Jesus also teaches that we are not to make a show of our prayerfulness to impress people. Rather we are to go into our room, shut the door, and pray to our Father. He also cautions us not to "heap up empty phrases as the Gentiles do."

◆ *The Lord's Prayer* (see Matthew 6:9–13; Luke 11:1–4). One day the apostles asked Jesus to teach them how to pray the way John taught his disciples. Jesus gave us the Lord's Prayer, also called the Our Father (*Pater Noster* in Latin). The Lord's Prayer is so precious to Christians that during the Rite of Christian Initiation for Adults, there is a special rite in which it is handed to the catechumens as a gift. In this prayer, Jesus allows us to approach the Lord and Master of the Universe as Father. This implies that we have an intimate relationship with God, that we come to God with a childlike trust, and that God is always accessible to us. It's significant that in this prayer we use the first person plural, approaching God as his family, not as an individual. The Our Father has seven petitions. The first three are related to God; we ask that his supreme reign be recognized by all. The last four petitions are for our needs: that we have daily sustenance, forgiveness of sins, freedom from temptation, and deliverance from evil. The prayer is a thoroughly Jewish prayer, with parallels in other Jewish writings. Both Matthew and Luke include versions of the Our Father prayer. The one we pray today is based on the longer version found in Matthew. However, Catholics do not add the doxology at the end of Matthew's version, which is not found in Luke or the earliest

Holy Land site...

The Church of the Pater Noster (Our Father) was built on the Mount of Olives in 1856 by Aurelia Bossie, Princess de la Tour d'Auvergne. She invited Carmelite sisters to live next to it. Excavations revealed a grotto thought to be where Jesus prayed. Today at the church at least 139 plaques are displayed, each with the Our Father in a different language including Braille, Tagalog, and Ojibway.

To clasp one's hands in prayer is the beginning of an uprising against the disorder of the world.

Karl Barth

versions of Matthew's Gospel. It has been added in the Mass, however, after the priest prays a prayer that elaborates on the last line of the Our Father. Here is Matthew's version of the Our Father: *Our Father in heaven, hallowed be your name. Your kingdom come. Your will be done, on earth as it is in heaven. Give us this day our daily bread. And forgive us our debts, as we also have forgiven our debtors. And do not bring us to the time of trial, but rescue us from the evil one. For yours is the kingdom, the power, and the glory, now and forever. Amen.*

Jesus, a Model of Prayer

As any good teacher, Jesus models what he teaches. He practices what he preaches. This is true in regard to prayer. For example, Luke mentions a time when "Jesus was praying alone, with only the disciples near him" (Luke 9:18), something that must have occurred often. Given Jesus' unique relationship with the Father, when he communed intimately with God, his awareness of God and the level of his contemplation were far above ours. Nevertheless, we can follow his example.

First of all, Jesus prays before major events in his life. Before embarking on his mission, he withdraws to the desert for prayer and penance. He prays before the theophany at his baptism. Prior to selecting the apostles, he goes to a mountain and spends the entire night in prayer. Before the multiplication of loaves and before walking on the sea, he prays. He prays in the garden before his death. Finally, while hanging on the cross, Jesus calls out to his Father.

Jesus also prays early and by himself: "In the morning, while it was still very dark, he got up and went out to a deserted place, and there he prayed" (Mark 1:35). After feeding the five thousand, he goes up a mountain by himself to pray. Besides praying alone, Jesus prays with others. He prays in the synagogues, in the Temple, and at Passover celebrations. When Jesus is transfigured, he has taken Peter, James, and John up a mountain to pray. At times Jesus prays spontaneously, as when he exclaims in what is known as "the joyful shout": "I thank you, Father, Lord of heaven and earth, because you have hidden these things from the wise and the intelligent and have revealed them to infants" (Matthew 11:25). And before raising Lazarus from the dead, Jesus looks upward and prays, "Father, I thank you for having heard me" (John 11:41). Also, following Jewish prayer customs, Jesus blesses the bread before multiplying it.

Jesus prays for others. He tells Peter, "I have prayed for you that your own faith may not fail; and you, when once you have turned back, strengthen your brothers" (Luke 22:32). And at the Last Supper he prays a lengthy prayer for all his disciples, including us.

for your spiritual health...

Take your spiritual pulse: Reflect on how your prayer life compares to Jesus' example. Decide on one way you will improve your prayer life, starting today.

Teachings on the Kingdom and Other Things

Jesus' teaching touched on a wide variety of human concerns:

- The kingdom that Jesus proclaims is present. He declares that because he casts out demons, the kingdom has come (see Luke 11:20). When Pharisees ask him when the kingdom is coming, Jesus replies, "The kingdom of God is among you" (Luke 17:21). Some translations have "within you." At the end of his life, Je-

Jesus meek and humble of heart, make my heart like yours.

sus explains to Pilate that his kingdom is not from this world (John 18:36). Jesus teaches that it's not prayer, prophesying, exorcising, or working miracles that gains heaven. Rather, it is doing the will of his heavenly Father. Jesus will welcome those who do the Father's will into the kingdom (see Matthew 7:21–23).

◆ Contrary to conventional wisdom, Jesus teaches that calamities are not always the result of sinfulness. He gives two examples: Pilate had some Galileans who were offering sacrifice slaughtered. And a tower at Siloam fell and killed eighteen people. Jesus asks whether those Galileans or those people in Jerusalem who were killed were bigger sinners than anyone else in the area. (Probably not.) Yet, Jesus reminds us that we still need to repent (see Luke 13:1–5).

◆ Jesus outlines a strategy for dealing with someone who has offended you. If someone sins against you, first try handling the matter privately by talking to the person alone. If the person doesn't listen, bring one or two others with you to speak to the offender. If this fails, then have the church talk to the person. If the person still is obstinate, have nothing to do with him or her (see Matthew 18:15–17).

◆ Jesus regards repairing relationships as a prerequisite for participating in religious rites. He says, "When you are offering your gift at the altar, if you remember that your brother or sister has something against you, leave your gift there before the altar and go; first be reconciled to your brother or sister, and then come and offer your gift" (Matthew 5:23–24). Only when we are right with other people will we be worthy to approach God our Father.

Jesus' Impact on Language

Some of our everyday expressions have their origin in Jesus' teachings. Here are some that are probably familiar to you:

- The left hand not knowing what the right is doing (see Matthew 6:3–4)
- The blind leading the blind (see Matthew 15:14)
- Casting your pearls before swine (see Matthew 7:6)
- The narrow gate (see Matthew 7:13–14)
- A millstone around your neck (see Mark 9:42)
- Going the extra mile (see Matthew 5:40–42)
- A good Samaritan (see Luke 10:25–37)
- The salt of the earth (see Matthew 5:13)

Paradoxes Stated by Jesus

- "Those who want to save their life will lose it, and those who lose their life for my sake, and for the sake of the gospel, will save it" (Mark 8:35).
- "Many who are first will be last, and the last will be first" (Mark 10:31).
- "I came…so that those who do not see may see, and those who do see may become blind" (John 9:39).
- "All who exalt themselves will be humbled, and all who humble themselves will be exalted" (Matthew 23:12).

trivial tidbit...

As a young student, St. Francis Xavier was motivated to follow Christ after St. Ignatius quoted to him Jesus' words, "What does it profit them to gain the whole world and forfeit their life?" (Matthew 8:36). The Greek word for "life" here means "one's true life."

✦ In a statement at odds with any meek and mild image of Jesus, he says, "Do not think that I have come to bring peace to the earth; I have not come to bring peace, but a sword" (Matthew 10:34). Jesus causes division, in nations and even in families, as is still seen today. He forewarns the disciples that if people have persecuted him, surely they will persecute them also.

✦ When ministry work kept the apostles too busy even to eat, Jesus tells them, "Come away to a deserted place all by ourselves and rest a while" (Mark 6:31). He encourages us to come to him when cares or work overwhelms us. He invites, "Come to me, all you that are weary and are carrying heavy burdens, and I will give you rest. Take my yoke upon you, and learn from me; for I am gentle and humble in heart and you will find rest for your souls. For my yoke is easy, and my burden is light" (Matthew 11:28–30). Taking up a yoke means following Jesus. Another interpretation of Jesus' metaphor is that his simple laws are easy to bear compared to the heavy, cumbersome regulations of the Jewish leaders. Still another way to view this statement is that the rest of Jesus is the Sabbath rest.

✦ On speaking carefully: "The tree is known by its fruit.... Out of the abundance of the heart the mouth speaks. The good person brings good things out of a good treasure, and the evil person brings evil things out of an evil treasure. I tell you, on the day of judgment you will have to give an account for every careless word you utter" (Matthew 12:33–36).

✦ Jesus teaches Nicodemus, "No one can see the kingdom of God without being born from above...without being born of water and the Spirit" (John 3:3, 5). He is referring not to John's baptism but to being born again through Christian baptism. The Spirit alive in us prepares us for the kingdom.

Jesus is the polar star of human freedom.

Pope Benedict XVI

◆ Jesus spells out his mission for Nicodemus: "God did not send the Son into the world to condemn the world, but in order that the world might be saved through him. Those who believe in him are not condemned, but those who do not believe are condemned already, because they have not believed in the name of the only Son of God" (John 3:17–18).

◆ Once Jesus asked if anyone would say to a servant who has come in from plowing or tending sheep, "Come sit at my table." He knows his audience will think this is absurd. Jesus continues, "Instead wouldn't the master tell the servant to prepare the meal and serve him? The servant would eat later." Just as the servant shouldn't expect rewards for doing what he is supposed to do, neither should we expect rewards for just doing our duty as children of God (see Luke 17:7–10).

◆ Jesus encourages his disciples to be accepting of everyone. John reports that when a stranger was casting out demons in Jesus' name, the disciples tried to stop him. Jesus corrects them, "Do not stop him.... Whoever is not against us is for us" (Mark 9:39–40).

◆ Another time, when Jesus and the disciples intend to pass through a Samaritan village, they are not allowed in because they are going to Jerusalem. James and John, the Sons of Thunder, are incensed and bent on retaliating. They ask Jesus if he wants them to command fire to come down and consume the village, as if they had power to do this! But Jesus scolds them. In the Acts of the Apostles we learn that later many Samaritans became Christians.

quick quote...

We have such a great God that a single of his words contains thousands of secrets.

St. Teresa of Avila

✥ Jewish prophets spoke of the Day of the Lord to refer to any future catastrophe that was a judgment against Israel, for example, the Babylonian exile. In Jesus' time, the Jews thought that when Jerusalem was destroyed, the world would end. They believed that this end would be cataclysmic, a singular intervention by God that would lead to the establishment of God's kingdom. Jesus taught that no one knows the hour of the final Day of the Lord except the Father (Mark 13:32). Like other Jews, Jesus seemed to think that it would be soon. When he describes the fall of Jerusalem, he speaks of the end of the world using language common to apocalyptic literature. This is writing that "reveals" the end of the world using symbols such as signs in the sun and the stars. These symbols are not to be taken literally.

quick quote...

Alexander, Caesar, Charlemagne, and I founded empires. But on what did we rest the creation of our genius? Upon force. Jesus Christ founded his empire upon love; and at this hour millions of men would die for him.

Napoleon Bonaparte

The teachings of Jesus that have filtered down to us in the Gospels are just a sampling and, in some cases, a condensed version. In Acts 20:35, Paul says, "We must support the weak, remembering the words of the Lord Jesus, for he himself said, 'It is more blessed to give than to receive.'" This saying of Jesus is nowhere in the Gospels. It makes us wonder what else we're missing that Jesus said as he addressed the crowds for hours. One consolation is that Jesus continues to speak today through his Church guided by his Spirit.

Nuggets from Jesus

Jesus was a master at aphorisms. The Gospels contain more than a hundred of them. Jesus probably repeated these short, provocative sayings often. They are memorable maxims that were easily passed on from one early Christian to another. Some of them could have been conventional wisdom sayings that Jesus incorporated into his own teaching. For example, when Jesus first preaches in Nazareth he uses a proverb: "Doubtless you will quote to me this proverb, 'Doctor, cure yourself!'" (Luke 4:23). And he warns against false prophets who are wolves in sheep's clothing (see Matthew 7:15), an image from one of Aesop's fables. Here are some more:

- "I am the light of the world. Whoever follows me will never walk in darkness but will have the light of life" (John 8:12).
- "The works that the Father has given me to complete, the very works that I am doing, testify on my behalf that the Father has sent me" (John 5:36).
- "Do not worry about tomorrow, for tomorrow will bring worries of its own. Today's trouble is enough for today" (Matthew 6:34).
- "If you continue in my word, you are my disciples; and you will know the truth, and the truth will make you free" (John 8:31).
- "Where two or three are gathered in my name, I am there among them" (Matthew 18:20).
- "Be perfect, therefore, as your Father is perfect" (Matthew 5:48). Luke has, "Be merciful, just as your Father is merciful" (Luke 6:36).
- "What is impossible for mortals is possible for God" (Luke 18:27).

- "All who take the sword will perish by the sword" (Matthew 26:52).

- "Strive first for the kingdom of God and his righteousness, and all these things will be given to you as well" (Matthew 6:33).

- "You cannot serve God and wealth" (Matthew 6:24).

- "Let anyone with ears to hear, listen" (Mark 4:9).

- "The last will be first, and the first will be last" (Matthew 20:16).

- "Make purses for yourselves that do not wear out, an unfailing treasure in heaven, where no thief comes near and no moth destroys. For where your treasure is, there your heart will be also" (Luke 12:34).

15 Teacher: Parable Teller

Jesus is called Teacher more than anything else in the Gospels. He teaches with genius and eloquence and holds people spellbound. They wake up early to hear him teach in the Temple. They crowd Jesus on the shore, compelling him to board a boat in order to be heard better. Thousands even go hungry as they listen to him for three days. Unlike other Jewish religious teachers, Jesus doesn't center his teaching on explaining the Torah. Rather, he employs common ordinary objects and experiences to deliver his messages about God's kingdom. And shrewdly he uses concrete situations to explain abstract concepts.

Often Jesus uses the Socratic method, posing questions to engage people and lead them to new insights, which was standard teaching practice at the time. In fact, much of Jesus' teaching included in the Gospels is prompted by questions from people, in particular, the scribes and Pharisees, who were his most challenging debate opponents.

Another characteristic of Jesus' teaching common to his people was hyperbole, or exaggeration, which has shock value, piques curiosity, and fixes his statements in people's minds. He calls a mustard seed the smallest seed. It's not. And he says it grows into the largest bush. It doesn't. He says that if a hand or foot is a source of sin we should cut it off. This is not to be taken literally. Neither is the statement that to follow him one must hate mother and father. He is just illustrating that discipleship must be a top priority. Jesus also talks about a field that will bear wheat a hundredfold, which is an impossibility. Another time Jesus says, "Until

The shortest distance between a human and truth is a story.

Anthony de Mello, S.J.

heaven and earth pass away not one letter, not one stroke of a letter, will pass from the law until all is accomplished" (Matthew 5:15).

Jesus as Storyteller

Jesus' most frequent and memorable teaching device was the parable. Parables are statements or stories that use natural images to convey supernatural truths. The word *parable* is from the Greek for "to throw alongside of." Some parables are one-sentence similes and metaphors; others are short stories. All are an English teacher's delight. The Gospels are mosaics of these stories and comparisons.

Who doesn't love a good story? Whether in print, on film, or just told live, stories capture interest and make a lasting impression. Jesus, a master teacher, was a born storyteller, skilled at making a point through stories and word pictures. His stories contain direct discourse, details, and the repetition of lines—techniques that appeal to young and old. Often there is a punch line. The Synoptic Gospels are enlivened by at least forty distinct parables that Jesus related. Naturally he repeated these parables in different towns, so the Gospel writers might have been working with several versions.

Parables are not complicated. They have simple plots, clear characterization, plain language, and common objects. However, this simplicity is deceptive. Like a riddle or a Rubik's cube, a parable teases people to figure out its meaning. To theologian John Shea, a parable is like a joke: You either get it or you don't.

Parables are sometimes surprising. Archibald M. Hunter defines a parable as "one of those stories in the

Bible which sounds at first like a pleasant yarn, but keeps something up its sleeve which suddenly pops up and knocks you flat." The parables show God acting in unexpected ways and turning commonly held notions upside down. Through parables Jesus lifts people to a new level of thinking and acting. He challenges them to make a response in their lives.

The Meaning of Parables

A parable has layers of meanings like an onion. The first level is what Jesus intended. Very often his parables were directed to his opponents and were means of defending his outreach to sinners. A second meaning is how the early Church saw the parables as it used them as tools to instruct Christians. A third meaning is how the evangelist interpreted the parables. These last two meanings sometimes made their way into the Gospels in the form of added conclusions or explanations of the parable. For example, after Mark's parable of the Sower and the Seed, a passage explains what each element in the story represents (see Mark 4:26–29).

Although the concrete images, situations, and expressions Jesus used were familiar to his immediate audience, to us they can be puzzling. So in part, our understanding of parables depends on our knowledge of Jesus' culture.

In organizing their material, the Gospel writers often grouped parables and sayings according to theme or a common object. Sometimes the evangelist attached another saying of Jesus to the parable, which cast it in a certain light. In this way the teachings are played off one another, like a kaleidoscope, chang-

big book search...

Parables have the characteristics of stories: setting, characters, plot, conflict, theme, dialogue, suspense, and sometimes irony. Like fairy tales and folk tales, parables often use repetition and the number three. Read a parable or two in your Bible looking for these features.

One teaching technique that Jesus had in common with other Jewish teachers was to go "from light to heavy." This means using one reality to introduce a greater one. For example, Jesus says, "If you, who are evil, know how to give good gifts to your children, *how much more* will your Father in heaven give good things to those who ask him!" (Matthew 7:11).

ing meanings and at times leading to confusion. Also some parables were fused together, so we have a parable within a parable.

At one time parables were analyzed as if they were allegories in which each person and object had a specific meaning. For example, in the parable of the Good Samaritan, St. Augustine saw the Samaritan as Jesus, the oil as grace, and so forth. However, the usual way to break open a parable is to search for one main lesson Jesus is conveying. It is also helpful to listen to the story with the ears of the heart in order to discover what God is telling us and our various communities today through the story.

Parables of the Kingdom

So what do the parables teach? Jesus used parables to reveal the mysteries of the kingdom of God, which was his vision of how the world should be. In this utopian kingdom, there are no enemies. There God's will holds sway, and therefore there is peace, justice, and joy. Jesus himself inaugurates the kingdom of God on earth. Because God is in him, and he is in us, the kingdom can be in us. These parables describe the kingdom in terms of growth, life, and values:

- *A Treasure* (see Matthew 13:44). Jesus compares the kingdom to a treasure that a man finds in a field to his great joy. This is not unusual because in those days of frequent wars people stashed their valuables in a jar and buried it. Perhaps the man was a farmer working for another man and in plowing land he discovers the treasure. By Jewish law he should have split it in half with the owner. Instead he sells all that he has to obtain enough cash to purchase the field and be entitled to that entire treasure. Compared to the joy of possessing the kingdom, other things pale in significance.

In Aramaic, the kingdom parables begin with an expression that means, "The kingdom is like the following case...." Our translations read, "The kingdom is like... (a particular thing)." For example, "the kingdom of heaven is like a man who sows seed." The kingdom here is not really comparable to a man but to the whole process of sowing seeds and getting results.

◆ *A Pearl* (see Matthew 13:45). Jesus teaches that the kingdom is like a pearl so fine that a merchant sells everything he owns, liquidates his business, in order to purchase it. He's willing to change his life completely just to possess the precious pearl. Clearly the message is that God's kingdom is worth giving up everything for, just as Jesus is worth leaving everything behind to follow.

◆ *Seeds* (see Mark 4:26–29). Jesus likens the kingdom to the growth of seeds. Someone scatters seed on the ground. As days and nights pass, in the darkness of the ground the seed mysteriously sprouts and develops until it produces a stalk, then a head, and finally ripe grain, which can be harvested. The sower doesn't have a clue how this happens. The same God who manages the growth of seeds guides the growth of his kingdom; we don't have to worry.

◆ *A Mustard Seed* (see Matthew 13:31–32). Jesus further compares the kingdom to a mustard seed, which is little bigger than a pinhead but can grow to be nine feet tall. Although it becomes a shrub and not a tree, Jesus says it becomes a tree large enough for birds to make their nests, or in Luke, large enough to shade many birds. This parable is interpreted to mean that the small kernel of the Church begun in Israel is intended to be the home and shelter for people of all nations. It's surprising that Jesus chooses a mustard seed for his comparison instead of a seed that becomes a mighty cedar, which was the Old Testa-

trivial tidbit...

Jesus refers to yeast another time in the Scriptures, but in a negative context. He says, "Beware the yeast of the Pharisees and Sadducees!" (Matthew 16:11).

ment symbol for Israel. Actually mustard shrubs were regarded as weeds, and Jewish law banned them from gardens. Similarly the nucleus of the kingdom was a small band of insignificant people.

◆ *Yeast* (see Matthew 13:33). In another kingdom parable, Jesus uses a homey example. He says that the kingdom is like leaven, or yeast, that a woman puts into three measures of flour. This is provocative and startling to its hearers on three counts. First, the image for God is a woman. Second, yeast is actually mold, a symbol of corruption. And third, a measure of yeast is an enormous amount. Three measures would yield enough bread to feed about a hundred people. The point of the parable, though, is quite clear. Just as a pinch of yeast spreads throughout the dough and changes it, increasing it to several times its size, so does the kingdom penetrate and transform the whole world. This parable, like that of the mustard seed, illustrates the universality of the kingdom. From a modest beginning with a small group of disciples in a small country, the kingdom of God will touch every nation on earth.

◆ *Wheat and Weeds* (see Matthew 13:24–30, 36–43). This parable and the one about a catch of fish are about the sorting of the good and bad at the final judgment. These parables teach that the Church must exercise patience as we wait for the kingdom of justice and peace. Jesus explains the kingdom by the story of a man who sows seed. An enemy comes when everyone is asleep and sows weeds among the wheat. Both the good plants and the weeds grow. The weeds are darnel, which are poisonous and resemble wheat.

Slaves ask the farmer if he wants them to gather the weeds. He says no because the roots of the wheat and weeds are intertwined and in the process of pulling up the weeds they will uproot the wheat too. But at harvest time the reapers will collect the weeds and bundle them to be burned. Then they will gather the wheat into his barn. The disciples ask Jesus to explain this parable. He says that the Son of Man is the sower, the field is the world, the good seeds are the children of the kingdom, the bad seeds are the children of the evil one, the enemy is the devil, the harvest is the end of time, and the reapers are angels. The angels will collect all those who cause sin and evildoers and throw them into the fire, but the righteous will shine like the sun in the kingdom of their Father.

✦ *A Catch of Fish* (see Matthew 13:47–49). In a similar parable to that of the harvest, Jesus compares the kingdom to a net thrown into the sea. The fishermen haul it in and sort the fish, putting the good ones into baskets and throwing out the bad. (To the Jews fish without scales, such as catfish, were unclean; and so when they were caught, they were thrown out.) Jesus says this is how the angels will sort the evil and the righteous.

✦ *An Open Party* (see Luke 14:16–24; Matthew 22:1–14). Several parables act as a guide to who will belong to God's kingdom. In Luke, Jesus tells the story of a man who invites many people to a banquet. When all is ready, as is the custom, the host sends a slave to deliver the second invitation. Those fortunate people who were invited give ridiculous excuses for not coming. One has purchased land and says he

trivial tidbit...

The fact that in some of Jesus' parables the characters are slaves doesn't mean that Jesus condones slavery. It just shows that he is a product of his time, when owning slaves was an acceptable practice throughout the world.

Jesus once taught that it is better not to invite to a meal friends and relatives who would be apt to invite you back. Instead invite the poor, the crippled, the lame, and the blind who can't repay you, for then you will be repaid at the resurrection (see Luke 14:12–14).

must go to inspect it. Another has bought five yoke of oxen and is going to try them out. A third maintains that he can't come because he is newly married. These invited guests are just plain rude. When the slave reports their responses, the insulted host becomes very angry. He sends the slave out to the streets to bring in the poor, the crippled, the blind, and the lame. After the slave does this, he informs the host that there is still room in the banquet hall. Then the master sends him out to the roads to compel others to come, saying that none of those invited will taste his dinner. Matthew offers a more violent version of this parable. A king is giving a wedding banquet for his son. He sends slaves to call those who had been invited, but they will not come. He sends another group to announce that the meal is prepared and everything is ready. Those invited just walk away, one to his farm, another to his business. Some even mistreat and kill the slaves. Enraged, the king sends troops who destroy the murderers and burn their city. Then he tells his slaves that those invited were not worthy, and so they should invite everyone they find, good and bad. Since it's highly unlikely that a king would kill people for not accepting his invitation, Matthew might have added that feature to represent Jesus and the Christian missionaries who were being killed. This parable again shows how Israel, the chosen people, sometimes rejected salvation and even killed the prophets, and so now all people are welcome into the kingdom. There is another parable nested within this one: The king notices one man who is not wearing a wedding robe and asks how he got into the feast without one. The man doesn't answer. The king orders his attendants to bind the man hand and feet and throw him out into the darkness. Jesus concludes the story by saying, "For many are called, but few are chosen." Some scholars think that the man without a clean white robe was rude, lazy, or proud because such robes were provided at feasts and he easily could have donned one. The underlying message is that we need to be clothed with good deeds and Christian qualities in order to participate in the feast of heaven.

◆ *Wicked Tenants* (see Matthew 21:33–41; Mark 12:1–12; Luke 20:9–16). Another parable illustrates in no uncertain terms that the kingdom will be given to a new people, those who believe. Jesus recounts that a landowner plants a vineyard, puts a fence around it, digs a wine press in it, and builds a watchtower. When he is going out of the country, he leases his vineyard to tenants. At harvest time, he sends slaves to collect his produce. The tenants beat one slave, kill another, and stone the third. The king sends more slaves than before, and they meet the same fate. Finally he sends his beloved son to the tenants. But by Jewish law, if a man had no heirs, his property went to his tenants. So the tenants throw the son out of the vineyard and kill him. Jesus asks what the owner of the vineyard would do; and the members of his audience, the Jewish leaders of his time, answer that he would put the tenants to death and find new tenants. Jesus reveals the point of the parable by saying to them, "The kingdom of God will be taken away from you and given to a people that produces the fruits of the kingdom." This parable is the story of Israel. The king is God, the slaves stand for the prophets, and the son is Jesus,

fyi...

The icon Christ the Teacher is a variation of the *Pantocrater* icon, the first icon of Christ. The Greek word means "all-powerful" and first referred to God. Christ holds the Gospel book in his left hand. His right hand is either in an orator's position or raised in blessing with the fingers forming ICXC, a Greek abbreviation for "Jesus Christ." These letters also appear divided on either side of his halo. In the halo there may be a cross with Greek letters that mean "I am who I am." The oldest extant Pantocrater dates from the sixth or seventh century and was uncovered in St. Catherine's Monastery in the Sinai Desert in 1962.

quick quote...

In the end we will all be judged on love.

St. John of the Cross

who would be killed outside the city walls of Jerusalem. The chief priests and the Pharisees know full well that they are depicted as the bad tenants in the parable. They would like to arrest Jesus, but they fear the people, for Jesus is as popular as a sports hero or movie star today. At the conclusion of this parable Jesus quotes Psalm 118:22: "The stone that the builders rejected has become the cornerstone (or keystone)." There is a play on words here because in Hebrew the words "son" (*ben*) and "stone" (*eben*) are similar.

◆ *The Two Sons* (see Matthew 21:28–32). Jesus tells a parable that succinctly captures the position of the Jewish leaders. He says that a man had two sons. The man tells the older son to go and work in the vineyard. This son replies, "I won't," but then reconsiders and goes after all. The father gives identical orders to the other son, who replies, "I'll go," but this son does not go. Jesus declares to the chief priest and elders that tax collectors and prostitutes are entering the kingdom ahead of them, because these sinners believed John, whereas the Jewish leaders did not. You can imagine how this statement shocked and infuriated the religious leaders. On another level, the parable has general application: It illustrates in story form the universal adage, "Actions speak louder than words."

◆ *Workers in the Vineyard* (see Matthew 20:1–16). In a parable that offends our sense of fairness, Jesus says that the kingdom of heaven is like a man who early in the morning hires laborers to pick grapes in his vineyard for the usual daily wage. Later, about nine o'clock, he goes again to the marketplace and hires others there. He agrees to pay them what is right.

Then he goes out again at noon, at three o'clock, and at five o'clock and each time hires workers with the same agreement. In the evening the man has his manager call the workers and pay them beginning with last. When those first hired witness the latecomers receiving a full day's wage, they expect to be paid more themselves. But all of the workers receive the same daily wage. Naturally those who worked all day grumble, "These last worked only one hour, and you have made them equal to us who have borne the burden of the day and the scorching heat." The landowner explains that he gave them what they agreed to, and so why should they care if he chooses to pay others differently? He asks, "Are you envious because I am generous?" Jesus concludes by saying, "So the last will be first, and the first will be last." This parable paints a picture of God whose loving mercy transcends human justice and logic and whose grace is sheer gift.

quick quote...

What must Jesus have been like if he came up with these stories and allowed us to grasp what God is like?

Gerald O'Collins, S.J.

What God Is Like

The parable of the Workers in the Vineyard included under "Parables of the Kingdom" also belongs in this section, because the owner is a caricature of God, who has incredible mercy towards all. Three other parables show that God has a heart for sinners. All three teach that God rejoices when a sinner returns. They explain why Jesus himself associated with sinners and even dined with them, to the dismay of the Pharisees and scribes. Jesus doesn't condemn sinners, and he never speaks harshly to them. Instead, he works for their well-being. He tells the critical Pharisees, "Those who are well have no need of a physician, but those who are sick.... I have come to call not the righteous but

A Judgment Scene

Jesus creates a dramatic scenario of the last judgment in which he clearly identifies himself with the poor (see Matthew 25:31–46). The passage is not strictly a parable. Jesus starts by describing the judgment scene found in the Book of Daniel. He says that the Son of Man will come in glory with all the angels. He will be seated on his throne with all nations—Jewish and Gentile—gathered before him. But then, Jesus adds a comic touch. He represents people as animals. He says that like a shepherd, he will separate people, putting the sheep on the right, which is the place of honor, and the goats on the left. To the sheep he will say, "Come, you that are blessed by my Father, inherit the kingdom prepared for you from the foundation of the world; for I was hungry and you gave me food, I was thirsty and you gave me something to drink, I was a stranger and you welcomed me, I was naked and you gave me clothing. I was sick and you took care of me, I was in prison and you visited me." Bewildered, these good people will ask when they did these things for him. The king will answer, "Just as you did it to one of the least of my family, you did it to me." Then he will say to those on his left, "You that are accursed, depart from me into the eternal fire prepared for the devil and his angels; for I was hungry and you gave me no food, I was thirsty and you gave me nothing to drink, I was a stranger and you did not welcome me, naked and you did not give me clothing, sick and in prison and you did not visit me." Then they will ask when it was that they neglected to do these things. The king will answer, "Just as you did not do it to one of the least of these, you did not do it to me." Then the bad will go to eternal punishment and the good will go to eternal life. In Jesus' eyes, love shown toward the little people is paramount.

sinners" (Matthew 9:12–13). Matthew finds this sympathetic, merciful Jesus described in Isaiah: "He will not break a bruised reed or quench a smoldering wick" (Matthew 12:20). Here are the three parables about what God (and therefore Jesus) is like:

❖ *The Lost Sheep* (see Luke 15:3–7; Matthew 18:12–14). Jesus captures his rescue mission of humanity in this touching parable. He asks, "Which one of you having a hundred sheep and losing one doesn't leave the ninety-nine and go after the one that is lost until he finds it?" (No doubt, many of his hearers wouldn't do this, but God does!) When the shepherd counted the sheep at the end of the day, he discovered that one was missing. He goes off to search for it, perhaps leaving the rest of the sheep in the care of another shepherd. Jesus says that when the shepherd finds the lost sheep, he lays it on his shoulders and carries it back with much joy. This is no mean feat, since a sheep could weigh about a hundred pounds and the terrain was rugged. The shepherd then calls his friends and neighbors to rejoice with him. Jesus says that there will be more joy in heaven over one sinner who repents than over ninety-nine righteous persons. Matthew doesn't call the sheep "lost" but one that has gone "astray," which is more descriptive of a sinner. The context of this parable in Matthew implies that church leaders are to search for members who have fallen away from the community.

trivial tidbit...

On Yom Kippur, the Day of Atonement, a scapegoat was released into the desert symbolically bearing the sins of all. The goat therefore became a symbol of evil. Sometimes the devil is depicted as having a goat's head.

trivial tidbit...

When a teacher asked her class who was unhappy when the prodigal son came home, one bright lad answered, "The fatted calf."

trivial tidbit...

Rembrandt's last painting was *The Return of the Prodigal Son*, now in a museum in St. Petersburg, Russia. In his book on this parable, Father Henri Nouwen pointed out that in this painting of the father embracing the son, one of the father's hands is masculine and the other is feminine.

✦ *The Lost Coin* (see Luke 15:8–10). In another parable Jesus compares God to a housewife who has ten silver coins and loses one. Some commentators think that the coins refer to the woman's personal property or dowry worn in her headdress or necklace to mark her as a married woman. Her husband won't be too happy at the loss. Others think that they signify how poor the woman was, since each coin (probably a drachma) was only a day's wage. Totally focused on finding her lost treasure, the woman lights a lamp in the dim house, sweeps the dirt floor with extreme care, and searches until she finds it. Then the woman calls her women friends and neighbors together to rejoice with her. Anyone who has lost something valuable and found it can identify with the woman's diligence in searching for the coin as well as her relief in finding it. Jesus again says that there is joy in the presence of God's angels over one sinner who repents.

The Parable That Contains the Entire Gospel

Certainly the parable of the Prodigal Son (see Luke 15:11–32) ranks at or near the top of a list of ten best-loved parables. It is the longest one that Jesus told, and some say that it contains the essence of the Good News. This parable might more accurately be named the Prodigal (Extravagant) Father, for it is a heartwarming story of a father's unconditional, all-forgiving love, the love God our Father has for us.

Jesus relates that a man has two sons. The younger one, itching to be free, demands and receives from his father his share of the inheritance. This is allowed by Jewish custom but is quite brash as it deprives the father of care in his old age. The boy's share could be a third of the property because we know that after Jesus' time the oldest son was entitled to twice as much as the younger children. In a few days the young man leaves for a distant country, most likely a Gentile one. There he squanders his money in dissolute living. When a famine occurs, he manages to get a job feeding pigs. There's no lower occupation for a Jew, because the Jews regard pigs as unclean. The boy is so hungry that he wishes he could eat the pods of the carob tree that are the pigs' food, but no one offers him any. Then the son comes to himself and realizes that his father's hired hands have more than enough to eat. He decides to return to his father and say, "Father, I have sinned against heaven and before you; I am no longer worthy to be called your son; treat me like one of your hired hands." He starts walking home.

While the boy is still far off, his father, spots him, which suggests that the grieving man has been scanning the horizon every day, hoping to spot his wayward son. Filled with compassion, the father lifts his long robes and runs to his son, something very undignified for a Middle-Eastern man to do. Before the lad even says a word, the father embraces and kisses him. When the boy begins his planned speech, the father interrupts him. The deliriously happy father not only takes his son back but restores his respect. He orders his servants to quickly bring out the best robe—not any robe, but the best one—and clothe his son in it, and to put a ring on his finger and sandals on his feet. Giving someone a robe is a sign of honor, a ring signifies authority, and shoes are worn by free people, not slaves.

Then the father tells his men to slaughter the fatted calf so that they can eat and celebrate. Meat was a rarity, saved for feasts. There's no scolding, and the father showers far more on the boy than he deserves, spending even more of the family money on him. Fr. Andrew Greeley puts a new spin on the story. He proposes that the prodigal son is not really sorry. His return is a matter of survival, and his speech is a manipulation of the father. And the boy will probably continue to live irresponsibly. If this is the case, the father's love is truly "prodigal."

During the celebration the older son comes in from the fields, where, no doubt, he's been working hard. He hears lively music and dancing and asks a slave what is going on. When he is informed of the good news, he becomes angry and refuses to go in. He will not eat with a sinner. The father, on learning this, leaves the celebration, comes out to him, and pleads. But the son, full of self-pity, complains bitterly, "Listen! For all these years I've been working like a slave for you, and I have never disobeyed your command; yet you have never given me even a young goat so that I might celebrate with my friends. But when this son of yours came back, who has devoured your property with prostitutes, you killed the fatted calf for him!" Notice that instead of "my brother" he says contemptuously "this son of yours." And he describes his relationship with the father in terms of slavery and obedience, not love. Trying to reason with his older son, the father replies, "Son, you are always with me, and all that is mine is yours. But we had to celebrate and rejoice, because this brother of yours was dead and has come to life; he was lost and has been found." Ironically, in being generous to one son, the father has alienated the other one.

In this moving parable the father represents God, who longs to welcome back sinners with open arms. God's love also embraces those righteous children who begrudge others God's mercy. The father in the story really has two wayward sons, and his great love encompasses both of them. The younger son has been compared to the Gentiles and the older son to the Pharisees who kept the letter of the law. Father William Burke has suggested that the reason we don't know how the story ends—did the older son go in to the party or not—is because we are all the older son, and we have yet to make up our minds whether or not we can tolerate a prodigal father like the one in the story, who is Jesus' idea of what God is really like.

16 Role Model: Qualities of Kingdom People

Some of Jesus' parables are morality stories that teach the qualities that members of God's kingdom should possess. Of course, Jesus is the ultimate role model for kingdom members, so in the final analysis these were stories about himself:

◆ *The Pharisee and the Tax Collector* (see Luke 18:9–14). Quite pointedly in one parable Jesus warns the Pharisees about being self-righteous. Two people went to the Temple to pray. One was a Pharisee, a religious leader, and the other was a tax collector, who was despised as a crook. The Pharisee prayed an egocentric prayer, praising himself rather than God. He said, "God, I thank you that I am not like other people: thieves, rogues, adulterers, or even like this tax collector. I fast twice a month; I donate a tenth of all my income." What the Pharisee claimed to have done is praiseworthy. He has gone far beyond what the law prescribed. Because prayers were prayed aloud, all in the Temple could hear how wonderful he was. Meanwhile the humble tax collector stood far off and didn't even dare to lift his eyes. Beating his breast, which was a sign of anguish, he begged, "God, be merciful to me, a sinner!" This sinner put all his hope in God. Jesus concludes that the tax collector went home justified, more pleasing to God, than the other man. Jesus then clinches the story's meaning with one of the reversals characteristic of God's kingdom: "All who exalt themselves will be humbled, but all who humble themselves will be exalted." He echoes the words of Mary's Magnificat in which she praises God because: "He has scattered the proud...and lifted up the lowly."

The Good Shepherd

Jesus calls himself the good shepherd and explains why (see John 10:1–16). A good shepherd lays down his life for his sheep, unlike a hired man who abandons the sheep and flees when a wolf comes. Jesus knows his sheep and they know him. They recognize his voice and follow him, but not the thieves who will steal and kill them. In expanding on this figure of speech, Jesus states his mission: "I came that they may have life, and have it abundantly." The shepherd metaphor calls to mind Psalm 23 in which God is a shepherd who leads his flock to green pastures and still waters and keeps them safe. In a typically Jewish mixing of metaphors, in the same breath Jesus calls himself the gate to the sheepfold. Through the gate the sheep enter home, where it's safe and peaceful, and where they're cared for and nourished. Likewise, through Jesus we have access to the Father and our true homeland, which is the kingdom of God.

trivial tidbit...

A shepherd carrying a sheep on his shoulders was the early Christians' commonest image of Jesus. The shepherd image also appeals to children, even though they usually aren't familiar with shepherds.

For insight into the relationship between a shepherd and his sheep, read the book *A Shepherd Looks at Psalm 23* by Phillip Keller.

Acting on the Word

A fundamental characteristic of Jesus' followers is that they live out God's word. Jesus taught, "Not everyone who says to me, 'Lord, Lord,' will enter the kingdom of heaven, but only the one who does the will of my Father in heaven" (Matthew 7:21). One day when Jesus is teaching, a woman in the crowd cries out, "Blessed is the womb that bore you and the breasts that nursed you," but Jesus contradicts her saying, "Rather blessed are they who hear the word of God and keep it." Another time when Jesus is informed that his mother and brothers want to see him, he responds, "My mother and my brothers are those who hear the word of God and do it" (Luke 8:20–21). Incidentally, these are not put-downs of Mary, for she, above all others, heard the word of God and kept it. The following two parables reinforce that we must hear and follow God's word:

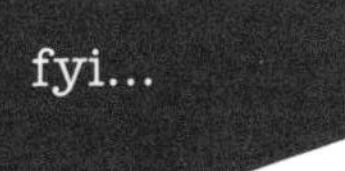

Parables are windows and mirrors. Like a window some parables allow us to peer through them to a vision of God and God's kingdom. Like a mirror some parables put before us a reflection of ourselves.

◆ *House Built on Rock* (see Matthew 7:24–27; Luke 6:47–49). Houses constructed high on rock are safer from rising waters than houses built low in the sand. Jesus says that whoever acts on his words is like a wise man who dug deeply and built his house on rock. When rain fell and floods and wind blasted his house, it stood strong. On the other hand, whoever doesn't act on God's words is like a foolish man who built his house on sand without a foundation. When the rains came, his house fell with a crash and was demolished. Similarly, when we build our lives on unstable things such as money, success, work, or physical appearance, then something like the diagnosis of cancer can cause it to come crashing down.

quick quote...

The bread in your cupboard belongs to the hungry; the coat unused in your closet belongs to the one who needs it; the shoes rotting in your closet belong to the one who has no shoes; the money which you hoard up belongs to the poor.

St. Basil the Great

✦ *The Seeds and the Soil* (see Matthew 13:3–9, 18–23; Mark 4:2–9, 14–20; Luke 8:4–8, 11–15). In those days people first cast seeds on the ground and then plowed. One of Jesus' parables is about the growth of seeds. He says that a sower sowed some seeds. Some seeds fell on the path and birds ate them. Other seeds fell on rocky ground where they had little soil and water. They sprang up right away but as soon as the scorching sun came up, not having roots, they withered. Other seeds fell among thorns that choked them. The picture of this farmer haphazardly tossing seed in the wrong places must have drawn chuckles from the crowd listening to Jesus. Luckily, other seeds fell on rich soil, grew tall and strong, and produced crops—some thirty, some sixty, even a hundredfold. Then Jesus declares, "Listen, anyone who has ears to hear." He proceeds to explain that the seed is the word. The seed on the edge of the path are people who hear the word, but Satan comes and carries it away. Those who receive the seed on rocky ground are those who hear the word with joy and believe for a while. But because they have no root, if a trial or persecution comes on account of the word, they fall away. Then there are those who have heard the word; but cares, riches, and pleasures choke it, so they produce nothing. But there are those who receive the seed in rich soil. They hear the word, accept it, and yield a large harvest. This story was tailored to the early Christians who, at the time the Gospel was written, were encountering resistance and undergoing persecutions. Scholars think that Jesus' original intent was to teach about the fabulous spread of the kingdom. Despite some setbacks, the seed flourishes, just as the kingdom will. It's possible that seed could produce a yield five times greater. For seed to produce thirtyfold would be miraculous. Sixtyfold and hundredfold would be outrageous.

◆ *The Children in the Marketplace* (see Matthew 11:16–17). Jesus uses the image of children playing in the street to describe the people of his time. He says that some children call out, "We played the flute for you, and you did not dance; we wailed, and you did not mourn." This mini-parable is difficult to interpret, but here is one reasonable explanation: A group of children is playing wedding and stand for Jesus, who teaches an easy way of religion. Another group of children is playing funeral and stand for John the Baptist, who called for asceticism. Just as the petulant children won't cooperate, the Jewish people don't respond to either John's or Jesus' invitation.

quick quote...

He [Christ] lived serenely,
as a greater artist
than all other artists,
despising marble and
clay as well as color,
working in living flesh.
That is to say, this
matchless artist...loudly
proclaimed that he
made...living men,
immortals.

Vincent Van Gogh

Praying with Perseverance

Jesus also uses parables to encourage us to pray and not lose heart. He promises, "Ask and it will be given you; search and you will find, knock and the door will be opened for you" (Matthew 7:7). Here are two parables by which Jesus teaches us to keep saying, "Please, please, please," until God answers. It's been proposed that the real focus of these parables is not the people begging but the willingness of the helpers to fill their request. In other words, these stories highlight God's graciousness in answering our prayers:

a cool website...

To boost your prayer life, go to Sacred Space at www.jesuit.ie/prayer.

◆ *The Persistent Friend* (see Luke 11:5–8). This parable is based on the fact that the Jews view hospitality as a serious obligation. Jesus says suppose a visitor arrives unexpectedly at midnight and you have no food

short prayer...

Lord Jesus Christ, who are the Way, the Truth, and the Life, we pray do not let us stray from you, the Way, nor distrust you, the Truth, nor rest in anything else but you, the Life. Teach us by your Holy Spirit what to believe, what to do, and where to take our rest. (Erasmus)

to offer him. You go to a friend's house, bang on the door, and ask him to lend you three loaves of bread. This is quite an intrusion, given that a family slept all in one room and so the knocking woke everyone up. Moreover the door is bolted. At first the disturbed neighbor will answer, "Don't bother me; the door is locked and my children are with me in bed. I can't get up and give you anything." Jesus correctly predicts that if you keep asking, even if friendship doesn't motivate the neighbor to answer the plea, eventually he will get up and give you what you need just so he and his family can sleep. It is significant that this parable in Luke comes immediately after Jesus teaches his disciples the Our Father, in which we pray, "Give us this day our daily bread." With Jesus' Father, you only have to ask to get what you need.

✦ *The Judge and the Widow* (see Luke 18:1–8). Another parable that urges continuous prayer is about a widow and a judge. This judge is a tough character who doesn't fear God (meaning he is corrupt) and has no respect for people. Nevertheless, with patience and perseverance the widow keeps asking him to grant her justice against her opponent, perhaps a male relative who is withholding money from her. This is bold of the widow because women did not have rights. For a while the judge simply refuses to comply. But eventually, despite his reputation for meanness, he grants her request just to keep her from wearing him out. The original Greek words here literally mean to keep her from "giving me a black eye." The imagery for the woman is that of boxing!

Wealth and the Wealthy

To the Jews, abundance was a blessing. Jesus is not against riches per se, but rather against their misuse and hoarding wealth at the expense of the poor. Jesus teaches that we ought to share the goods of the earth. He even conjures up a preposterous image to make his point. He says that it is as difficult for a wealthy man to enter heaven as it is for a camel, the largest animal in Palestine, to pass through the "eye of a needle." Here are two parables with the same lesson:

◆ *The Rich Fool* (see Luke 12:16–21). One day a man asks Jesus to order his brother to split the inheritance with him. Jesus refuses to take up his cause and instead warns him to be on guard against greed. Then Jesus reinforces this advice with a parable related to the adage "There are no pockets in shrouds." Jesus says that a rich man had a great harvest and pondered where to store all his crops. He decided to tear down his barns and build larger ones to store all his grain and possessions. Then the wealthy man said to himself that he had enough goods to last many years. He could relax, eat, drink, and be merry. But God said to him, "You fool! This very night your life is being demanded of you. And all your things, whose will they be?" Jesus comments that rather than storing up treasures for ourselves, we need to be rich towards God. The rich man neglected to thank God for his crops. Also, in his self-talk, he was self-centered. His speech was full of "I's." If the rich man had shared his goods with the poor, then he would have had a claim to the treasure of heaven. As it was, he committed idolatry, worshiping his goods.

trivial tidbit...

Some scholars think that the needle in Jesus' comparison was a gate in Jerusalem called the *Needle*. Others propose that Jesus was referring to a thick fisherman's rope called a *camel*. There's no reason why Jesus couldn't literally have meant a large camel and a tiny needle in a funny hyperbole.

for your spiritual health...

You might decide it's time to weed out your clothes and other possessions. Don't just give away what you don't "need." Consider giving at least something from your abundance that would really be a sacrifice for you.

Most Jews before the time of Jesus thought that the dead went to Sheol, an underground realm where everyone existed like shadows. Later, around the time of Jesus, some Jews began to believe in an afterlife and regarded Sheol as the place where the good waited "in the bosom of Abraham" for resurrection while the bad were in torment. In the Greek translation of the Bible, Sheol is called Hades. It is different from Gehenna, the name Jesus used for hell, a permanent place of punishment. Gehenna, was a valley near Jerusalem where garbage was burned and where human beings, including children, had once been sacrificed to an idol.

✦ *The Rich Man and the Poor Man* (see Luke 16:19–31). Jesus, the champion of the poor, employs a parable to open our eyes to their plight. He says there was a rich man who dressed in purple, the color of royalty, and expensive fine linen undergarments. This man never had to worry about where his next meal was coming from. In fact, he feasted sumptuously every day. Tradition calls him Dives, from the Latin for "wealth." His mansion was surrounded by a wall, and at his gate lay a poor, starving man named Lazarus who was covered with sores that dogs used to lick. Lazarus longed to eat just the scraps that fell from the man's table, but the rich man never noticed him. Riches can dehumanize a person. The dogs take better care of the beggar than Dives does. Incidentally, Lazarus is the only person Jesus ever names in a parable. His name means "God helps." The poor man died and was carried by angels to be with Abraham. The rich man too died but went down to Hades, a place of torment and flames. From there Dives looked up, and far away he saw Abraham with Lazarus in peace next to him. He called to Abraham, begging to let Lazarus dip his finger in water to cool his tongue. The burning pain was so great that a glass of water wasn't necessary; just a few drops would bring relief. Although he had never helped Lazarus, now Dives looked to him for help. Abraham responded to Dives, "Child, remember that during your life you received good things, while Lazarus received evil, but now he is comforted but you are in agony. Besides, between you and us there is a great chasm so no one can cross sides." The rich man then pleaded with Abraham to send Lazarus to his house to warn his five brothers so that they would not end up suffering like him. He's treating Lazarus like a lackey, but at least Dives showed concern for people other than himself. However, Abraham replied, "They have Moses and the prophets to listen to." The man insisted, "If someone goes to them from the dead, they will repent." But Abraham said, "If they don't listen to Moses and the prophets, neither will they be convinced even if someone rises from the dead." This point is proved later when another man named Lazarus does come back from the dead, but instead of repenting, the Jewish leaders only become more intent on killing Jesus, who had brought Lazarus back to life.

trivial tidbit...

Most scholars think that the expression "the bosom of Abraham" comes from the practice of eating while reclining. At the heavenly banquet Lazarus, who was next to Abraham, is lying near his breast, the highest place.

Showing Mercy

Two of Jesus' parables illustrate that—just as God extends loving mercy to us—so we, God's children, ought to be merciful. They put flesh on a conversation Peter and Jesus have. Peter asks Jesus how often he should forgive someone and probably thinks he is being magnanimous in suggesting as many as seven times. Jesus replies with a hyperbole, "Not seven times, but, I tell you, seventy-seven times" (Matthew 18:22). Some translations have seventy times seven. In either case because to the Jews seven is the perfect number, Jesus means that kingdom people forgive unceasingly. Their hearts encompass all people, including those perceived as foes. Here are two "mercy parables":

◆ *The Friendly Samaritan* (see Luke 10:25–37). A lawyer, an interpreter of Jewish law, addresses Jesus as "Teacher" and asks what he must do to receive eternal life. Jesus, using the Socratic questioning method, asks him what Scripture says. The lawyer quotes, "You

Santo Niño de Atocha (Holy Child of Atocha) aids prisoners, travelers, miners, and immigrants. Legends began when Atocha, Spain, fell to Muslims. Jailed Christians were denied food except what children brought. Women prayed to Our Lady. A child in pilgrim's clothing began bringing food to prisoners. On the statue of Our Lady of Atocha, the shoes of the Child Jesus she held were worn and dirty. Replaced, they became soiled again. In Fresnillo, Mexico, miners were trapped. Their wives praying in church saw that the child from the Our Lady of Atocha statue was gone. When the miners emerged, they said a child gave them water and showed them the way out.

shall love the Lord your God with all your heart, and with all your soul, and with all your strength, and with all your mind; and your neighbor as yourself." Jesus says he is correct. But then the man, perhaps to justify himself for asking a question that was so simply answered, poses another question: "Who is my neighbor?" In response, Jesus relates one of his most memorable parables, the parable that has added to our language the expression "a good Samaritan." He teaches that the acid test of our love of God is love of neighbor. Jesus says that a man going from Jerusalem to Jericho was attacked by robbers who stripped him, beat him, and left him half dead. The road was about sixteen miles long through an uninhabited region and so dangerous that it was nicknamed "the path of blood." A priest going down the road saw the poor man, but passed by on the other side. A Levite, another official priest, also noticed the victim and passed by on the other side. Perhaps these two men ignored the injured man because contact with him could have rendered them unclean, that is, unfit for ritual. Or maybe they were afraid to stop or weren't sure how they could help. But then a Samaritan came near, saw the man, and was moved with pity. Using his supplies, he poured oil and wine on the man's wound and bandaged them, perhaps with cloth torn from his own clothes. Then he hoisted the beaten man onto his own animal and held him there as he walked to an inn. There he cared for the victim all night. The next day the Samaritan paid the innkeeper two *denarii*. (A *denarius* was a day's wages.) The Samaritan promised, "Take care of him and when I come back, I will repay you whatever more you spend." This offer protected the victim from falling into debt to the innkeeper. In essence, the Samaritan gave the innkeeper a blank check. This rescuer went far beyond the minimal help the situation called for. Jesus concludes by asking, "Which of these three was a neighbor to the man who fell into the hands of the robbers?" The lawyer can't even bear to say "Samaritan." He replies, "The one who showed him mercy." And Jesus commands, "Go and do likewise." He has stretched the Jews' concept of "neighbor," which was limited to fellow Jews, to include anyone in need, even an enemy.

◆ *The Unforgiving Servant* (see Matthew 18:21–35). Jesus teaches that the kingdom of heaven demands forgiveness through a parable that is an enactment of the request in the Our Father "forgive us our trespasses as we forgive those who trespass against us." Once a king was settling accounts with his slaves. One slave owed him ten thousand *talents*, an exorbitant amount equivalent to billions of dollars. (A talent was worth more than fifteen years' wages. Herod's annual income, for example, was nine hundred talents.) Of course, the slave couldn't pay; and so the king ordered that he, his family, and all his possessions be sold to make the payment. The slave knelt and begged, "Have patience with me and I will pay you everything." Out of pity, the king forgave his debt. The slave didn't have to pay anything. This king is an image of God whose goodness is boundless. On his way out the slave met another slave who owed him just a hundred *denarii*. (A *denarius* was the usual one-day wage.) The newly forgiven slave seized his fellow slave by the throat and demanded, "Pay what you owe." The debtor fell down

trivial tidbit...

The Jews listening to the parable of the "good" Samaritan had to be stunned that Jesus made their longtime foe the hero of the story and someone to imitate. They were even more shocked if they realized that the kindhearted Samaritan was meant to be an image of God who has mercy on us and pays our bills. In particular, the priestly Sadducees who heard this parable must have been incensed at hearing the priest and Levite cast as the bad guys.

for your spiritual health...

Figure out a way that you can "cross to the other side of the road" to come to the aid of someone in need in your life. Now do it.

and begged, "Have patience with me, and I will pay you." But the merciless slave threw him into prison until he could pay his debt. Although the king had forgiven his large debt, the slave wouldn't even give his debtor an extension on a very small debt. Other slaves witnessed the scene and took action against this evil. Distressed, they reported it to the king. The king summoned the slave and said, "You wicked slave! I forgave you all your debt because you pleaded with me. Should you not have had mercy on your fellow slave, as I had mercy on you?" In anger the king handed him over to be tortured until he paid his entire debt, which was impossible, so he would be tortured for life. Jesus remarks, "So my heavenly Father will also do to you, if you do not forgive your brother or sister from your heart." The good God forgives us a multitude of sins, making up for them with the gift of his beloved Son. It's only right that we "pay it forward" and pass on the favor to others.

"Always Prepared" Parables

Members of the kingdom are always ready for the coming of the Lord. Like other Jews, Jesus believed in a future catastrophic day. He warns people to be awake and alert for it. Jesus declares that the Son of Man will come unexpectedly, just as how in Noah's day the flood took people by surprise. Jesus underscores the need for watchfulness as well as for conversion and repentance in several parables: the parable of the Faithful or Unfaithful Slaves, the parable of the Ten Bridesmaids, and the parable of the Ten Talents and its variation about the king. These are called "crisis parables" or "parables of urgency" because they are about situations that require immediate action in order to be saved. In these crisis parables some people take advantage of their opportunity and make good decisions, while others don't:

◆ *The Faithful or Unfaithful Slave* (see Matthew 24:45–51; Luke 12:35–38, 42–48). Jesus contrasts two slaves. He poses the example of a faithful slave who, when his master returns home, is found at work. This slave is rewarded. He will be put in charge of everything. On the other hand, a wicked slave says, "My master is delayed," and stupidly takes advantage of the situation. He beats the other slaves and eats and drinks with drunkards. This slave will be punished when his master returns unexpectedly. In Luke's Gospel Jesus tells a more colorful story about anticipating the master's return. He says, "Be dressed for action and have your lamps lit; be like those who are waiting for their master to return from the wedding banquet, so that they may open the door for him as soon as he comes and knocks." These slaves, Jesus says, will be blessed because the master will seat them for a meal and serve them. That a master would wait on his slaves is highly improbable, as improbable as God preparing a heavenly banquet for his creatures!

◆ *The Ten Bridesmaids* (see Matthew 25:1–13). Jesus sheds light on the kingdom of heaven through a story about bridesmaids. A Jewish bridegroom would go to his bride's house and escort her to his house where the ceremony would take place. The two were accompanied on the way by people with lights and burning torches. In Jesus' parable ten bridesmaids took their lamps and went to meet the bridegroom. Five brides-

quick quote...

If you haven't any charity in your heart, you have the worst kind of heart trouble.

Bob Hope

trivial tidbit...

In one parable Jesus compares himself to a thief! He says that if a house owner knew the hour a thief was coming, he would not let his house be broken into. So we also must be ready, "for the Son of Man is coming at an unexpected hour" (Luke 12:39–40).

maids were foolish and irresponsible and took no oil, while five were wise and took flasks of oil. When the bridegroom was delayed, all the women fell asleep. At midnight came a shout, "Look! Here is the bridegroom! Come out to meet him." All the bridesmaids trimmed their lamps. The foolish ones said to the wise, "Give us some of your oil, for our lamps are going out." But the wise replied, "No! There will not be enough for you and for us; you had better go to the dealers and buy some." While the foolish women were gone, looking for a dealer who was open at midnight, the bridegroom arrived. The women whose lamps were burning brightly escorted him to the banquet, and the door was shut. Later the unprepared bridesmaids came and called, "Lord, Lord, open to us." But he replied, "Truly I tell you, I do not know you." This expression means, "I don't want to have anything to do with you." Perhaps the bridegroom was peeved that only half the honor guard accompanied him and his bride. At the end of the parable Jesus comments, "Keep awake therefore, for you know neither the day nor the hour." This may have been a conclusion added by Matthew. The point of the story is really not to stay awake but to be prepared. After all, both the foolish and the wise bridesmaids fell asleep. It's thought that originally the five foolish bridesmaids stood for the Jewish leaders and the five wise for Christians. The foolish ones who did not accept the Messiah would have no part in the messianic banquet. Applied to us Christians, this parable is a caution to always be prepared to meet Jesus, whether he comes at our death or at the end of the world or in the ordinary activity of daily life.

✦ *Three Servants and the Talents* (see Matthew 25:14–30; Luke 19:11–27). Another parable that teaches preparedness is about a man going on a journey who entrusted his property to his slaves, with the understanding that they would invest it. To one he gave five *talents*, to another two, and to another one. (A talent is the wage for fifteen years, a huge amount to entrust to a slave.) The slave with five talents traded them at once and made five more. The one with two talents did likewise and made two more. But the slave with one talent played it safe. He dug a hole and hid his master's money out of fear. The law of the time apparently stated that if entrusted money was stolen from a house, the servant had to pay it back, but if it was stolen from the ground he didn't have to. After a long time the master returned. The one with five talents presented him with the five plus five more. His master said, "Well done, good and trustworthy slave; you have been trustworthy in a few things, I will put you in charge of many; enter into the joy of your master." To the one who doubled his two talents, he said the same. Then the slave with one talent said, "Master, I knew that you were a harsh man, so I was afraid and hid your talent. Here you have what is yours." He handed over the one coin. The master replied, "You wicked and lazy slave. You should have invested my money and on my return I would have received my own talent with interest." Then he ordered, "Take his talent and give it to the one with ten talents and throw him into the outer darkness." Luke's rendition of this parable has another one embedded in it that refers to Jesus' rejection by the Jews. In his parable the master is a nobleman who wants to be a king. He goes off to

quick quote...

Make ready for the Christ, whose smile, like lightning, sets free the song of everlasting glory that now sleeps in your paper flesh like dynamite.

Thomas Merton, OCSO

In Luke's parable, which is about pounds rather than talents, the noblemen gives ten servants each a coin. But as the tale unfolds, there are only three servants. Someone attributed this discrepancy to "redactor's fatigue." In other words, the editor attempted to align the story more with the other parable but didn't do a thorough job. Coincidentally, the word *talent* that means money in the parable is the word for "gift" or "skill" in English. Our definition dovetails with a theme recognized in the parable: Work for the kingdom with passion and dedication, using all your gifts with ingenuity.

plead for royal power. His citizens hate him and do not want him to rule over them. A delegation goes to protest his kingship, but in vain. When the newly-appointed king returns, he has his enemies killed. Commentators suggest that this addition is rooted in a real event. The Jewish historian Jeremias reports that in 4 B.C., Herod Archelaus journeyed to Rome to get his kingship over Judea confirmed. A Jewish embassy of fifty persons also went to Rome to resist his appointment. Archelaus was not given all the territory he had hoped for and was declared an ethnarch, not a king. When he returned to Judea, he retaliated by slaughtering a great number of Jews.

❖ *The Barren Fig Tree* (see Luke 13:6–9). Another parable concerns a person who had a fig tree in his orchard. When he found no fruit on the tree, he told the gardener, "For three years now I have found no fruit on this tree, so cut it down. Why should it deplete the soil?" The gardener suggested, "Sir, let it alone for one more year, until I dig around it and fertilize it. If it bears fruit next year, well and good; but if not, you can cut it down." The gardener is an image of Jesus, our constant intercessor, who has unfailing hope in us.

❖ *The Crafty Steward* (see Luke 16:1–9). Jesus tells one parable that at first glance seems to promote dishonesty. A rich man had a manager who was accused of squandering his property, so he fired him. The manager wondered what he would do to keep food on the table. He wasn't strong enough to dig and was ashamed to beg. Then he decided on a way to ingratiate himself with people so that they would welcome him into their homes. He summoned the master's debtors one by one. He asked the first, "How much do you owe my master?" The man answered, "A hundred jugs of olive oil." (This was about 900 gallons.) The manager said, "Make it fifty." He asked another, "How much do you owe?" The man replied, "A hundred containers of wheat." (This was about a thousand bushels.) He said to him, "Make it eighty." These numbers are extravagant, a typical feature of oriental storytelling. Of course, the master could not ask his creditors, who were grateful for their bargains, to refund these goods. The ending of the parable has a humorous twist. When the master found out how the manager had cheated him, instead of being angry, he praised him for using his wits. Picture the rich man slapping his knee and exclaiming, "That rascal!" It seems that the manager cheated his master for his own self-interests. A kinder interpretation is that he sacrificed some of his own profit on the deals, not his master's money. In either case, the point Jesus is making is that disciples ought to be clever, decisive, and determined in their ministry. Some see in this parable a warning to the Jews to act quickly and prudently as they face a crisis: their imminent destruction.

fyi...

Jesus delivers a lesson on being shrewd another time when he exhorts his followers to be as gentle as doves but as sly as serpents (Matthew 10:16).

trivial tidbit...

In 2006, a badly fragmented apocryphal Gospel of Judas, discovered in Egypt in the 1970s was in the news. Due to mistranslations it was thought to reveal that Jesus favored Judas with secret knowledge and directed Judas to hand him over in order to further the work of salvation. This interpretation of the manuscript has been discredited.

17 The Word: Parables in Action

The teachings of Jesus echo in a profound way the message woven all through the Old Testament: the spectacular truth that God loves us. Jesus' very existence is the greatest proof of this love, and his actions match his words, for he is none other than God, the Word made flesh.

Jesus is like a walking parable. Looking at him and listening to him, we learn what God is like and what God wants for us. The following accounts of Jesus' interactions with people are lessons in themselves. The first four reveal God reaching out in concern and love to sinners and outcasts. They are recommended readings for the celebration of the sacrament of Penance, where Jesus definitively says to us, "Your sins are forgiven. Go, sin no more."

◆ *Zacchaeus Out on a Limb* (see Luke 19:1–10). Zacchaeus has two strikes against him. Not only is he a wealthy chief tax collector, viewed as an obnoxious scoundrel by his own people, but he is short. One day Jesus is passing through Jericho, the city of palms. Zacchaeus is dying to get a glimpse of this popular teacher, but he is too short to see over the crowd. A resourceful man, he runs ahead and climbs a sycamore tree on the route. This is not our kind of sycamore tree but rather a Mediterranean one that bears a fruit like a fig. Although this tree has low, wide-spreading branches, it still must have been a sight to see Zacchaeus

trivial tidbit...

Jericho is one of the oldest continuously inhabited cities in the world. Archaeologists have excavated twenty successive communities, the earliest dating back to 9,000 B.C. In the Old Testament the walls of Jericho came "tumbling down" when the Hebrews, led by Joshua, paraded around it blowing trumpets and shouting.

scramble up it. He sacrifices his dignity for a view of Jesus. Apparently Jesus sees the latent good in the tax collector. Approaching the tree, Jesus looks up and, addressing him by name, announces, "Zacchaeus, hurry and come down, for I must stay at your house tonight." The man is elated that Jesus presumes to be welcome at his house, as though they already were two good friends. He shimmies down the tree. But the disapproving crowd grumbles, "He is going to be the guest of a sinner." Jesus is scandalizing them. With instant compunction, Zacchaeus stands and promises Jesus, "Look, half of my possessions, Lord, I will give to the poor; and if I have defrauded anyone of anything, I will pay back four times as much." This restitution far exceeds the twenty percent that Mosaic Law required. Then Jesus proclaims, "Today salvation has come to this house, because he too is a son of Abraham. For the Son of Man came to seek out and to save the lost." The merciful heart of Jesus goes after sinners even when they are hiding and even when they are up a tree. Although Zacchaeus' spontaneously offers to make restitution, it's notable that Jesus doesn't demand it. The Jews reinstated sinners only after they did penance, made restitution, offered a Temple sacrifice, and recommitted themselves to the Law. Jesus simply welcomes sinners back and at most warns them not to sin again. He constantly spurs on people to be their best selves.

✥ *Misery Meets Mercy* (see John 8:2–11). The earliest Greek versions of John's Gospel that have been found do not contain the following story. One morning when Jesus is seated teaching people in the Temple, the scribes and Pharisees carry out a scheme concocted to charge him with something. A woman is a pawn in their plan. They bring her to Jesus and make her stand before everyone. They say, "Teacher, this woman was caught in the very act of committing adultery. In the law Moses commanded us to stone such women. Now what do you say?" Notice that although the woman is caught "in the act," her guilty partner is not apprehended. Jesus bends down and writes on the ground with his finger. The accusers keep pressing Jesus for his judgment, while the woman listens, quaking in fear, her fate in his hands. Finally Jesus straightens up and pronounces, "Let anyone among you who is without sin be the first to throw a stone at her." This is a clever answer. Jesus bends down and begins to write again. One by one, beginning with the elders, Jesus' enemies slink away until he is alone with the woman, who must have been mortified as well as terrified. Tongue in cheek, he asks, "Woman, where are they? Has no one condemned you?" She responds, "No one, sir." Then Jesus, the only one present who is technically eligible to stone her, says, "Neither do I condemn you. Go your way and sin no more." St. Augustine poetically described this encounter as "misery meets mercy." This is the only time the Gospels mention that Jesus wrote, but no one knows what he wrote. Some conjecture that he listed the sins of the men in the crowd, or perhaps the names of their mistresses! More important than knowing the undisclosed words is knowing that Jesus gave the woman another chance to live a good life and in the process foiled his enemies again.

trivial tidbit...

In a "wicked version" of the Bible published in 1716, a careless printer had Jesus say to the adulterous woman, "Go your way and sin on more."

quick quote...

God is love the way an emerald is green. He is "I love."

Simone Weil

Holy Land site...

Today, Jacob's well still produces fresh water. It is in a lower chapel in an Orthodox church in Nablus, a town north of Jerusalem that is in the region still referred to as Samaria today.

◆ *A Woman Who Loves* (see Luke 7:36–50). A Pharisee named Simon once invited Jesus to dine at his house. When Jesus arrives, the customary rituals to welcome guests are omitted, but Jesus overlooks this rudeness and stays. While he is eating, a sinful woman who has heard Jesus was there enters the house. At a feast the doors were usually left open so that the popularity and prestige of the host could be observed. The woman, who was probably a prostitute, carries an alabaster jar of ointment. Scandalously unveiled and with hair unbraided, she makes her way to where Jesus reclines and stands behind him at his feet. She is weeping, her tears spilling from her face onto his feet, which she dries with her hair. She kisses Jesus' feet, which is an expression of grateful love, and anoints them with the precious ointment. We don't know what prompted this woman's abandoned display of love. Perhaps she had an encounter with Jesus previously, or maybe she had just heard him teach and was moved by his parables about God's mercy and love for sinners. We may wonder what emotions the woman's actions evoked in Jesus' heart—certainly not embarrassment or dismay, but rather a tender sympathy. He was fully aware of the cause of her tears. Simon, the host, reasons that if Jesus were really a prophet he wouldn't allow a woman to touch him, especially a wanton one like her. Jesus, of course, is not afraid to break taboos. He defends the woman by posing a riddle to Simon: "A certain creditor had two debtors; one owed five hundred *denarii*, and the other fifty. (A *denarius* was a day's wages.) When they couldn't pay, he canceled the debts for both. Now which of them will love him more?" Simon grudgingly answers, "I suppose the one for whom he canceled the greater debt." Jesus says, "Right." Then he contrasts Simon and the woman on three points, and in each case the woman puts Simon to shame. In a searing reply to Simon, Jesus charges, "Do you see this woman? I entered your house; you gave me no water for my feet, but she has bathed my feet with her tears and dried them with her hair. You gave me no kiss, but from the time I came in she has not stopped kissing my feet. You did not anoint my head with oil, but she has anointed my feet with ointment." Then Jesus assures the sobbing woman, "Your sins are forgiven. Your faith has saved you. Go in peace." The others at the table murmur, "Who is this who even forgives sins?"

❖ *Jesus in Glory on a Mountain* (see Matthew 17:1–8; Mark 9:2–8; Luke 9: 28–36). Jesus invites Peter, James, and John to come up a mountain alone with him to pray. To Jews, a mountain was the place of revelation and communion with God. Luke relates that the three apostles are overcome by sleep, perhaps because they have climbed a mountain and spent hours in prayer. But suddenly they are wide-awake, because Jesus has been "transfigured," made resplendent in a way that showed his divinity. His face shines like the sun, and his clothes are dazzling white. Moses and Elijah appear and talk with him. These two figures from the Old Testament are charismatic Jewish personages. Moses represents the Law and Elijah the prophets. Luke lets us know that the three speak about the "departure" Jesus is about to accomplish in Jerusalem, a euphemism for his passion and death, his exodus. Peter, overcome with awe at this supernatural

short prayer...

Merciful Jesus, I trust in you.

Holy Land site...

Although modern scholars conclude that it's more likely that the transfiguration took place on Mount Hermon or even Mount Carmel, tradition holds that Mount Tabor was the site. A road with hairpin curves leads to the top of Mount Tabor, where a basilica commemorates the event.

fyi...

The Greek word for transfiguration is *metamorphosis*. Jesus' transfiguration foreshadows the resurrection, when Jesus undergoes the change from mortal human life to new, glorified life.

Other Versions of the Woman Who Anointed Jesus

The other Gospels tell stories that are similar to the one in Luke. The purpose of their accounts, however, is not to show the value of contrition but to hint at Jesus' death. In Matthew 26:6–13 and Mark 14:3–9, Jesus is dining at the house of Simon the leper when a woman breaks open an alabaster jar and pours costly oil on his head, much the way that we pour champagne on the heads of victors. This is an extravagant gesture, but love does such things.

In John 12:1–8, Jesus is dining at the house of Lazarus, and Martha serves, which is no surprise. Their sister Mary anoints Jesus' feet with expensive perfume, and the fragrance fills the room. Although a few drops will do, she uses an entire pound. In all three Gospels, when observers (John's Gospel says Judas) criticize the waste of oil and argue that it could have been sold and the money given to the poor, Jesus explains that this anointing is in preparation for his burial. In Matthew and Mark, Jesus not only defends the woman but predicts that people will hear of her throughout the world wherever the good news is told. His prediction proves true.

experience, wants to prolong it. He exclaims, "Lord, it is good that we are here. If you wish, I will make three tents here, one for you, one for Moses and one for Elijah." He may have been thinking of the shelters the Israelites constructed for the Feast of Tabernacles in remembrance of their desert sojourn. While Peter is speaking, a bright cloud, the sign of God's presence, overshadows all of them. A voice from the cloud proclaims, "This is my beloved Son with whom I am well pleased. Listen to him!" God the Father declares his love and approval of his Son and commands us to listen to Jesus, who is a greater mouthpiece for him than either Moses or Elijah. The three apostles, trembling, fall to the ground face down until Jesus comes and touches each one, saying, "Get up, and do not be afraid." The apostles look up and see no one but Jesus. On the way down the mountain Jesus tells them not to say anything about the vision until after he is raised from the dead. Some scholars think this epiphany occurred after the resurrection. Others argue that it lacks post-resurrection characteristics. As it appears in the Gospel, the transfiguration in which Jesus is glorified and affirmed by the Father serves to strengthen the three apostles, and Jesus himself, for facing a future ordeal not on a mountaintop but on a hill, Calvary.

quick quote...

Although the transfiguration was remarkable, the greater wonder is that Jesus was able to hide his glory every day.

Archbishop Fulton Sheen

big book search...

Read 2 Peter 1:16–18, where Peter recalls the revelation he received on the mountain. Write a statement of how you might have felt had you been there.

✦ *Martha and Mary, Two Different Ways* (see Luke 10:38–42). When Jesus and the apostles come to Bethany, Martha welcomes Jesus into her home, so she was most likely the oldest. Her sister Mary sits at the Lord's feet and listens to him, while Martha bustles about preparing for the meal. Martha, probably

The Samaritan Woman Who Thirsts

En route to Galilee from Judea, instead of skirting Samaria as most Jews do, Jesus travels through this land of "sinners." (See John 4:5–42.) The Gospel states that Jesus *had* to pass through, as though it were ordained that he meet this particular woman there. About noon Jesus, exhausted by the journey, is resting by Jacob's well in Samaria while the disciples are fetching food in the city. A Samaritan woman comes to the well to draw water, although women usually gathered there in the morning. Jesus startles her by requesting, "Give me a drink." Aware that Jews don't speak to Samaritans, share utensils with them, or talk to women in public, she asks, "How is it that you, a Jew, ask a drink of me, a woman of Samaria?" Instead of refusing to speak to Jesus and leaving, she too breaks with convention and converses with him. Jesus replies that if she knew who he was, she would have asked him for living water. The well is fed by an underground spring, and this moving water is referred to as "living water." However, Jesus is figuratively referring to eternal life. The woman takes his words literally and retorts that he has no bucket and the well is deep. How will he get that living water? She asks if he is greater than Jacob and his sons. Jesus replies with a riddle: "Everyone who drinks of this water will be thirsty again, but those who drink of the water I give will never be thirsty. It will become in them a spring gushing up to eternal life." The woman, still on the literal level, asks for this water so that she may never thirst again or have to come to the well again. First, though, she needs to come face-to-face with her sin.

Jesus, who knows all our secrets, plays a bit with the woman. He says, "Go call your husband, and come back." But the woman answers with an ambiguous half-truth, "I have no husband." Jesus zeroes in on the whole truth and says, "You are right, for you have had five husbands, and the one you are living with now is not your husband." The woman, impressed that he knows all about her, respectfully says, "Sir, I see that you are a prophet," and abruptly changes the subject. She introduces a theological topic, remarking that Samaritans worship on their mountain while Jews say people must worship in Jerusalem. Jesus explains that salvation is from the Jews and soon people will worship neither on the mountain nor in Jerusalem but in spirit and truth. Once the spirit of the risen Lord is released on earth, worship will never be the same. The woman says, "I know the Messiah is coming," and Jesus admits, "I am he." This is the first time that Jesus states that he is the Messiah. It is noteworthy that it is to a Samaritan and a woman.

The disciples return and are thunderstruck to find Jesus speaking with a Samaritan—and a woman at that. The conversation has left the Samaritan woman so flustered that when she departs, she leaves her water jar behind. Perhaps this forgotten jar symbolizes that her life is changed. She has received living water, grace, personally from Jesus. And she has finally found the love she has thirsted for. The woman returns to the city and, buoyed up by her life-giving encounter with Jesus, she now fearlessly goes about in public. She becomes an evangelizer to her people, non-Jews. She tactfully invites them, "Come and see a man who told me everything I have ever done! He can't be the Messiah, can he?" Other Samaritans walk out to the well to see Jesus.

In the meantime the disciples urge Jesus to eat something, but he replies, "I have food to eat that you do not know about." Then he explains, "My food is to do the will of him who sent me and to complete his work." With his whole being Jesus is dedicated to the Father and to doing the Father's work. This is what gives him life and energizes him. When the Samaritans arrive, they ask Jesus to stay with them, and he does for two days. Many are persuaded to believe that he is the Savior of the world, not only on the word of the woman but because of his words.

This story illustrates just how Jesus does the Father's will. He courts the outcast again, playfully sparring with a woman so immoral and alienated that she can't fetch water with the other women but must venture out in the scorching noonday sun. And she's a Samaritan no less! Ironically neither Jesus nor the woman has had a drink of water. They have both been refreshed by their conversation.

trivial tidbit...

The Orthodox Church honors the Samaritan woman as St. Photini, a name which means "the enlightened one." They believe that she converted her five sisters and two sons, and preached the good news until the day she was martyred.

after grumbling for a while, comes over to Jesus and asks in an accusing tone, "Lord, do you not care that my sister has left me to do all the work by myself? Tell her then to help me." But instead of rescuing Martha, Jesus pinpoints the real trouble. He says, "Martha, Martha," repeating her name, a sign of loving friendship, "you are worried and distracted by many things. There is need of only one thing. Mary has chosen the better part, which will not be taken away from her." For centuries this story has been used to teach that a life of prayer, listening to the Lord, supersedes a life of activity. In actuality both prayer and action are ways to serve the Lord. As someone said, "Being and doing are sisters." If Martha hadn't prepared the meal, the three wouldn't have eaten. The problem seems to be the way Martha was carrying out her tasks: worried and distracted. Perhaps she was trying to do too much, preparing an eight-course meal instead of simple fare. Ideally our action will be combined with prayer so that it is carried out in faith and calmly. It's been proposed that the untold ending of the story is that after the meal both Jesus and Mary get up and do the dishes! Another interpretation of this pericope focuses on Mary's sitting at Jesus' feet in the typical fashion of a male disciple. Jesus could be teaching that the one thing necessary for every follower is to listen to him. It could also mean that women have as much right as men to be disciples of Jesus.

❖ *Children as Models* (see Matthew 18:1–5, 19:13–15; Mark 10:13–16; Luke 18:16–17). People like to present their babies to be kissed and held by political VIPs. One day people brought their children and infants to Jesus in hopes that he would lay his hands on them and pray. The disciples sternly order the parents to leave Jesus alone. Instead of thanking the disciples for protecting him, Jesus is indignant and reprimands them, saying, "Let the little children come to me, and do not stop them; for it is to such as these that the kingdom of heaven belongs. Whoever does not receive the kingdom of God as a little child will never enter it." Then, to the parents' delight, this bachelor prophet takes the children up in his arms, lays his hands on them, and blesses them. Another time the disciples ask Jesus who will be the greatest in heaven. Jesus calls over a little child. We can picture Jesus putting his hands on the child's shoulders and presenting him to the crowd. Jesus says, "Unless you change and become like children, you will never enter the kingdom of heaven. Whoever becomes humble like this child is the greatest in the kingdom of heaven. Whoever welcomes one such child in my name welcomes me" (Matthew 18:1–5). Jesus makes children a flesh-and-blood parable illustrating what a member of the kingdom is like: simple, dependent, and humble. Children are helpless, so everything is a gift to them. Similarly, the kingdom of God is sheer gift to its members. Especially in Jesus' culture, children were nobodies. They had no rights and were not self-important. In Jesus' kingdom the highest places go to the nobodies.

trivial tidbit...

There is a tradition that the child Jesus used in his demonstration was St. Peter's son. Another tradition holds that he was the future St. Ignatius of Antioch.

◆ *A Widow's Penny* (Mark 12:41–44; Luke 21:1–4). One day Jesus notices something that he turns into a springboard for a lesson in generosity. He has just denounced the scribes for seeking honor, for devouring

quick quote...

The path of trusting love is to count on our heavenly Father for everything in a spontaneous movement of abandonment, like that of children, remaining convinced of our radical nothingness, but nevertheless sure of his paternal goodness, if necessary with boldness.

Blessed Teresa of Calcutta

widows' houses, and for saying long prayers just to impress people. A widow serves as a foil to them. Jesus sits in the Court of Women area of the Temple and watches people deposit money in the thirteen trumpet-shaped treasury chests. Many rich people donate large amounts. Then a poor widow comes along and deposits two small copper coins, the lowest coin in circulation. Making use of this teachable moment, Jesus summons his disciples. Either Jesus knows the woman or else he has the power to divine her situation. He explains to the disciples that the widow gave more money than all the rest because while others donated from their abundance, she sacrificed everything she had to live on. She trusts God to provide the bread for her next meal.

A Lesson in Humility

Once when Jesus notices guests choosing the places of honor, he teaches, "When you are invited to a wedding banquet, don't sit in the place of honor, in case someone more distinguished than you has been invited. For then the host may say to you, 'Give this person your place,' and then in disgrace you would head for the lowest place. Instead, when you are invited sit at the lowest place so that your host may say to you, 'Friend, move up higher,' and you will be honored. All who exalt themselves will be humbled, and those who humble themselves will be exalted" (Luke 14:8–11). How well Jesus understands human nature.

18 Lawgiver: Moral Code and Beatitudes

As we might expect, most of the ethical teachings of Jesus are found in Matthew, who presents him as another Moses, who was the original "lawgiver." Jesus always emphasized that he was not abolishing the old law. He taught that his followers will be able to draw out from the storehouse of morality both old and the new. When asked how to be perfect, he answers, "Keep the commandments." When asked how to attain eternal life, he responds with the Jewish Shema, "Love God," and with another Jewish law, "Love your neighbor." However, Jesus requires even more from his followers than simple adherence to rules. At the Last Supper he commands that we are to show the utmost love, namely the same love that he shows us. And we know the demands and beauty of Jesus' total and unconditional love. It compelled him to come to earth as a human being and to lay down his life for us. As part of his mission on earth, Jesus spells out for us in word and deed how we too can show this divine love in our lives. The moral laws that Jesus dictates go far beyond what the Jewish law required. They describe an ideal way of living. In setting forth this new moral code, Jesus was more than a new Moses. He was Yahweh.

Holy Land site...

The Mount of the Beatitudes, north of the Sea of Galilee, is said to afford the most magnificent view of it. On the mount stands a church built in 1938 to replace a fourth-century Byzantine church. In its eight-sided cupola are windows, each with the first line of a beatitude. Though this mount is only surmised to be the setting for the Sermon on the Mount, its slope does form a natural amphitheatre. When visiting the Holy Land, both Pope Paul VI and Pope John Paul II left stoles there, which are displayed to this day.

The Beatitudes as Right Attitudes

In the beatitudes, Jesus hands us the blueprint for living a happy life. How ironic that he teaches us to avoid what the world prizes as keys to a happy life: possessions, power, and prestige. Both Matthew and Luke give us a set of beatitudes. (See Matthew 5:3–11; Luke 6:20–26.) Although the beatitudes listed by Matthew are referred to as the "eight" beatitudes, there are really nine, but the last two are very similar. Each beatitude declares a certain kind of person to be *blessed* (which means "happy"), and then promises a reward, mostly some expression that means participation in the eternal life of God. This format was a common teaching device. Luke offers an alternate version of four beatitudes and then pairs each one with a woe that describes an opposite kind of person. Moreover, Luke's beatitudes are in the second person: "Blessed are *you* poor."

Matthew's beatitudes are the grand opening of the first of five long sermons (collections of Jesus' teachings) called the Sermon on the Mount. Jesus, like Moses, is seated. Luke's beatitudes are in the Sermon on the Plain, and Jesus stands. As you read Matthew's version here, notice that the beatitudes are a portrait of Jesus himself.

✦ Blessed are the poor in spirit, for theirs is the kingdom of heaven. "Poor in spirit" here means acknowledging one's total dependence on God.

✦ Blessed are those who mourn, for they will be comforted. Kingdom people grieve over the sin and evil in the world.

♦ Blessed are the meek, for they will inherit the earth. The meek and humble will be raised up, just as Mary's "Magnificat" states. Jesus exhorts us to imitate his meekness.

♦ Blessed are those who hunger and thirst for righteousness, for they will be filled.

♦ Blessed are the merciful, for they will receive mercy. This means we are to forgive and love, especially the needy.

♦ Blessed are the pure in heart, for they will see God. The pure in heart are the good people, the ones who live the law of love.

♦ Blessed are the peacemakers, for they will be called children of God.

♦ Blessed are those who are persecuted for righteousness' sake, for theirs is the kingdom of heaven.

♦ Blessed are you when people revile you and persecute you and utter all kinds of evil against you falsely on my account. Rejoice and be glad, for your reward is great in heaven, for in the same way they persecuted the prophets who were before you.

quick quote...

Jesus founded a new kingdom where the poor are happy, where peace is the principle for living together, where the pure of heart and those who mourn are raised up and comforted, where those who hunger and thirst after justice have their fill, where sinners can be forgiven, where all are brothers and sisters.

Pope Paul VI

Raising the Bar

Jesus said, "In everything do to others as you would have them do to you" (Matthew 7:12). This guiding principle for moral living, the ethic of reciprocity, the law of love, is found in most faith traditions. However, usually it is expressed negatively (Do not do...), which is sometimes called the "silver rule." Jesus' moral vision is much more proactive.

In Matthew, Jesus lays out his laws using the for-

quick quote...

Christianity has not been tried and found wanting. Christianity has been found difficult, and left untried.

Gilbert K. Chesterton

mula, "You have heard that it was said…, but I say to you." Jesus is quite radical in that he demands more of people than the old law did. In fact, he holds up an unattainable ideal when he says, "Be perfect, therefore, as your heavenly Father is perfect" (Matthew 5:48). In the first six cases that follow, Jesus has intensified the old law, usually extending it to govern our inner spirit too. In the last four, he gives examples of things to avoid:

◆ *Anger.* Old law: Forbids murder. Jesus: Anger, insulting another, and name-calling will all be punished. Jesus focuses on the interior motivation for murder: anger. Moreover, he teaches that if you are about to offer your gift at the altar and remember that someone has something against you, leave your gift and first be reconciled. Also, if someone accuses you, try to settle out of court. (See Matthew 5:21–26.)

◆ *Adultery.* Old law: Forbids adultery. Jesus: Anyone who looks at a woman with lust has already committed adultery. Again Jesus gets at the root of the matter that leads to adultery. Speaking in typical oriental fashion, he makes the dramatic statement that it is better to tear out your eye, lose a member of your body, and cut off your right hand if they cause you to sin, rather than have your whole body go to hell. (See Matthew 5:2–32.)

◆ *Divorce.* Old law: Accepts divorce and decrees only that a certificate of divorce be given. Jesus: Bans divorce, (except, Matthew says, in case of unchastity). Whoever marries a divorced woman also commits adultery. (See Matthew 5:31–32.) Mark has Jesus add, "What God has joined together, let no one separate" (Mark 10:9).

◆ *Oaths.* Old law: Forbids false oaths but says to carry out vows. Jesus: No one should swear; you should always speak the truth, so that simply making a statement should be sufficient. He refers to oath formulas in which the Jews swore by heaven, earth, Jerusalem, or their heads. (See Matthew 5:33–37.)

◆ *Retaliation.* Old law: An eye for an eye and a tooth for a tooth (meaning you cannot extract from someone who harmed you more than the harm done to you). Jesus: "If someone strikes you on the right cheek, turn the other also; and if anyone wants to sue you and take your coat, give your cloak as well; if anyone forces you to go one mile, go also a second mile. Give to everyone who begs from you and do not refuse anyone who wants to borrow from you" (Matthew 6:38–42).

◆ *Enemies.* Old law: Love your neighbor and hate your enemy. Jesus: "Love your enemies and pray for those who persecute you, so that you may be children of your Father in heaven; for he makes his sun rise on the evil and on the good, and sends rain on the righteous and on the unrighteous. For if you love those who love you, what reward do you have?" (Matthew 5:44–46).

◆ *Flaunting Piety.* Jesus teaches that those who are religious just to be seen by others will not be rewarded. He says that when giving alms we should not let our left hand know what our right hand is doing. When we pray, we should go into our room and shut the door. When we fast, we should do it secretly. (See Matthew 6:1–18.)

trivial tidbit...

In the Bible as a whole there are 250 beatitudes declared by various people.

quick quote...

Forgive, and you will be forgiven; give, and it will be given to you. A good measure, pressed down, shaken together, running over will be put into your lap.

Jesus of Nazareth
(Luke 6:37–38)

for your spiritual health...

Renew yourself by the practice of making a daily examination of conscience as a means to become a better, more Christlike person.

◆ *Riches.* Jesus advises that instead of storing up treasures on earth, store up treasures in heaven that will be safe from rust, moths, and thieves. He observes, "Where your treasure is, there your heart will be also" (Matthew 6:21). He also says that no one can serve two masters and therefore we cannot serve God and wealth (see Luke 16:13), a truth borne out powerfully by the plight of the current world economic crisis, which was caused by greed.

◆ *Judging.* Jesus recommends not judging others so that we may not be judged. He cleverly asks, "How can you say to your neighbor, 'Let me take the speck out of your eye,' while the log is in your own eye?" (Matthew 7:4) This is one example of how Jesus uses word pictures to convey an abstract lesson in a memorable way.

◆ *Giving Scandal.* Jesus teaches, "If any of you put a stumbling block before one of these little ones who believe in me, it would be better for you if a great millstone were fastened around your neck and you were drowned in the depth of the sea" (Matthew 18:6). To show the gravity of this crime, Jesus uses a strong image, for the Jews considered death without burial abhorrent. Moreover, if the millstone excavated at Capernaum is an indication of the size and weight of what Jesus had in mind, there would be no chance of survival.

The Challenge of Jesus

Jesus realizes that what he asks is pretty daunting. He exhorts us, "Enter through the narrow gate; for the gate is wide and the road is easy that leads to destruction, and there are many who take it. For the gate is narrow and the road is hard that leads to life, and there are few who find it" (Matthew 7:13–14). The road to heaven is not a six-lane highway, but a rough, narrow road that leads to a narrow gate.

On the other hand, Jesus has lifted the heavy burden of the ritual laws from peoples' backs. As he said, his yoke is easy. His followers are not bound to the multiple Sabbath regulations and dietary traditions. Pharisees once ask the disciples why they don't fast the way John the Baptist's disciples do. Jesus answers that there's no need for the wedding guests to fast when the bridegroom is present. Bridegroom is a joyous metaphor Jesus chose for himself. It is not unusual, for Yahweh in the Old Testament is presented as Israel's husband, a spouse who is loving even in the face of infidelity. Jesus is also a bridegroom in his parable of the Ten Bridesmaids. In the last book of the Bible, Jesus and the new Jerusalem (the Church) are compared to a husband and bride (see Revelation 21:2, 9). So, this image has overtones of the messianic banquet where Jesus will preside someday with all those who live his Way in loving fidelity.

Jesus employs two practical images to highlight the newness of the way of life he is inaugurating. These images were probably drawn from what he learned from his parents at home. First Jesus points out that no one sews unshrunk cloth on an old cloak or the patch will tear the old cloth. Secondly he uses the example that no one puts new wine into old wineskins. Otherwise when the wine ferments and emits gas, the old, brittle skins will burst and the wine will be lost. (See Mark 2:21–22.)

All people are called to holiness. (Those who are canonized, offcially declared saints, have lived lives of heroic virtue.) The presence of the Holy Spirit in someone is indicated by the fruits of the Holy Spirit: charity, joy, peace, patience, kindness, goodness, generosity, gentleness, faithfulness, modesty, self-control, and chastity. (See Galatians 5:22-23.)

19 Prophet: Facing Opposition

Jesus' life is the prime example of the adage "No good deed goes unpunished." In light of his wondrous feats and remarkable teaching, you would think that everyone would have hailed him as a hero. Indeed, it was once observed that the whole world is running after him, and Luke reports a time "when the crowd gathered by the thousands, so that they trampled on one another" (Luke 12:1). Jesus was the last and greatest prophet in Israel. A prophet is a messenger of God who is intoxicated by God and protests against flawed religion and social injustices. He or she works to make God's vision for the world a reality. Two disciples describe Jesus as "a prophet mighty in deed and word" (Luke 24:19). After the multiplication of loaves, the people say, "This is indeed the prophet who is to come into the world" (John 6:14). They want to make Jesus king, but instead of cooperating, he disappears. His enormous popularity was probably one of the very things that triggered antipathy in the hearts of some. For it made the religious leaders prey to that green-eyed monster, jealousy. It also caused Jewish authorities to fear that Rome would crack down on the potentially dangerous crowds. What's more, Jesus was never concerned about being politically correct. He flouted cultural customs, broke Jewish laws, and made seemingly blasphemous claims, actions that enraged the scribes and Pharisees. Hatred of Jesus became a tidal wave that swelled until it destroyed him.

for your spiritual health...

A prophet's role is to comfort the afflicted and to afflict the comfortable. Think of one way that you have been or could be a prophet, or call to mind someone you have observed acting like one.

The Fate of Prophets

Few people take kindly to criticism. As the Old Testament prophets, who spoke for God, called for repentance, they exposed people's faults and were often killed for their efforts. John the Baptist, a New Testament prophet, met with the same fate. Jesus knew his life was in danger from the beginning, but that didn't stop him from preaching the truth and a new social order. Some of his parables, such as the parable of the Wicked Tenants, were blatant descriptions of the unfaithful Jewish leaders. They realized he was speaking about them, but they were afraid to arrest him because of the crowds. Jesus' words and actions obviously rankled them in several ways.

Recall that already at the beginning of Jesus' ministry his neighbors in his hometown object violently to his assertion that he wouldn't be working mighty deeds in Nazareth. They attempt to throw him off a cliff. People have a hard time accepting that someone they know is suddenly acting like a prophet. They ask, "Is not this the carpenter, the son of Mary?" (Mark 6:3). Jesus' relatives are no more supportive of him. When Jesus is so consumed by his mission that he doesn't eat, they think that he is out of his mind. One day a delegation of his relatives travels to Capernaum to bring home Jesus, whom they must have viewed as the black sheep of the family.

Throughout his public ministry, Jesus dealt with skeptical people. For example, he casts a demon out of a mute man, who Matthew says was also blind. (See Matthew 12:22–29; Luke 11:14–22.) When the man can hear and see again, some people accuse Jesus of curing him by Beelzebul, the ruler of the demons.

Calmly Jesus appeals to common sense and reasons with them that he couldn't be an agent of Satan, for whom casting out a demon would be counterproductive. Jesus points out that a kingdom divided against itself cannot stand. If Satan is divided, how will his kingdom stand? Furthermore, Jesus asks the people if he casts out demons by Beelzebul, by whom do their exorcists cast them out? On the other hand, if Jesus casts out demons by the finger of God, then the kingdom of God has come. Then patiently through a story Jesus teaches that the power of God is mightier than Satan's. He says that a strong man fully armed guards his castle safely until a stronger man overpowers him (Luke adds "ties him up") and takes his armor and possessions. Besides dealing with the skeptical people, Jesus also had to suffer the loss of the many disciples who became disenchanted with him and quit following him.

trivial tidbit...

The Jews called Satan Beelzebul, a name derived from Baal the Prince, who was a pagan god of the people surrounding them. Probably originally in jest, they changed Baal to Beelzebub, which means "the lord of the flies."

Sabbath Scandals

Keeping holy the Lord's Day, the Sabbath, is God's commandment. By observing the Sabbath, the Jews were imitating God, who rested on the seventh day after the work of creation. Scripture states that the penalty for working on the Sabbath is death (Exodus 31:15). Jewish leaders interpreted the Law in a collection of 613 rules. Thirty-nine main headings had to do with what is forbidden on the Sabbath. These include sewing more than two stitches, harvesting more than two ears of corn, walking more than 1,000 yards, and carrying anything heavier than a fig. These laws made observing the Sabbath more of a burden than the day of rest that God intended it to be. By

trivial tidbit...

Muslims acknowledge Jesus as a prophet, but they don't believe he is God. For them, Adam was the first prophet and Muhammad was the last.

action and word, Jesus tried to reinstate the original meaning of the Sabbath, thereby incurring the wrath of those Jews who enforced their manmade regulations as vigorously as they did God's Law.

One day as Jesus is walking through fields of grain, the disciples pluck some grain and rub them in their hands to remove the chaff. The Pharisees ask Jesus why they were acting unlawfully and working on the Sabbath. Jesus reminds them that David and his companions unlawfully once ate special bread meant only for priests. (Twelve loaves of bread were kept in the Meeting Tent where God was present. They were then consumed by priests. Once when David and his followers were hungry, the priest gave the sacred bread to him.) Jesus instructs the Pharisees, "The Sabbath was made for humankind, and not humankind for the Sabbath" (Mark 2:27). In Matthew, Jesus tells the Pharisees they have not understood what God says to the prophet Hosea, "I desire mercy and not sacrifice."

As already seen, Jesus "worked" miracles on the Sabbath. In the process he broke other Sabbath laws, for instance by making clay for the blind man's eyes and ordering a paralyzed man to work by carrying his mat on the Sabbath. After some Sabbath miracles, Jesus used examples of rescuing an animal on the Sabbath (which was allowed) to lead the Jewish teachers to see that human need was above the law. He also pointed out that circumcisions were done on the Sabbath, so why shouldn't he cure a man's whole body? (See John 7:21–23.) His words usually fell on deaf ears. The Jewish authorities concluded that anyone who violated the Sabbath as Jesus did could not be a man of God.

Ignoring Washing Rules

The Jews had numerous washing rituals. These were not for the purpose of hygiene. Rather they were the Pharisees' attempt to extend the ritual practices of the Jewish priests to the people as a whole because they were a priestly people. Mark explains that the Jews don't eat unless they thoroughly wash their hands, they don't eat anything from the market unless they wash it, and they have many other traditions regarding washing cups, pots, and kettles (see Mark 7:3–4). To the Pharisees' dismay, Jesus and his disciples do not always conform to these traditions.

One day Pharisees and scribes ask Jesus, "Why do your disciples break the tradition of the elders? For they do not wash their hands before they eat." Jesus turns the tables and asks why they break God's commandments for the sake of their traditions. He gives the example of someone who disobeys the commandment to honor mother and father by giving to God money that should go to support the parents. Then Jesus calls a crowd over and teaches, "It is not what goes into the mouth that defiles a person, but what comes out of the mouth." In other words, it is sin—not eating with unwashed hands—that defiles a person. Purity of the heart is what matters. When the disciples tell Jesus that the Pharisees are offended by what he says, Jesus responds, "Let them alone. They are blind guides of the blind. And if one blind person guides another, both will fall into a pit" (Matthew 15:1–20). The self-righteousness of the Pharisees is toxic.

Korban means a sacrifice offered to God. The scribes and Pharisees taught that by korban, offering money or property to God, a son could cancel any claim his parents had on it.

quick quote...

Jesus not only challenged the politics of purity but advocated the politics of compassion.

Marcus Borg

big book search...

Jesus upheld the prophet Micah's pithy summary of what God expects of us. Read Micah's oft-quoted words in Micah 6:8.

Criticism

Despite the signs that point to Jesus as the Messiah, the religious leaders of his time fail to recognize him, and Jesus refuses to give them more signs. When the scribes and Pharisees ask for a sign, Jesus says, "An evil and adulterous generation asks for a sign, but no sign will be given to it except the sign of the prophet Jonah. For just as Jonah was three days and three nights in the belly of the sea monster, so for three days and three nights the Son of Man will be in the heart of the earth" (Matthew 12:38–40). Jesus goes on to say that the Ninevites (the Assyrians who conquered Israel and were called to repentance by Jonah) as well as the queen of the South (from Africa, who journeyed to listen to Solomon) will both condemn this generation because something greater than Jonah and Solomon is here. In other words, even enemies and foreigners will condemn the Jews for their obtuseness. (See Matthew 12:38–42.)

Later Jesus repeats this accusation, cleverly referring to nature. He says, "When there's a red sky at night, there will be fair weather. If there's a red sky in the morning, it will be stormy. You know how to interpret the sky but not the signs of the times" (Matthew 16:2–3).

Another time a Pharisee invites Jesus to dine and is amazed when Jesus doesn't wash before he goes to the table. At that, Jesus bursts forth with blistering criticisms of the Pharisees. (See Luke 11:37–53; Matthew 23:1–36.) Today, we take such violent condemnations by Jesus with a grain of salt, knowing that the evangelists were writing at a time when Pharisees were beating and killing Jewish Christians. In Luke's account, Jesus accuses the Pharisees of cleaning the outside of the cup and the dish while they themselves are full of greed and wickedness inside. He goes on to exclaim, "You fools!" and he lists the Pharisees' crimes: tithing but neglecting justice and the love of God, and loving to have the seat of honor and to be greeted with outward demonstrations of respect. Jesus says that the Pharisees are unmarked graves that people walk over without realizing it. Contact with a tomb made one unclean, so Jesus is saying here that the Pharisees, who are so concerned about cleanliness, are themselves unclean.

When the scribes protest that his comments also insult them, Jesus gives them a tongue-lashing too. Among other things, he accuses them of loading people with burdens and not lifting a finger to ease them. He says they take away the key of knowledge from people and walk around in long robes, devouring widows' houses and saying long prayers for the sake of appearance. (See Luke 20:46–47.)

Matthew has Jesus aim even more colorful language in public at both Pharisee and scribes as a group. His charges are called the *seven woes*. Six of the seven accusations begin with "Woe to you, scribes and Pharisees, hypocrites." Jesus says, "You cross sea and land to make a single convert, and you make the new convert twice as much a child of hell as yourselves" (Matthew 23:15). These leaders paid attention to minor things and neglected justice, mercy, and faith. Jesus captures this fault in a vivid metaphor: "You strain out a gnat but swallow a camel" (Matthew 23:24). He compares the leaders to whitewashed tombs, which look beautiful on the outside but inside are full of bones and filth.

trivial tidbit...

Jews at the time of Christ painted tombstones white so that people wouldn't accidentally touch them and become "unclean."

quick quote...

If Jesus Christ were to come today, people would not even crucify him. They would ask him to dinner, and hear what he has to say, and make fun of it.

Thomas Carlyle

Jesus calls the Pharisees and scribes snakes and brood of vipers. After such lambasting, is it any wonder that they turned hostile and lay in wait to catch him in something he might say wrong that would show that he was not from God?

Blasphemy

This was the biggie that got Jesus in the most trouble. The Jews believed in one invisible God. Consequently for Jesus to claim God's powers was blasphemy. In the incident of plucking corn on the Sabbath, Jesus makes two loaded statements. He asserts, "Something greater than the temple is here" (Matthew 12:6) and "The Son of Man is lord even of the sabbath" (Mark 2:28). In other words, this young man was equating himself with God. Such blasphemous statements made the Pharisees see red. To them Jesus was a megalomaniac. When Jesus then says, "My father is still working, and I also am working," they become determined to kill him, because calling God his Father was equivalent to making himself equal to God. And how could there be two Gods? (See John 5:17–18). Jesus scolds the Jews for not believing John the Baptist, who testified for him. He says that the works the Father has him do also testify to his legitimacy. So, in his mind, do the Scriptures and Moses. Jesus states that they refuse to come to him to have life, and he bluntly charges, "You do not have the love of God in you" (John 5:42).

When Jesus teaches, he uses the expression "I say to you." In the original text, the people are not "astounded" to hear him speak this way but "alarmed." This is because the Torah, God's law, was the ultimate authority, and here was a man claiming that authority. In fact, the Jews had a saying that wherever there were two or more of them and the Torah, God was present. Jesus paraphrases it: "Wherever two or three are gathered in my name there I am in their midst" (Matthew 18:20).

Another time when Jesus heals the paralytic and says to him, "Your sins are forgiven," the scribes and Pharisees wonder, "Who is this who is speaking blasphemies? Who can forgive sins but God alone?" (Luke 5:21).

Jesus tries to expand the Jewish leaders' thinking by asking, "How can they say that the Messiah is David's son? For David says in the book of Psalms, 'The Lord said to my Lord, "Sit at my right hand, until I make your enemies your footstool."' David calls him Lord, so how can he be his son?" (Luke 20:41–44). Jesus doesn't provide the answer, but after the resurrection it's clear that he, the Son of David, is Lord of all.

quick quote...

There is more hunger for love and appreciation in this world than for bread.

Blessed Mother Teresa of Calcutta

The Wrong Crowd

The Pharisees and scribes saw themselves as the righteous ones. They avoided contamination by contact with undesirable people like sinners, tax collectors, prostitutes, lepers, and the like. Jesus, on the other hand, associated with this motley group of untouchables and shook up the established social order. In his stories, Jesus made tax collectors and Samaritans his heroes, showing that he was for the underdog. He acted freely, not bound by culture and transcending its taboos. Innumerable times Jesus touched people considered unclean, or "dirty," and let them touch him, thereby polluting himself. To the Jews, dining with

trivial tidbit...

Mark 11:16 notes that Jesus wouldn't let anyone carry anything across the Temple. People were accustomed to taking a shortcut through the Temple, and Jesus made it clear that this bordered on the sacrilegious.

someone expressed mutual acceptance and a bond of kinship. The table was a "little temple." Jesus dared to eat with crooks and riffraff. Based on the hostility he aroused by his inclusive meals, someone once quipped that Jesus ate himself to death! And he still eats with sinners today—all of us.

Setting the Trap to Arrest Jesus

Jesus further antagonizes the Jews by predicting the fall of Jerusalem. Approaching this city one day, he actually breaks downs and weeps at the thought of its destruction, for he loves it. Jesus foretells, "Your enemies will set up ramparts around you and hem you in on every side. They will crush you to the ground, you and your children within you, and they will not leave within you one stone upon another" (Luke 19:41–44). Later, when some people were speaking about the beautiful stones of the Temple and the gifts offered there, Jesus predicts that one day "not one stone will be left upon another. All will be thrown down" (Luke 21:6). Both the Temple and the holy city Jerusalem were supreme icons for the Jews. They stood for everything their religion and culture deeply cherished. To hear someone talk about the complete destruction of these icons was abominable. The "kill the messenger" practice would prove to be in effect.

The Jewish leaders connive to trap Jesus in his speech so that they can hand him over to the authorities. Each time they try something, however, Jesus cleverly foils their schemes. One day, for example, Pharisees and Herodians (Luke has "spies" instead of Herodians) approach Jesus. (See Luke 20:20–26.) They ask him if it is lawful to pay taxes to the emper-

The Cleansing of the Temple

Jesus' cleansing of the Temple has been called his "temple tantrum." (See Matthew 21:12–13; Mark 11:15–18; Luke 19:45–46; John 2:13–22.) For the Synoptics, this action by Jesus is the immediate catalyst that puts into motion the plot to eliminate him. In John's Gospel, however, this disturbing event is placed at the beginning of Jesus' ministry, where it sets the Jewish leaders against him from the very start. Through this act, Jesus takes on the religious establishment directly, hitting them where it hurts—in the pocketbook. In the Temple courtyard people sold animals for the sacrifices and moneychangers exchanged coins that bore pagan images for coins that were acceptable for donation. One day Jesus becomes so incensed at the commercialism and sometimes shady business going on in the holy place where God was present that with eyes flashing he fashions a whip out of cords and drives the sellers and moneychangers, along with the sheep and cattle, completely out of the Temple. He pours out the moneychangers' coins and overturns their tables. He shouts at those selling doves, "Take these things out of here! Stop making my Father's house a marketplace!" (John 2:16). Imagine the chaos: animals bleating, cattle bellowing, birds panicking, vendors yelling, and coins clinking and rolling on the floor. In the Synoptic Gospels, Jesus quotes Scripture: "My house shall be called a house of prayer; but you are making it a den of robbers."

This revolutionary and violent act of Jesus in the holy Temple shocks the Jewish leaders on two counts. First of all, to them Jesus is acting way out of bounds. Who is he to determine what goes on at the Temple? It's surprising that they didn't have temple guards arrest him immediately. Perhaps his crowd of followers was too large. Second, this is the kind of incident that the Jews wanted to avoid at all cost. It might attract the attention of the Romans, who were ready to enforce peace with brutality if necessary.

fyi...

Verbal arguments between Jesus and hostile groups like the scribes and Pharisees are called *controversy dialogues*.

or. This is a loaded question. If Jesus answers yes, the crowd who looked to him as a Messiah to save them from the Romans would turn against him. If Jesus answers no, he can be reported to Rome as an insurrectionist. Aware of their cunning, Jesus unmasks their hypocrisy. He orders, "Show me a *denarius*." It seems that his adversaries do carry this foreign coin, which is inscribed, "Tiberius Caesar, Son of the divine Augustus, great high priest" and displays his image. Possessing this coin indicates that they give allegiance to Rome and also that they have no scruples about the Jewish ban on images. Jesus asks, "Whose head and title does it bear?" The men answer, "The emperor's." Jesus, perhaps with a wink to the apostles, coolly slips out of their trap. He says, "Then give to the emperor the things that are the emperor's and to God the things that are God's." This cryptic answer has been interpreted in different ways. It has been seen as a basis for separation of church and state. It can mean that we are to obey the state, but the state is subject to God's authority. In any case, Jesus' answer serves the purpose. The questioners are baffled and silenced. Jesus has bested them.

Another time Sadducees, who don't even believe in the resurrection, ask Jesus a trick question about it. (See Luke 20:27–40.) According to Jewish law, when a man dies leaving a wife with no children, his brother may marry her and have children for him. The Sadducees pose an extreme hypothetical case, mocking belief in the resurrection. They say suppose that a woman's husband dies and leaves her childless. She marries in turn his seven brothers who each die and leave her childless. When the woman dies, who will be her husband? This is a ludicrous situation calculated to make Jesus look foolish. Jesus has two obvious options. He can align with the Sadducees' thinking and deny resurrection, or he can say that the woman will be married to all eight men, which was polyandry and against Jewish law. Jesus settles the question and eludes the Sadducees' web by responding that in the next age there will be no marriage. (In Mark 12:24 and Matthew 22:30 he says that people will be like angels, who are pure spirits.) Jesus goes on to explain that there will be a resurrection because Moses calls God "the God of Abraham, Isaac, and Jacob" and "the God of the living." Consequently these patriarchs must still be alive. Some of the scribes admit that Jesus has spoken well. They don't dare ask him any more questions.

Finally, Jesus himself pinpoints another reason why he rouses such antipathy when he says, "The world…hates me because I testify against it that its works are evil" (John 7:7). That hatred will soon boil over into a supreme work of evil, when innocence itself is betrayed and crucified in the person of Jesus of Nazareth.

Apologetics is the field of theology that presents reasons for the faith and defends the faith against objections. Christian apologists of note are C.S. Lewis, G.K. Chesterton, and Cardinal John Henry Newman.

20 King: Beginning of the End

Jerusalem was the City of David where that royal ancestor of Jesus had his palace. The Book of Revelation presents an image of Christ riding on a white horse and crowned with a diadem. On his robe and on his thigh are the names *King of kings* and *Lord of lords* (Revelation 19:16). But in stark contrast to the mighty hero of Revelation, Jesus enters Jerusalem meekly on a donkey. In this holy city Christ, the true king, will lay down his life for his people. The hour is drawing near.

At the Festival in Jerusalem

Jesus stays in Galilee because he knows that the Jews are looking for an opportunity to assassinate him. He is at the top of their most wanted list. When the festival of Booths (Tabernacles) approaches, Jesus sends his brothers to Jerusalem for it. He explains that he isn't going, for the world hates him. But then Jesus secretly goes to the festival after all. (See John 7:1–52.)

During the festival Jesus is a main topic of conversation. The people are divided about him. Some say he is a good man, maybe even a prophet, while others denounce him as a deceiver. About the middle of the festival, Jesus goes to the Temple and teaches so well that the Jews marvel at his knowledge. Jesus asserts that his teaching is from the one who sent him. Then he boldly confronts the Jew-

fyi...

The Infant of Prague devotion centers on Jesus as child and king. The statue is a crowned child holding a globe topped by a cross and blessing us. The original eighteen-inch-high statue is wax-covered wood. It was brought from Spain and given to the Discalced Carmelite Fathers in Prague in 1628. After a war, Fr. Cyril found it with rubbish and heard Jesus say, "The more you honor me, the more I shall bless you." This statue, in the Church of Our Lady of Victory, has over seventy sets of clothing.

ish leaders and asks, "Why are you looking for an opportunity to kill me?" (John 7:19). The people debate thus about whether or not Jesus is the Messiah:

- Maybe the authorities won't arrest him because they realize he is the Messiah.
- No one knows where the Messiah comes from, but we know where this man is from.
- When the Messiah comes, will he do more signs than this man?
- Scripture says the Messiah comes from Bethlehem not Galilee.
- He has a demon and is out of his mind.
- Can a demon open the eyes of a blind man?

The Pharisees and the chief priests send Temple police to arrest Jesus. In the meantime Jesus informs the people that he will be with them just a while longer and then will go to the one who sent him. He says they will search for him but not be able to find him, for they can't go where he will be. They don't know what to make of this puzzling statement and wonder if Jesus intends to go out to teach the Greeks.

Each day of the festival there is a ceremony to thank God for rain for the harvest and to pray for rain the coming year. The chief priest fills a large gold pitcher with water from the Pool of Siloam, walks around the altar with it, and pours it into silver basins that lead to the foot of the altar. On the last day of the festival he circles the altar seven times. Against this backdrop on this last and greatest day, Jesus cries out, "Let anyone who is thirsty come to me, and let the one who believes in me drink." To those who believe in him, Jesus promises living water flowing from within. He is referring to the Holy Spirit, who will come after Jesus is glorified.

Impressed by Jesus' words, the police observe, "Never has anyone spoken like this," and they return without him. The Pharisees mock the police for siding with the crowd that doesn't know the law the way they do. Then the Pharisee Nicodemus, however, who has personally spoken with Jesus, dares to remind the others that the law doesn't judge people without a hearing. The Pharisees also mock Nicodemus, saying, "You are not from Galilee too, are you?" The tension heightens.

Light of the World

Each day of the Feast of Tabernacles, four enormous golden candelabras are lit in the Court of the Gentiles to symbolize God's presence with his people. The light illumines the whole city of Jerusalem, and men holding torches dance and sing around the candelabras all night on this festival of joy. Taking his cue from this dramatic background, Jesus calls himself the light of the world and claims that anyone who follows him will have the light of life. He speaks about his Father. He also declares, "When you have lifted up the Son of Man, then you will realize that I am he" (John 8:28). He says that sin enslaves people, but the Son makes them free. He is the light that no darkness can overcome.

trivial tidbit...

In Holman Hunt's popular nineteenth-century painting called "Light of the World," Jesus is knocking at a door overgrown with weeds. He wears a crown of thorns and carries a lantern. The door has no handle or doorknob, not by mistake but to convey that Jesus can't enter our hearts unless we open them.

trivial tidbit...

In 1990, archaeologists unearthed an ornate limestone ossuary from the first century that has the name Caiaphas written on it twice. The ossuary might have contained the bones of a 60-year-old man believed to be Caiaphas, who was high priest for nineteen years.

Later that same trip, Jesus explains that his disciples know the truth and the truth will make them free. (See John 8:31–59.) The people argue that they are not slaves because Abraham is their father. Jesus replies that if they were Abraham's children, they would not be trying to kill him. They then claim that God is their father. Jesus says that if this were true, they would love him because he was sent by the Father. Rather, the devil is their father. If they belonged to God, they would believe his true words. They counter, "Are we not right in saying that you are a Samaritan and have a demon"? (John 8:48). When Jesus says, "Whoever keeps my word will never see death" (John 8:51), they argue that Abraham and the prophets died. Is Jesus greater than they are? Jesus asserts that the Father glorifies him and he knows the Father and keeps his word, so Abraham rejoiced to see his day. Flabbergasted, the people say, "You are not yet fifty years old and have you seen Abraham?" Jesus responds, "Before Abraham was, I am." At this seemingly outrageous blasphemy, the Jews pick up stones to throw at Jesus, but he hides and departs from the Temple.

At the Feast of the Dedication

Jesus is back in Jerusalem for the feast of the Dedication (Hanukkah). (See John 10:22–42.) As he walks in the Temple, some of the people ask him pointblank if he is the Messiah. Jesus answers, "I have told you and you do not believe." He says that his works testify to him. His sheep know his voice and follow him, and he will give them eternal life. When Jesus states, "The Father and I are one," the crowd again prepares to stone him. Jesus asks for which of his good works are they going to stone him, and they reply, "For blasphemy." The authorities try to arrest him again, but he escapes and goes to the land across the Jordan River. While he is there, many people believe in him, which must have been consoling after the poor reception given him in Jerusalem.

It is during this trip that Jesus receives word of the death of Lazarus in Bethany, which is not far from Jerusalem. After Jesus raises Lazarus from the dead, the chief priests and Pharisees and the council hold a joint meeting to discuss how to deal with the problem of Jesus. (See John 11:45–12:11.) They fear that if everyone believes in Jesus, the Romans will destroy their Temple and their nation. The high priest Caiaphas makes a statement that proves prophetic (but not for the reasons he thinks): "It is better for you to have one man die for the people than to have the whole nation destroyed."

Meanwhile Jesus hides in Ephraim near the wilderness like a fugitive. This is the second time he is fleeing for his life. As Passover approaches, people wonder if Jesus will come to Jerusalem. The Pharisees order that anyone knowing his whereabouts should report it so that they can arrest him. Jesus travels again to Bethany where his friends give a dinner for him. Martha serves, and Lazarus is at the table with Jesus. While he is in Bethany, a crowd gathers to see him as well as the resuscitated Lazarus. Some people had actually witnessed the raising; others had heard about it. Getting wind of this, the chief priests plot to put Lazarus to death too as a step in curbing Jesus' popularity (see John 12:9–11).

If anyone comes to me, I want to lead them to Him.

Edith Stein

How fitting that we celebrate the feast of Christ the King on the last Sunday of the liturgical year, before Advent. In 1969 Pope Paul VI made this feast, which was instituted in 1925, a solemnity and gave it a new title: Our Lord Jesus Christ, King of the Universe.

trivial tidbit...

A prophecy describes the king as coming "riding on a donkey, on a colt, the foal of a donkey" (Zechariah 9:9). Matthew seems unaware that Jewish poetry repeats ideas using synonyms. So, in his account of the entrance into Jerusalem, Jesus rides on both a donkey and a colt! (See Matthew 21: 6-7.)

Judas, a Tragic Figure

The Sanhedrin had decided to hold off doing anything about Jesus until after the Passover when his supporters would return home. But then a fortuitous visit from one of Jesus' closest followers enables them to act swiftly. Luke states that Satan entered into Judas. Judas goes to the chief priests and asks, "What will you give me if I betray him to you?" (Matthew 26:15). They pay him thirty pieces of silver, a paltry sum, the price of a slave, and Judas begins to look for a chance to turn Jesus in.

Ever since the apostle Judas Iscariot delivered Jesus into the hands of his enemies, his name has been synonymous with traitor. Parents no longer choose this once-popular name for their children, and traditional art gave him a black halo. We might wonder why Judas just didn't simply walk away from Jesus, as many other disciples did. Several theories have been advanced about the motive for Judas' despicable act:

- Judas was simply greedy. In John 12:6 we learn that he was a thief. He was in charge of the common purse and stole from it.

- In Judas' opinion as a zealot, Jesus was taking too long to come forth as the Messiah, and so he tried to force Jesus' hand to openly begin his rule. Presumably, Judas never thought that Jesus would actually be killed, since Jewish leaders had no power to execute.

- Judas was angry because Jesus had publicly rebuked him for criticizing the anointing by Martha's sister Mary at Bethany.

◆ Judas had become disillusioned with Jesus.

◆ Judas never understood the identity of Jesus and feared that Jesus' enemies were closing in on him, so he struck a deal with them to save his own skin.

◆ Like Caiaphas, Judas feared that the crowds Jesus drew would call down Rome's wrath, and so it was better that this one man die than that Israel endure more oppression.

Matthew states that after Jesus was condemned, Judas regretted what he'd done. Judas returns to the chief priests and admits, "I have sinned in betraying innocent blood." They retort, "What's that to us?" Judas throws down the coins in the Temple and goes and hangs himself. The priests use the blood money to purchase the potter's field for a cemetery for strangers (see Matthew 27:5–10). Acts 1:16–20 reports a different death: Judas dies and his body bursts open when he falls in a field he has bought with the blood money. Jesus commented at the Last Supper that it would have been better if Judas had not been born. The poet Dante places Judas in hell in the lowest level, which is for betrayers. Sadly, Judas didn't know Jesus well enough to realize that even he would have been forgiven if he had just asked.

trivial tidbit...

During the Middle Ages in Germany and Switzerland on Palm Sunday, a wooden carving of a man on a donkey mounted on wheels was pulled through the streets. The figure was called a *palmesal*, literally "palm-ass" in German.

Hailed as King

The day after Caiaphas decides that Jesus must die, thousands of Jews flock to Jerusalem to prepare for the Passover. Jesus begins his death march. (See Matthew 21:1–11; Mark 11:1–11; Luke 19:29–40; John 12:12–19.) On his way to the city, Jesus directs two disciples to enter a village and bring back a colt or

fyi...

Today on Passion Sunday (Palm Sunday) Christians process, waving palms. This practice dates from at least the late fourth century when the pilgrim Etheria described seeing a procession in a Jerusalem church. Ashes from the palms are used the next year for marking foreheads with crosses on Ash Wednesday.

a cool website...

Christians today weave blessed palm into various shapes and display them in their homes. See www.italiansrus.com for a tutorial in palm weaving.

young donkey that they will find tethered there. He instructs them that if anyone asks why they are doing that, they are to respond, "The master has need of it." The disciples do as told. Then they throw their cloaks over the colt for a saddle, help Jesus mount it, and all proceed to Jerusalem. Conquering kings rode stallions, great warhorses, into a city, not donkeys, which are ungainly beasts of burden. Riding a young donkey is a humble act that shows that Jesus comes in peace.

When word gets around that Jesus is coming into the city, people break off palm branches and go to meet him, shouting, "Hosanna. Blessed is the one who comes in the name of the Lord—the King of Israel." *Hosanna* means "God save us." Matthew reports that the whole city was shaken (as by an earthquake). The Pharisees, seeing Jesus become a national hero, tell him to order his disciples to stop; but Jesus replies, "If these were silent, the stones would shout out" (Luke 19:39). People spread their cloaks and branches before him as they did for their kings. The Pharisees bemoan to one another, "You see, you can do nothing. Look, the world has gone after him!" (John 12:19). Unintentionally, their statement, too, is prophetic.

In John's Gospel, some Greeks ask to see Jesus, an inkling that his Way will spread to the Gentiles. (See John 12:20–32.) At this time Jesus speaks as he does in the agony in the garden, an event John omits: "Now my soul is troubled," and "Should I say, 'Father, save me from this hour?'" and "Father, glorify your name." At that, a voice from heaven declares, "I have glorified it, and I will glorify it again." People suppose that this was thunder or an angel speaking.

Jesus explains that the voice was for their sake, not his. He claims, "When I am lifted up from the earth, I will draw all people to myself."

Despite Jesus' many signs, people still don't believe in him (see John 12:36–43). Many, even some of the Jewish authorities, do believe but don't confess it for fear of being banned from the synagogues. John says, "For they loved human glory more than the glory that comes from God" (John 12:43). Jesus poses the same challenge to us today. We can choose to believe or not to believe, depending on whether we love human glory or God's glory more.

When John was writing his Gospel, Christians were being banned from synagogues. which might have prompted him to mention banning in his account of Jesus.

21 Bread of Life: The Last Supper

We must eat to live. In all cultures this necessary task is associated with friendship and celebrations. Making someone a meal or taking them out to dinner is an expression of love. And what's a party without food? At least once Jesus provided a miraculous picnic for thousands of people. This was only a prelude—an appetizer—for the special feast he first held for his friends on the night before he died, a meal called the Last Supper, which is perhaps the most famous meal in history. For twenty centuries this same meal has nourished millions of people who have celebrated it as the Eucharist.

The Passover Connection

The most dramatic saving event for the Jewish people was the Exodus, which commenced with a meal of unleavened bread and lamb. Ever since then, the Jews have commemorated the Exodus each year by sharing the same solemn meal, called the Seder meal, which includes four cups of wine. The Seder takes place during the feast of Passover. This name recalls how when the firstborn of each Egyptian family died during the last of the ten plagues, the Israelites were spared because they had marked their doors with the blood of a lamb as a signal for death to "pass over." Later, as they trekked through the desert, God again saved his people by sending manna, bread from heaven.

At feasts in first-century Israel, people ate reclining on cushions around a low table. They rested on their left sides with their feet away from the table and ate with their right hands. Scholars theorize that the table for the Last Supper was U-shaped and that Jesus was in the place of honor on the left side, flanked by John and Judas, while Peter was at the far end of the opposite side. Scripture doesn't mention women being present at the meal, but it would have been very like Jesus to invite them.

In the Synoptic Gospels' accounts of the last meal Jesus ate with his apostles, lamb isn't mentioned and the four cups of wine apparently aren't drunk. Nevertheless, these Gospels indicate that it was a Passover meal. This would be fitting, because Jesus' passing over from death to life was another saving event, the saving of all creation. Unique as always, John's Gospel, has the meal take place on the day before the Passover. This too is appropriate because it means that Jesus' sacrifice on the cross occurred simultaneously with the sacrifice of the lambs for the Passover meal. Scholars have long debated whether the Last Supper was a Passover meal. Today the tendency is to think that John is technically correct, but again it is not important to the deeper meaning of the story.

Jesus obviously wants the final meal with his friends to run smoothly because it is his farewell to them. (See Luke 22:7–13; Mark 14:12–16.) Orchestrating this monumental event must have been bittersweet for him. He charges Peter and John with preparing the meal. When they ask where it will be, Jesus directs them to go to the city, presumably Jerusalem, where a man carrying a water jar will meet them. He would be easily spotted, because usually it's women who carry the clay pots. The apostles are to follow the man into a house where they are to say to the owner, "The teacher asks you, 'Where is the great room where I may eat the Passover with my disciples?'" The owner will escort them to a large upper room already furnished. There they are to prepare the Passover meal. The two apostles depart and find everything just as Jesus had described. They prepare the meal, probably with the help of some of the women disciples.

Eucharist, a Farewell Gift

Then, Jesus performs an act that we Catholics recall each time we participate in Mass (see Luke 22:14–20; Mark 14:22–25; Matthew 26:26–29). While Jesus is at table with the apostles, he declares, "I have eagerly desired to eat this Passover with you before I suffer." He takes a loaf of bread, gives thanks, breaks it, and gives it to the apostles, saying, "This is my body which is given for you. Do this in memory of me." He does the same with the cup, saying, "This is my blood of the covenant which is poured out for many for the forgiveness of sins." All of the apostles drink from it. Jesus says, "I will never again drink from the fruit of the vine until I drink it new with you in my Father's kingdom." Through these actions Jesus assumes the role of priest and offers God the supreme sacrifice of his life. He also creates a way that he can always remain with his disciples to strengthen and unite them.

At this meal Jesus inaugurates a new covenant, or new testament. Abraham sealed his covenant with a sacrifice of blood (see Genesis 15), and Moses sealed the Israelites' covenant with God by sprinkling them with the blood of the sacrifice (see Exodus 24:3–8). So too Jesus' new covenant is sealed with blood—his own precious blood, for he himself is the sacrifice.

Catholics interpret the words "This is my body" and "This is my blood" literally. We believe that Jesus is present at each Mass, offering himself to the Father again for us. Through the priest and the power of the Holy Spirit, the bread and wine become for us his body and blood. At Communion, Jesus comes to us, bringing us divine life and uniting all of us who share this life into one body, which is his mystical body.

trivial tidbit...

Leonardo da Vinci's famous painting of the Last Supper, finished in 1498, portrays the moment when Jesus reveals that he will be betrayed. The masterpiece is painted onto an entire wall of a monastery in Milan.

fyi...

In the thirteenth century the priest began to elevate the sacred host at Mass. The idea spread that looking at the host was beneficial. This gave rise to Exposition of the Blessed Sacrament, adoration before the sacred host in a holder called a monstrance.

Holy Land site...

Although an older room in St. Mark's Syrian Orthodox Church is a more probable site of the Last Supper, tourists are shown an upper room in Jerusalem. It is called the Cenacle, from the Latin word for "dinner." Below it is the supposed tomb of King David. The Cenacle, built over an old church, dates back to the twelfth century.

trivial tidbit...

Some scholars think that the foot washing was baptism for the apostles because their baptisms aren't described elsewhere.

The Eucharist is the centerpiece of Catholic life. It is a foretaste of the heavenly banquet.

The Eucharist in Paul

The words of the institution of the Eucharist are also found in a letter of Paul: "The Lord Jesus, on the night he was betrayed, took bread, and when he had given thanks, he broke it and said, 'This is my body that is for you. Do this in remembrance of me.' In the same way, he took the cup also, after supper, saying, 'This cup is the new covenant in my blood. Do this, as often as you drink it, in remembrance of me' " (1 Corinthians 11:23–25). This shows that the words of consecration we use today were present in the Church in its earliest recorded days.

Washing of the Feet and the Betrayal Predicted

John's Gospel does not give an account of the institution of the Eucharist. However, it does let us know of one striking event at the Last Supper that the Synoptics don't mention—the washing of the feet (see John 13:2–18). Luke places the disciples' squabbling about who is greatest at this supper. Jesus' action in John is a lesson that logically follows that argument. Jesus gets up, removes his outer robe, and ties a towel around himself as a servant might do. He pours water into a basin and with his holy hands begins to wash the disciples' feet and wipe them with the towel. One after the other he kneels before them and does this demeaning chore, which among Jews was only carried out by a pagan, not even by a Jewish servant. When Jesus comes to Peter, the head of the apostles protests, "You will never wash my feet." Jesus replies, "Unless I wash you, you have no share with me." Peter then, with his typical over-the-top exuberance, exclaims, "Lord, not my feet only but also my hands and my head!" Jesus then states that only feet need be washed for, having bathed, the disciples are clean, but not all (referring to Judas). What is implied here is that the apostles all have taken the ritual baths required before celebrating Passover. Judas, however, is spiritually unclean.

Jesus dons his robe again and returns to the table. Then he spells out the message of this parable in action. Just as he, their Lord and Teacher, has washed their feet they ought to wash one another's feet. How poignant that Jesus washed Judas' feet that night too!

Sometime during the supper, Jesus is troubled in spirit and reveals to the apostles that one of them will betray him (see Matthew 26:20–25; Mark 14:17–21; Luke 22:21–23; John 13:21–30). The apostles, including Judas, all ask, "Surely not I, Lord?" Peter motions or nods to the "beloved" disciple next to Jesus, traditionally thought to be John, to ask Jesus who it was. This disciple inquires, "Lord, who is it?" In John's Gospel, Jesus replies that it is the one to whom he will give a piece of bread after dipping it in the dish. Then he dips the bread and hands it to Judas. (In Mark and Matthew Jesus says, "He who dips his hand into the dish with me." In Luke, Jesus says, "His hand is with me on the table.") In essence, it seems that Jesus is offering Judas an opportunity to halt his treachery and be one with him again, but all

short prayer...

O Sacrament most holy, O Sacrament divine, all praise and all thanksgiving be every moment thine!

fyi...

The first food and drink consumed on the moon were communion elements. In 1969, when Edwin "Buzz" Aldrin left the lunar module Eagle to walk on the moon, he first took out a piece of bread and a tiny chalice of wine. He asked everyone listening in to think of the moon landing and give thanks. Then Aldrin consumed the communion his pastor had given him from his church, Webster Presbyterian, in Texas.

big book search...

The letter to the Hebrews presents Jesus as the new, eternal priest. Read Hebrews 4:1–5:10, 7:26–8:6, 9:23–26.

in vain. In Matthew's Gospel, Jesus declares that it would have been better for his betrayer not to have been born. Then Judas has the gall to ask, "Surely not I, Rabbi?" and Jesus replies, "You have said so." In John's Gospel, Jesus orders Judas, "Do quickly what you are going to do." Because Judas kept the communal purse, the others assume that Jesus is sending him out to buy something for the festival or to give to the poor. Judas leaves immediately, and John makes the terse, foreboding statement, "It was night." It is unclear whether Judas was present for the institution of the Eucharist. Notice that he was the first one ever to leave Mass early!

At one point during the meal Jesus foretells that the apostles will desert him (see Matthew 26:31–35; Mark 14:26–31; Luke 22:31–34; John 13:36–38). Peter vehemently protests that even though all others desert him, he will follow Jesus to prison and to death. But Jesus punctures this bravado by revealing that Peter will deny even knowing him three times before the cock crows. According to Matthew and Mark, this conversation occurs after the hymn is sung and the group goes out to the Mount of Olives. They also note that all the disciples insist that they will die with Jesus rather than deny him. Brave words but empty, considering what ensues that night. However, although the apostles, except for John, desert Jesus at his death, eventually all but John die for him.

Farewell Discourse

In John's Gospel, Jesus speaks at length to the disciples at the Last Supper. He addresses them tenderly as "little children." Then he presents his new commandment of love and promises the Holy Spirit who will come to help them. In conclusion, in chapter 17, known as the "high priestly prayer," Jesus prays for Church unity modeled on the unity of the Trinity: "That they may be one as we are one, I in them and you in me, that they may become completely one" (John 17:23). He prays this prayer "for all who will believe" in him. In other words Jesus prayed for us at the Last Supper!

The repetition and at times awkward structure in this last discourse indicate that John probably wove together sermons and sayings that Jesus had said on other occasions, perhaps including after Easter. Some of this last discourse relates to the fledgling Church. Chapters 14 through 17 of John contain some of the most inspiring and most quoted lines in Scripture. Here are a few salient sayings:

- "I give you a new commandment, that you love one another. Just as I have loved you, you also should love one another. By this everyone will know that you are my disciples" (John 14:34–35). The identifying trait of the followers of Jesus is to be their outstanding love for one another.

- "Do not let your hearts be troubled. Believe in God, believe also in me. In my Father's house there are many dwelling places. If it were not so, would I have told you that I go to prepare a place for you?" (John 14:1–2). Jesus assures us that there is another life beyond this one where we will live with God.

- "I am the way, and the truth, and the life. No one comes to the Father except through me" (John 14:6). Jesus is the way to truth and to life.

big book search...

Read John 14–17 imagining Jesus speaking these words to the disciples at the Last Supper. Then reread them as Jesus speaking them directly to you.

trivial tidbit...

The "Holy Grail" referred to in romance literature beginning with the twelfth century and still sought in films today is either the dish used for the paschal lamb or the chalice at the Last Supper. In some versions of the legend St. Joseph of Arimathea received the Holy Grail from Christ.

for your spiritual health...

Make a habit of occasionally participating at a Mass on a weekday, perhaps to celebrate an event or to give special thanks for something.

◆ "Those who love me will keep my word, and my Father will love them, and we will come to them and make our home with them" (John 14:23). The same intimate union that Jesus enjoys with the Father is possible for all who follow Jesus.

◆ "The Advocate, the Holy Spirit, whom the Father will send in my name, will teach you everything, and remind you of all that I have said to you" (John 14:26). So often, even on that last night, the apostles do not understand. Jesus promises his Spirit who will enlighten them. This Spirit will be a way that Jesus will still be with them. *Paraclete* is the Greek word for "advocate." It means someone who is on your side.

◆ "No one has greater love than this, to lay down one's life for one's friends" (John 15:13). Jesus doesn't regard us as servants but as his friends. He proves his love by the ultimate sacrifice—his very life.

◆ "If you ask anything of the Father in my name, he will give it to you" (John 16:23). These words and similar ones are repeated at least six times in the last discourse. This is why our Mass prayers often conclude with variations of "We ask this in the name of Jesus the Lord."

◆ "In the world you face persecution. But take courage; I have conquered the world!" (John 16:33). Jesus has conquered all evil. Keeping this in mind helps us bear persecutions with patience and hope.

Knowing the terrors that are coming later that night, Jesus instills hope in the hearts of the apostles. He uses a feminine metaphor in promising them a happy outcome: A woman is in pain during labor, but then she forgets her anguish in the immense joy of having brought a human being into the world. In the same way, the apostles will grieve when Jesus leaves them, but he will return, turning their sorrow into a joy that no one can take from them (see John 16:19–22). Jesus also foretells that it is the time of his ordeal, when his disciples will scatter, leaving him alone. But then he affirms, as if reminding himself, "Yet I am not alone because the Father is with me" (John 16:32).

After this supper when Jesus has offered himself to the Father, he goes out to confront and embrace the cross of his bloody sacrifice, which is his destiny and our salvation.

Vine and Branches

During the Last Supper Jesus says, "I am the vine, you are the branches. Those who abide in me and I in them bear much fruit" (John 15:5). These words, which have been called the most beautiful in the Gospel, are Jesus' image for our close relationship with him. Jesus develops the thought in an extended metaphor. The Father is the vine grower. He cuts off branches that don't yield fruit. Healthy branches he prunes so that they yield even more fruit. The key to being a healthy branch is to stay united with Jesus, the life-giving vine.

trivial tidbit...

Since the fourteenth century many composers have produced the form of musical composition called a mass, which is musical settings for these Mass prayers: the Kyrie, Gloria, Credo, Sanctus, and Agnus Dei. Bach composed five masses, and Mozart composed nineteen. More recently Leonard Bernstein and Dave Brubek also wrote masses.

22 Redeemer: Passion

Jesus was born to die. What he referred to as his "hour" was the culmination of his mission on earth, and it was his finest hour. Jesus willingly took our place, as the Father wished, and became the sacrificial lamb for our sins. He clearly explained, "I lay down my life in order to take it up again. No one takes it from me, but I lay it down of my own accord.... I have received this command from my Father" (John 10:17–18). In those days, slaves and prisoners could be freed if someone paid the ransom price to redeem them. The price of our ransom from enslavement to sin was the blood of Jesus. His death and resurrection conquered sin and redeemed us.

Beyond redeeming us, Jesus' suffering brought another benefit. Harold Kushner wrote the book *Why Bad Things Happen to Good People* in which he grappled with the age-old mystery of suffering. Because Kushner is a Jewish rabbi, one consoling element is missing in his book, namely, that because God suffered and died all suffering has been infused with meaning. Because Jesus, who is God, submitted to pain and experienced death to redeem the world, by uniting our sufferings to his we can make our own suffering redemptive as well. For example, St. Paul rejoices in his sufferings and says, "I am completing what is lacking in Christ's afflictions for the sake of his body, that is, the church" (Colossians 1:24). Another beautiful aspect of the redemption is that by his passion and death Jesus identified with all innocent victims and those who suffer. In summary, as St. Catherine of Siena noted, "The crucifix is an infinite declaration of love."

The cross first appeared in art on a mid-fourth-century tomb. Crucifixes (the cross with a body) are rare until the seventh century. Protestants favor the cross without the body as a witness to belief in the Resurrection.

for your spiritual health…

When making the Sign of the Cross do it carefully, mindful of what it signifies.

It is important to remember that the Father did not "rejoice" in his Son's suffering. The Father suffered along with his Son. What father wouldn't? Such was their love for us that God experienced the human condition of suffering and death. We can never say that God does not understand what we have to go through.

Prophecies of Suffering and Death

Repeatedly, Jesus foretells his death and resurrection, and the apostles repeatedly fail to comprehend:

- After Peter acknowledges that Jesus is the Messiah, Jesus says that he must undergo great suffering at the hands of the Jewish leaders and be killed, but three days later he will be raised (see Matthew 16:21–23; Mark 8:31–33; Luke 9:22). Peter takes Jesus aside and objects, "God forbid it, Lord! This must never happen to you." Unwittingly he is echoing Satan's temptations to choose an easier way of being Messiah. Jesus scolds Peter, saying, "Get behind me, Satan! You are a stumbling block to me; for you are setting your mind not on divine things but on human things." So Peter the Rock has become the stumbling stone.

- After the transfiguration Jesus tells the apostles that the Son of Man will suffer and be raised from the dead (see Matthew 17:9, 12; Mark 9:9, 12).

- Later, in Galilee, Jesus teaches his disciples that he is to be betrayed into the hands of his enemies and killed and that in three days rise again (see Matthew 17:22–23; Mark 9:30–32; Luke 9:44–45). The disciples don't understand and are afraid to ask about it, probably out of dread.

◆ Another time, walking to Jerusalem, Jesus took the twelve aside and foretold that in Jerusalem he will be handed over to the Jewish leaders who will condemn him to death and hand him over to the Gentiles (see Matthew 20:17–19; Mark 10:32–34). They will mock him, spit upon him, flog him, and crucify him, and three days later he would be raised. Luke comments that the apostles do not grasp what he was saying (see Luke 18:31–32).

◆ Jesus often refers to being lifted up, a euphemism for crucifixion. Jesus teaches Nicodemus: "Just as Moses lifted up the serpent in the wilderness, so must the Son of Man be lifted up, that whoever believes in him may have eternal life" (John 3:14). Jesus informs the Jews that he is going away, and he says, "When you have lifted up the Son of Man, then you will realize that I am he, and that I do nothing on my own, but I speak these things as the Father instructed me. And the one who sent me is with me; he has not left me alone, for I always do what is pleasing to him" (John 8:28–29). Again he declares, "I, when I am lifted up from the earth, will draw all people to myself" (John 12:32).

◆ Jesus tells Philip and Andrew, "The hour has come for the Son of Man to be glorified.... Unless a grain of wheat falls into the earth and dies, it remains a single grain; but if it dies, it bears much fruit" (John 12:23–24). Jesus is the wheat that dies but then rises and offers himself as bread to the world.

◆ When Pharisees warn Jesus that Herod wants to kill him, Jesus replies, "Listen, I am casting out demons and performing cures today and tomorrow, and on

quick quote...

The crucifix is an infinite declaration of love.

St. Catherine of Siena

trivial tidbit...

Between 73 B.C. and 71 B.C., about 120,000 slaves, led at least in part by a slave named Spartacus, rebelled against Rome. Some 6,500 of them were crucified along the Appian Way, and their bodies were left hanging as a warning.

quick quote...

Jesus did not come to do away with suffering or remove it. He came to fill it with his presence.

Paul Claudel

Holy Land site...

On the Mount of Olives olive trees still grow, although the original ones were probably destroyed during the fall of Jerusalem in 70 A.D. There, where Jesus supposedly prayed, the Basilica of the Agony stands over a fourth-century church. The new church is also called the Church of All Nations because it was financed by sixteen nations. Inside of the church is an enormous rock encircled by a wrought iron crown of thorns.

the third day I finish my work. Yet today, tomorrow, and on the next day I must be on my way, because it is impossible for a prophet to be killed outside of Jerusalem" (Luke 13:32–33).

Jesus resolutely sets his face to Jerusalem, where lethal danger awaits him. His enemies are closing in on him. Now the hour has come.

The Agony in the Garden

After the Last Supper, Jesus and the eleven apostles go outside (see Matthew 26:36–46; Mark 14:32–42; Luke 22:39–46). Guided by the full moon, they cross the Kidron Valley to the Mount of Olives to a garden named Gethsemane, which is Hebrew for "oil press." John informs us that they often met there. So Judas knew where to find Jesus. According to Mark and Matthew, Jesus directs the apostles to sit while he prays, but he takes Peter, James, and John apart a little way with him. Mark reports that in the face of his own martyrdom, Jesus is overcome with horror and dismay. He confides to the three apostles that he is so grieved he could die. He tells them, "Remain here, and keep awake." Jesus looks to his friends for moral support as he faces his terrible destiny.

Jesus walks a little farther on from the apostles. Then, in Matthew and Mark, Jesus throws himself on the ground prostrate, while in Luke he kneels. Jesus fears death as much as any of us. (If he didn't, he wouldn't be human.) He prays, "Abba, Father, for you all things are possible; remove this cup from me; yet, not what I want, but what you want." Although Jesus dreads his future, he abandons himself to his Father's will. He gives free assent to his fate. He knows that the Father works all things for the good. Jesus' prayer serves as a model for all prayers of petition.

When Jesus returns to his three friends, he finds them asleep. Filled with the big meal (that included four cups of wine if it was a Passover meal) and lulled by the quiet, dark garden, they have dozed off. Disappointed, Jesus reproves Peter, "Simon, are you asleep? Could you not keep awake one hour? Keep awake and pray that you may not come into the time of trial; the spirit indeed is willing, but the flesh is weak." Jesus leaves again and prays the same words as before. Again he goes to the three apostles, and again he finds them asleep. Embarrassed, they don't know what to say. This happens a third time.

Luke does not have Jesus call apart the three apostles, but Jesus finds all eleven of them sleeping, and this happens just once. A passage added later to Luke states that an angel appears to strengthen Jesus. It also reports that Jesus' sweat fell like blood. This is a rare phenomenon called *hematohidrosis* that people under extreme stress may experience, something that a doctor such as Luke would note. Certainly assuming the weight of all the sins of all the human beings who ever lived or will live caused Jesus unparalleled agony. He was dying to atone for atrocities such as the Holocaust, the My Lai massacre, the Rwanda and Darfur genocides, the terrorist attacks of 9/11 and others; for slavery and human trafficking; for abortions and adultery; for corporate crime; and for all of our personal sins, serious and petty, as well as for the sins yet to be committed in the centuries beyond our lifetime. Perhaps too Jesus suffered from realizing that despite his heroic efforts, people would still make choices that

trivial tidbit...

In 1727, Johann Sebastian Bach wrote "The St. Matthew Passion," a musical setting of the passion as found in chapters 26 and 27 of the Gospel of St. Matthew. The work, which is almost five hours long, is called "the majestic cathedral of music" and the "pinnacle of sacred music."

quick quote...

Alone of all creeds, Christianity has added courage to the virtues of the Creator.

G.K. Chesterton

Devotion to the Sacred Heart centers on the total love of Jesus, human and divine. St. Margaret Mary Alacoque, a Visitation nun in France, promoted this devotion at Jesus' direction in visions she had from 1673 to 1675. He also requested that a Communion of reparation be made on the first Friday of every month for nine consecutive months.

The Suffering Servant

The prophetic writings of the book of Isaiah describe a mysterious figure who is known as "the suffering servant." He is an innocent person who suffers for his people. While Jews believe that he represents the people Israel as a whole, Christians identify this person with Jesus. If you read the four Songs of the Servant, you will see how closely they match Jesus and his act of redemption. They are Isaiah 42:1–9; 49:1–6; 50:4–10; and 52:13–53:12. Here are three excerpts:

"I gave my back to those who struck me, and my cheeks to those who pulled out the beard; I did not hide my face from insult and spitting" (Isaiah 50:6).

"He was wounded for our transgressions, crushed for our iniquities; upon him was the punishment that made us whole, and by his bruises we are healed" (Isaiah 53:5).

"They made his grave with the wicked and his tomb with the rich, although he had done no violence and there was no deceit in his mouth" (Isaiah 53:9).

would bar them from entering into eternal life. No wonder he sweat blood!

The Capture of Jesus

Now Jesus is ready to face his destiny (see Matthew 26:47–56; Mark 14:22–52; Luke 22:47–53; John 18:1–11). Suddenly he announces, "The hour has come; the Son of Man is betrayed into the hands of sinners. Get up, let us be going. See, my betrayer is at hand." Jesus doesn't try to escape. Even as he speaks, Judas arrives, leading soldiers and police from the chief priests and Pharisees. They bear lanterns and torches and are armed with swords and clubs. In the Synoptics, Judas approaches Jesus and kisses him, the prearranged sign to identify Jesus, an act that makes the treachery all the more sinister. In Luke, Jesus comments on the incongruity of the kiss. He asks, "Judas, is it with a kiss that you are betraying the Son of Man?" In Matthew we wince to read that Jesus addresses Judas as "friend," and says, "Do what you are here to do." How the human heart of Jesus must have ached at his friend's betrayal.

Men roughly grab hold of Jesus and arrest him. From this point on, he allows himself to be in the power of others. The disciples ask if they should strike with a sword, and one of them cuts off part of the right ear of the high priest's slave. Jesus commands, "Put your sword back into its sheath, for all who take the sword will perish by the sword. Do you think that I cannot appeal to my Father, and he will at once send me more than twelve legions of angels? Am I not to drink the cup that the Father has given me?" Rather than praising his disciples for attempting to defend

trivial tidbit...

At the end of the Last Supper in the Gospel of Luke, Jesus tells the disciples they must have a sword, even if they have to sell their cloak to get one. They say they have two swords, and Jesus says it is enough (see Luke 22:36–38). It is hard to imagine what Jesus had in mind, unless he wanted to show that it is possible to have arms to defend ourselves but still not use them.

Holy Land site...

Pilgrims pray the Stations of the Cross (*Via Dolorosa*) in Jerusalem. They follow the path laid out in the fourteenth century based on sites identified by Empress Helena in the fourth century. The first two stations are in the Antonia Fortress, seven are on the street amid the hubbub of the market, and five are in the Basilica of the Holy Sepulcher.

him, Jesus warns against violence, which only breeds further violence. The disciples don't realize yet that Jesus has a special relationship with the Father, who could, even now, send 72,000 troops of angels to his defense. And despite his prophecies, they don't understand how his life and mission is to play out.

Touching the slave's ear, Jesus heals it, an act of compassion before those who have no compassion for him. He questions the crowd, "Have you come out with swords and clubs as if I were a bandit? When I was with you day after day in the temple, you did not lay hands on me. But this is your hour, and the power of darkness!"

All of the disciples desert him and flee, leaving Jesus to face his enemies and his fate alone. Mark includes the detail that a young man wearing only a linen cloth follows Jesus. The soldiers catch him, but he squirms out of their grasp and, leaving behind the cloth, runs off naked.

In John's account of the capture, Jesus is in command of the entire situation. There is no kiss. Jesus simply asks, "Whom are you looking for?" The crowd answers, "Jesus of Nazareth." When Jesus declares, "I am he," they step back and fall to the ground, a dramatic detail in keeping with John's emphasis on the divinity of Jesus. Then Jesus protects his disciples. He says, "If you are looking for me, let these men go." John lets us know that Peter is the one who used the sword and that his victim's name was Malchus. According to Luke, the men who capture Jesus mock and beat him. Maliciously, they blindfold him and ask him to prophesy who struck him.

The Mysterious Streaker

Various theories are proposed about the identity of the young man who escaped in the garden (see Mark 14:51–52). One conjecture is that he was John Mark, the evangelist himself, in whose house the Last Supper was perhaps held. John Mark, the theory goes, was in bed and heard commotion, so he came out in his night attire to investigate. Another hypothesis is that the young man was Lazarus. This is based on the word used for the man's linen cloth: It is the same as for a burial cloth. Also it makes sense that Lazarus, a good friend of Jesus, would follow him longer than the apostles did. The fact that the soldiers apprehend him and not the apostles supports this idea. On the symbolic level, it's thought that the man represents either Jesus, who will soon rise from the tomb leaving the burial cloths behind, or those who are baptized and then clothed with a white garment. The fact that the night was too cold for a young disciple to be wearing only a cloth instead of his tunic and cloak suggests that the event is symbolic.

fyi...

The Divine Mercy devotion originated with St. Faustina Kowalska, a Polish nun. In February 1931, Jesus appeared to her with one hand blessing and the other touching his garment at his heart, from which two rays, one red and one pale, came forth. Jesus told Faustina to have an image made of him like this with the words "Jesus, I trust in you." He also asked that a feast be dedicated to the Divine Mercy on the Sunday after Easter. At Faustina's canonization in 2000, Pope John Paul II instituted Divine Mercy Sunday.

Holy Land site...

St. Peter of Gallicantu (which means "cockcrow") in Jerusalem is a dazzling church built on Mount Zion in 1931 to commemorate Peter's denials and remorse. A golden rooster tops its church dome. It's thought that this church stands over Caiaphas' house. Prison-like chambers where Jesus could have been held lie beneath it. Steps in its courtyard almost certainly date back to the time of Jesus. At the sight of these steps, astronaut Neil Armstrong (the first man to walk on the moon) commented, "This is where the real giant step for mankind took place."

A Kangaroo Court

Unlike John the Baptist, who was imprisoned for a while before he was executed, Jesus is killed with extreme haste (see Matthew 26:57–68; Mark 14:53–65; Luke 22:66–71; John 18:12–14, 19–24). The Gospels differ in the events leading up to Jesus' death. There are as many as six interrogations, and during them no one ever speaks up to defend Jesus. He is painfully alone throughout his ordeal. According to Matthew and Mark, Jesus is taken that night to the high priest Caiaphas and the rest of the Sanhedrin, while Luke says that this meeting occurs in the morning. Since the Sanhedrin never convened at night, Luke might be correct. Or this could have been a preliminary hearing, to be followed by an official one the next day. In any case, it is a kangaroo court. Charges are trumped up to warrant a death sentence. People give false testimony, but it doesn't agree. Some accuse Jesus of saying he would destroy the Temple, a garbled quoting of his words. Finally Caiaphas asks Jesus to defend himself, but Jesus remains silent. Then Caiaphas asks, "Are you the Messiah, the Son of the Blessed One?" In Mark, Jesus replies, "I am." (Matthew and Luke have him say, "You have said so.") Jesus goes on to quote the prophet Daniel: "You will see the Son of Man seated at the right hand of Power and coming with the clouds of heaven.' " Outraged, Caiaphas tears his garments, a symbol of extreme distress, and exclaims, "You have heard his blasphemy! What is your decision?" All agree that Jesus deserves death. Then some of them spit on Jesus. The guards take Jesus and beat him.

In John's Gospel, that night Jesus is taken first to

Annas, the former high priest, who questions him about his teaching. Jesus replies that he has spoken openly to all in the synagogues and in the Temple. He says, "I have said nothing in secret. Why do you ask me? Ask those who heard what I said." At that, a policeman strikes him in the face and sneers, "Is that how you answer the high priest?" Jesus responds, "If I have spoken wrongly, testify to the wrong, but if I have spoken rightly, why do you strike me?" Then Annas sends Jesus bound to Caiaphas, but John doesn't describe this meeting.

According to John, at first after Jesus is arrested, Peter and another disciple bravely shadow him and his captors. Peter's courage sets the scene for his downfall (see Matthew 26:69–75; Mark 14:66–72; Luke 22:54–62; John 18:15–18; 25–27). Because the anonymous disciple knows the high priest, he goes into the high priest's courtyard behind Jesus. This disciple says a few words to the woman guard at the gate, and Peter is allowed to enter. All four Gospels report that Peter joins a group gathered around a charcoal fire, for it is cold. Three times people identify Peter as one of Jesus' disciples. Either they've seen him with Jesus or his Galilean accent gives him away. (The Gospels vary in naming the accusers: the woman guard, two servant-girls, bystanders, and a slave related to Malchus.) Each time that Peter is associated with Jesus, he lies and denies it, claiming that he doesn't even know Jesus. Matthew and Mark say that Peter even curses and swears. At Peter's third denial, a cock crows. Luke says that at that moment the Lord—beaten, bound, and in custody—turns and looks at Peter. Their eyes meet, and no doubt Peter reads in Jesus' eyes com-

trivial tidbit...

Romans divided night hours into watches. At the third watch, from twelve to three in the morning, which was called *cockcrow*, a trumpet was sounded. Some scholars think that Peter's cockcrow referred to this watch.

trivial tidbit...

In the ninth century a pope decreed that churches should have a rooster on their spires in memory of Peter. These weathervanes are still seen in European towns and came to be known as *weathercocks*. A weathercock also means a fickle person, someone who changes with the wind.

Holy Land site...

Today the Sisters of Zion Convent is where the Antonia Fortress built by Herod once stood. It houses two chapels: the Chapel of the Condemnation and the Chapel of the Flagellation. Under it is the Chapel of the Lithostrotos ("paved square"), presumed to be where Pontius Pilate judged Jesus. Archaeologists, however, have dated the Lithostrotos to the time of Emperor Hadrian (76–138 A.D.).

passion, love, and pity. The big fisherman goes out and weeps bitterly. This terse sentence is surely one of the most moving in Scripture. There is a legend that Peter's copious tears carved furrows in his face.

The Scene before Pilate

Early in the morning the Jewish leaders have Jesus taken to the Roman *procurator* (governor) of Judea, Pontius Pilate (see Matthew 27:1–2, 11–26; Mark 15:1–15; Luke 23:1–5, 13–25; John 18:28–40). They do not have the power to carry out a death sentence and therefore must appeal to Rome. Ordinarily the Roman governor was not headquartered in Jerusalem, but to forestall riots and uprisings during the Passover he had moved there.

John notes that Pilate comes out to meet with the Jews, because entering his Gentile headquarters would make them unclean and unable to eat the Passover meal. In Luke, the Jewish leaders tell Pilate that Jesus forbade people to pay taxes to the emperor and claimed to be the Messiah, a king. Pilate asks Jesus pointblank, "Are you king of the Jews?" and Jesus answers, "You say so." Pilate states that he finds no basis for accusing Jesus, but the Jewish leaders insist that Jesus stirs up the people throughout the land, beginning with Galilee. In Mark and Matthew, Jesus doesn't defend himself against any accusations, which amazes Pilate.

In John, Pilate engages Jesus in conversation. Jesus explains, "My kingdom is not from this world," and claims that if it were, his followers would have fought for him. Pilate asks, "So you are a king?" And Jesus replies, "You say that I am a king. For this I was born,

A Strange Visit to Herod

Luke alone includes an appearance of Jesus before Herod Antipas (see Luke 23:6–12). When Pilate learns that Jesus is from Galilee, he realizes there is a way he can weasel out of handling the case. Pilate sends Jesus to Herod, ruler of Galilee, who is also in Jerusalem for the Passover. Herod is the fickle man who sentenced John the Baptist to death. Jesus once referred to him as "that fox," a Jewish expression meaning a worthless person. Herod was glad to receive Jesus. He had been wanting to see him in hopes of witnessing him perform a miracle. Herod questions Jesus at length, while the Jewish leaders vehemently accuse him. But Jesus remains silent. Then Herod and his soldiers mock Jesus and deck him out in an elegant robe. Stymied by the situation, Herod sends Jesus back to Pilate. Luke reports that, ironically, that day the two rulers, former foes, become friends. Even as a powerless prisoner, Jesus brings about reconciliation, a sign of the kingdom.

quick quote...

I am convinced that neither death, nor life, nor angels, nor principalities, nor present things, nor future things, nor powers, nor height, nor depth, nor any other creature will be able to separate us from the love of God in Christ Jesus our Lord.

Romans 8:35–39

In some early manuscripts, Barabbas's first name is Jesus. This, along with the fact that there is no historical evidence of the custom of releasing a prisoner on Passover, leads some scholars to think that Barabbas is an addition derived from the crowd calling for "Jesus, Son of God."

and for this I came into the world, to testify to the truth. Everyone who belongs to the truth listens to my voice." Then Pilate asks his famous philosophical question, "What is truth?" Little did he realize that the young man before him is the way, the truth, and the life. Again Pilate goes to the Jewish leaders and tells them that he finds no case against Jesus.

Matthew and Mark comment that Pilate realizes that Jesus has been handed over by the Jewish leaders out of jealousy. All four Gospels tell of another captured Jew, Barabbas, an insurrectionist or a robber who has committed murder. His name "Bar Abbas" means "Son of the Father," and he is a foil for Jesus, the real Son of the Father. The Gospels state that it was the custom to free a Jewish prisoner at Passover as a political favor. Pilate offers to free either Barabbas or Jesus. The crowd, blinded into a frenzy of hate by their religious leaders, chooses to free the terrorist Barabbas and calls for the gentle Jesus to be crucified. (Matthew includes the detail that Pilate's wife, called Claudia Procula according to tradition, sends him a message warning him not to have anything to do with Jesus because of a troubling dream she's had.) Pilate literally washes his hands of the affair before the crowd and declares, "I am innocent of this man's blood; see to it yourselves." The people answer, "His blood be on us and on our children," a chilling self-condemnation. According to Luke, Pilate really wants to release Jesus, so he again tries to reason with the crowd, but they shout, "Crucify him!" Imagine the anguish Jesus feels when he hears the people he loves calling for his death. A third time Pilate declares that he finds no grounds for the death sentence, but he fears that the people are on the brink of rioting. So he yields to their demands. For Pilate the end justifies the means.

Torture before Execution

Jesus now enters into what we call his passion (see Matthew 27:26–31; Mark 15:15–20; Luke 22:63–65; John 19:1–16). John's presentation of the passion is the most dramatic. After the crowd chooses Barabbas, Pilate has Jesus flogged. A scourging was usual before a crucifixion. For flogging, the victim's hands were tied to a pillar. The Romans used a whip made of from three to twelve leather straps, each tipped with shards of bone and metal. This tore the skin and caused much blood loss. Scourging was not only a form of torture but actually was intended to shorten the time of crucifixion. Where Jewish law set a limit of thirty-nine lashes; the Romans had no limit. Judging from Jesus' weakness and comparatively quick death, his scourging was severe. Flogging was not done to Roman citizens except for deserters.

In a parody of a coronation, the soldiers weave a crown or helmet of thorns and ram it onto Jesus' head. The wicked thorns pierce his skull, and blood flows down his face. The soldiers dress Jesus in a robe of purple, the color of royalty. (Matthew says a scarlet military cloak.) They shout, "Hail, King of the Jews!" and strike him on the face. Matthew and Mark place this mockery after the decision has been made to crucify Jesus. They include that the soldiers kneel down in homage, strike Jesus with a reed, and spit on him. Luke adds the detail that the soldiers blindfold Jesus and taunt him to prophesy which of them struck him.

trivial tidbit...

The oldest depiction of a crucifixion is second-century anti-Christian graffiti scratched into a wall in Rome. It says, "Alexander worships his god" and shows a crude picture of a boy before a man nailed to a cross. The man has the head of an ass.

Pilate may have had reason to be nervous about Jesus causing a rebellion. Tiberius had given Sejanus power to rule the empire, but in 31 A.D., after Sejanus proved to be a traitor, Tiberius had him executed along with other suspects. Pilate had most likely been appointed procurator by Sejanus.

quick quote...

We proclaim Christ crucified, a stumbling block to Jews and foolishness to Gentiles.

1 Corinthians 1:23

To the Roman soldiers, Jesus was just another prisoner to have fun with. Unwittingly the game they were playing was the actual truth: Jesus was king of the Jews and in fact the soldiers' king as well.

In John's account, after the flogging, Pilate then has Jesus, bruised and bloody, brought out before the people, perhaps to play on their sympathy. Pilate declares, "I'm bringing him out because I find no case against him." Jesus appears with the crown of thorns and robe, and Pilate says, "Behold the man." (This is *"Ecce homo"* in Latin.) The mob still calls for crucifixion. They say that according to their law Jesus ought to die because he claimed to be the Son of God. At this Pilate becomes even more afraid. Perhaps he is thinking how the Roman gods Jupiter and Mercury sometimes took the form of human beings. He asks Jesus where he comes from, but Jesus doesn't answer. So Pilate prods, "Do you not know that I have power to release you, and power to crucify you?" Jesus responds, "You would have no power over me unless it had been given you from above; therefore the one who handed me over to you is guilty of a greater sin." Pilate continues to try to release Jesus, but finally the Jews cry out that if he lets Jesus go, he is against the emperor, for Jesus claims to be king. This accusation of treason is the turning point. Pilate brings Jesus outside and sits on the judge's bench. He says, "Here is your King!" The people again cry, "Crucify him!" Pilate asks, "Shall I crucify your King?" The chief priests shout, "We have no king but the emperor," and Pilate caves in and hands Jesus over to be crucified for the crime of treason.

From his capture in the garden until his sentencing the next day Jesus has been tortured and humiliated. He knows that the worst is yet to come. Although he had the divine power to put a halt to this whole disaster instantly, Jesus perseveres, the faithful Son of the Father and the lover of us all, who accepts the violence aimed at him rather than returning the hatred in kind.

quick quote...

I live through the mercy of Jesus to whom I owe everything and from whom I expect everything.

Blessed Pope John the XXIII

23 Savior: Death on a Cross

Two days after the terrorist attack of September 11, 2001, in the rubble of the World Trade Center, a workman discovered large steel beams in the shape of a 20-foot-high cross. The cross was blessed at Ground Zero in October of that year and was still standing when Pope Benedict visited the site in April of 2008. In August of 2009, a 14-foot cross made of steel from the World Trade Center was dedicated where United Airlines Flight 93 crashed in Pennsylvania on September 11, 2001.

For more than 400 years, Lithuanians have placed carved wooden crosses outside their homes and businesses, where passersby would stop and say a prayer. When Lithuania became part of the Soviet Union, this cross-crafting was severely restricted. But the city of Siauliai kept up the custom of placing crosses on one particular hill as a resistance symbol, and survivors of the Siberia work camps added crosses in memory of friends who had died in the camps. Soviet soldiers bulldozed this hill three times. Then in 1991, Lithuania once again became independent, and today more than 20,000 crosses of all sizes stand on the Hill of Crosses.

We Catholics display crucifixes on our walls and wear crosses of gold and silver around our necks. So accustomed are we to the cross that we sometimes forget the

Crucifixion originated with the Persians about 400 B.C. The word *excruciating* comes from the Latin for "from the cross." Rome carried out executions near a major city gate so that they would be seen by many people and deter crime and rebellion. Only runaway slaves and rebels were crucified. Emperor Constantine forbade the inhuman practice around 400 A.D.

horror it originally represented. For good reason did Jesus dread his death. Crucifixion was the most agonizing, degrading, and gruesome means of execution. Only love motivated Jesus to go through with it.

Why is the cross so meaningful worldwide? Why has it become the symbol of Christianity? By enduring this excruciating death, Jesus saved us from sin and evil. Because of him, we now know that our own deaths and those of our loved ones are only the door to a new and unending life. That is why on Good Friday, the priest processes with the cross and sings three times, "Behold the wood of the cross on which has hung our salvation," and after each time we genuflect and respond, "Thanks be to God!"

Carrying the Cross

In Roman times, those to be crucified were forced to carry the horizontal beam of their crosses to the place of crucifixion outside the city walls. Jesus is supposed to carry his crossbeam to the hill named Golgotha, the Place of the Skull (see Matthew 27:32–34; Mark 15:21–23; Luke 23:26–32; John 19:16–17). In Latin the word *skull* is *calvarum*, from which the word *Calvary* was derived. Jesus' path takes him through the narrow streets of Jerusalem, the ones most frequented so that as many people as possible can see his humiliation and be persuaded not to imitate his crime. Two criminals, either revolutionaries or robbers, are paraded through the city with him. Along the way, spectators, including his adversaries, jeer at Jesus. Every step is sheer torture.

Jesus has been awake all night and has endured beatings and a scourging that could have put him into shock. Naturally carrying the sixty- or seventy-pound rough beam of wood across his lacerated shoulders is more than he can manage. There's a chance that he will die before being crucified. The Synoptic Gospels report that the soldiers recruit a passerby named Simon of Cyrene, a town in northern Africa, to carry the wood. They lay the beam on Simon, and he walks behind Jesus. Luke records that many people follow Jesus, including numerous women who are crying. Jesus addresses the women, "Daughters of Jerusalem, do not cry for me, but weep for yourselves and for your children." And he predicts the destruction that will soon befall the city.

According to tradition as reflected in the devotion of the Way of the Cross, Jesus falls three times on the way to Calvary. This is credible because of his weakened condition and loss of blood. With each fall, Jesus' tortured body is racked with pain as it hits the hard path. Perhaps the soldiers spur him on with lashes from their whips.

Mark and Matthew relate that when the grotesque procession reaches Calvary, the soldiers offer Jesus wine mixed with vinegar or myrrh as a sedative. According to Mark, Jesus refuses it. He chooses instead to drink the cup of suffering to the dregs. He will die keenly sensitive to the full measure of pain his sacrificial death entails.

The Crucifixion

The Gospels simply say Jesus was crucified at nine o'clock in the morning (see Matthew 27:35–37; Mark 15:25–26; Luke 22:33–34; John 19:18–25). The gory details are apparently too horrific for the

trivial tidbit...

One of the oldest works of Old English literature is the poem "The Dream of the Rood," which dates at least from the early eighth century. In the poem a man recalls a dream in which he speaks with the rood (cross). The cross has served its Lord well. It too was pierced with nails, and now it is decked with jewels. The cross tells the dreamer to spread the news of redemption.

a cool website...

On Good Friday in 1991, Pope John Paul II presented new stations of the cross based on Scripture. These can be prayed by going to www.usccb.org/nab/stations.shtml.

quick quote...

The cross was not only a stumbling block to the Jews and foolishness to the Gentiles. It is a permanent mystery for Christians.

Jürgen Moltmann

short prayer...

We adore you, O Christ, and we bless you because by your holy cross you have redeemed the world.

Veronica's Veil

The story of Veronica wiping the face of Jesus with her veil on the way to Calvary and then finding it imprinted with and an image of his holy face dates from the Middle Ages. An older story is that the woman with the flow of blood who was cured by touching Jesus' clothes was named *Veronica* (Bernice in Greek), which means "true image." Veronica's veil, supposedly one revered in the Middle Ages, is kept in a chapel in St. Peter's Basilica. It is taken out and shown once a year on the evening of Passion Sunday. Through the centuries artists have made copies of Veronica's veil. In 1999, a priest announced that in a monastery in Italy he had found Veronica's veil, which he proposed had been stolen from the Vatican in 1506. Although this veil differs from those venerated in the Middle Ages, Pope Benedict XVI visited it in 2006. Devotion to the Holy Face of Jesus began in 1844, based on paintings of the face on Veronica's veil. Now the face on the Shroud of Turin is used for this devotion.

evangelists to recount. However, we know what crucifixion involves. Soldiers strip Jesus. His clothing clings to his body with blood and sweat, so as it is peeled away it reopens his wounds. To avoid being offensive, our crucifixes depict Jesus wearing a loincloth. In reality, part of the punishing humiliation of crucifixion was hanging completely naked for all the world to see. Although it's been proposed that the Romans considerately allowed crucified Jews to wear loincloths, this is not likely. Next the soldiers stretch out Jesus' arms on the horizontal beam and hammer long nails through his wrists. Nails through the palms, as art usually shows, would tear through the flesh and not hold up the body. Jesus is to die with arms outstretched, embracing the world. Then the soldiers hoist the horizontal beam up and onto a vertical beam already standing in place. This jarring movement causes Jesus extreme pain. The soldiers then pound one or two nails through his feet. The pain from the metal piercing through muscle, bone, and nerves has to be incredible. The two criminals are crucified with Jesus, one on either side. Even in death, sinners are his companions.

It was the custom to write on a placard the crime of the one condemned. On the way to execution this placard was hung around the neck of the crucified or carried before him. Then it was posted above his head on the cross itself. John tells us that for Jesus, Pilate sarcastically had the inscription "Jesus of Nazareth, the King of the Jews" written in Hebrew, Latin, and Greek. Chief priests protested and told Pilate to write instead, "This man said he was King of the Jews." But Pilate replies, "What I have written I have written."

trivial tidbit...

Only one crucified body has ever been found. In 1968, the bones of a man in his twenties named Johohanan were discovered in an ossuary in Jerusalem. Through the side of the heel bone there was a nail containing fragments of olive wood. The implication is that this man was nailed to a cross through the sides, not the front, of his feet. Scholars surmise that after the man died, the soldiers couldn't remove this nail because it was bent.

a cool website...

Near St. Peter's Basilica in Rome, the Bridge of Angels (*Ponte Sant'Angelo*) spans the Tiber River. Along this bridge are ten large statues of angels, each holding something related to the passion of Jesus. Go to www.belief.net.com/features/bridgeofangels for meditations on the passion.

The "INRI" at the top of our crucifixes are the initials of the Latin words *Jesus, Nazarenus, Rex, Judaeorum.* Latin uses *I* for *J*, hence "INRI."

Four soldiers divide Jesus' clothes among them: his headcloth, sandals, belt, undergarment, and cloak. However, since the tunic was seamless and probably of good quality, perhaps woven by Mary, they decide to cast lots for it. So when Jesus dies, he owns nothing at all.

The Blood of the Lamb

In the Old Testament, the Israelites were saved from death by the blood of the sacrificed lamb marking their doorposts. This is a clear foreshadowing of Jesus, the lamb of God, whose blood redeemed the world and saved us all from everlasting death. The Passover lamb had to be a blue-ribbon lamb: unblemished and with no broken bones. Jesus, too, was the spotless lamb, whose legs were not broken. The prophet described the suffering servant with the same image: "Like a lamb that is led to the slaughter, and like a sheep that before its shearers is silent, so he did not open his mouth" (Isaiah 53:7). Scripture gives a vision of heaven where a multitude stands before God and the lamb. They are identified with the paradox, "These are they who...have washed their robes and made them white in the blood of the lamb" (Revelation 7:14). The one sacrifice of Jesus replaced all of the sacrifices in the Temple. Christians no longer practiced animal sacrifice.

The Design of the Sign

There have been many crosses designed over the centuries. Some reflect a particular meaning or historial experience; others are named for the person who was crucified on a cross in that shape. Here are some examples.

1 2 3 4 5

6 7 8 9 10

11 12 13 14 15

1. The **Latin Cross** or the **Tau Cross** are most probably the shape of Jesus' cross. Romans had criminals carry just the cross bar to their place of execution.
2. The **Tau Cross** is in the shape of a "T."
3. The **Greek Cross** is used by the Red Cross.
4. The **Jerusalem Cross** (evangelization cross) originated with the Crusades as a protection for crusaders. It is made of four Tau crosses that meet in the center and four Greek crosses to represent the four corners of the world.
5. **St. Peter's Cross** is an upside down Latin Cross, named for St. Peter who asked to be crucified upside-down, declaring he wasn't worthy to die as Jesus did.
6. **St. Andrew's Cross** is x-shaped like the one on which St. Andrew was martyred.
7. **The Russian Orthodox Cross** has a top bar to represent the INRI sign and a lower bar for the footrest on Jesus' cross.
8. **The Calvary Cross** stands on three steps that symbolize Mount Calvary where Jesus died.
9. **The Passion Cross** ends in points like nails or swords to indicate suffering.
10. **The Papal Cross** has three crossbars which stand for the pope's tiara (triple crown) or the two men crucified with Jesus.
11. **The Patriarchal Cross** has a small bar for the INRI sign the Romans nailed to Jesus' cross.
12. **The Celtic Cross** of the British Isles has a circle to symbolize eternity or the unity of Christians around the cross.
13. **The Maltese Cross** was used by Spanish royal families on their coats of arms. Its eight points represent the Beatitudes.
14. **The Hope Cross** is an anchor, a symbol of the hope the cross gives us.
15. **The Budded Cross** has three knobs representing the Trinity at each end.

God weeps with us so that someday we can laugh with him.

Jürgen Moltmann

big book search...

Look up prophetic Psalm 22 and read it to see how closely it parallels Jesus' crucifixion. Pay special attention to how it ends.

God thirsts to be thirsted for.

St. Gregory Nazianzen

Seven Last Words

Before dying, Jesus is suspended on the cross for six hours (see Matthew 27:38–50; Mark 15:27–37; Luke 23:32–46; John 19:25–30). This is the sacrifice he offered the night before: "This is my body.... This is my blood." In addition to the pain of his wounds, Jesus, naked, could have suffered from the bitter cold that forced the people in the courtyard to build a fire. Perhaps worse than the physical torment is the mental anguish of the seeming failure of his mission.

During the long hours on the cross, Jesus speaks to the people around him. The Gospels preserved the most memorable of his dying words. Luke says that from the cross Jesus prays a prayer in keeping with his teaching "Pray for your persecutors" (Matthew 5:44). Even as his torture is in progress, Jesus pleads, "Father, forgive them. They know not what they are doing." He intercedes for all who have taken part in his suffering and death. That includes us. Not long after this prayer of Jesus, when St. Stephen, the first Christian martyr, is being stoned to death, he repeats Jesus' words. On the cross Jesus lives out his teaching "Love your enemies."

Scholars say that on the cross Jesus was only about a foot off the ground. Looking down from the cross, Jesus can see his mother, his aunt, who is Mary's sister or cousin, Mary the wife of Clopas, and Mary Magdalene. Matthew adds that Mary the mother of James and Joseph, and the mother of the sons of Zebedee were present. Perhaps Jesus' most heart-wrenching pain is knowing how much his beloved mother is suffering by witnessing his horrible death. Beside Mary stands the man identified only as the disciple whom

Jesus loved. Jesus says to his mother, "Woman, here is your son," and to the disciple, "Here is your mother." And from that hour the disciple takes Mary into his home. Tradition holds that the disciple was St. John, who would have been the only apostle we know about who stayed with Jesus to the end. It's believed that this disciple represents all of us, and at that moment Jesus is giving us his mother Mary to be our mother, a marvelous bequest.

The Synoptics tell how Jesus is still mocked while on the cross. His opponents are there gloating. The Jewish leaders, the soldiers, and passersby taunt him: If he is the Messiah, the king of the Jews, he should come down from the cross; he saved others, but can't save himself; he was going to destroy the Temple and build it in three days, he should save himself. They don't understand that the true Messiah *can't* come down from the cross. Author Frederick Buechner observed that the true miracle of the cross was that there was no miracle.

Mark and Matthew agree that the two criminals also deride Jesus. But Luke offers a different version in which even in the throes of death Jesus is healing sinners. When one criminal tells Jesus to save himself and them, the other criminal rebukes him, saying that they are getting what they deserve whereas Jesus is innocent. This man of faith pleads, "Jesus, remember me when you come into your kingdom." And Jesus replies, "Truly I tell you, today you will be with me in Paradise" (Luke 23:39–43). So the one criminal comes down in history known as the good thief who "stole" heaven.

trivial tidbit...

The criminal who is promised the kingdom is called St. Dismas and the other one is Gestas, according to the twelfth-century apocryphal *Gospel of Nicodemus*.

fyi...

Tradition says that Dismas was on Jesus' right side. On Eastern crosses that have three bars, the third bar is a footrest that is slanted up to Jesus' right. Some say this represents Dismas going to heaven. For the same reason, Eastern churches make the Sign of the Cross from right shoulder to left, sometimes touching the right shoulder higher.

Holy Land site...

The Basilica of the Holy Sepulcher is over the place where tradition says Jesus died (and also says that Adam's skull is buried). Christian factions that lay claim to this church are often in conflict, so its keys are entrusted to Muslim families!

John records two other "words" of Jesus. He says that Jesus declares, "I am thirsty." Someone dips a sponge on a branch into a jar of sour wine and holds it up to him. John specifies that the branch was hyssop, reminiscent of the hyssop that was used to sprinkle the lamb's blood on the doorways to save the Israelites from death in Egypt. Jesus takes the wine and then says, "It is finished" (*"Tetelestia"* in Greek). After this cry of victory, he bows his head and gives up his spirit.

The Synoptic Gospels report Jesus' death differently. They state that from about noon until three darkness is over the land. The Synoptics also relate that the curtain in the Temple is torn in two. This curtain separated the people from the Holy of Holies where God was present and where only the high priest was allowed to go once a year. The tearing of the curtain symbolizes that Jesus' death gives everyone access to God. According to Mark and Matthew, Jesus cries out, *"Eli, Eli, lema sabachthani?"* which means "My God, my God, why have you forsaken me?" It is the cry of a desperate, broken man, someone who is experiencing the terror of being abandoned by God, what theologian Martin Buber called "the eclipse of God." When bystanders hear these words, they think Jesus is calling for Elijah and wait to see if Elijah would come to save him. Although the cry conveys that Jesus is despairing on the cross, actually he is quoting from Psalm 22, which ends on a note of hope. Finally Jesus cries out loudly. Luke notes that he prays, "Father, into your hands I commend my spirit," which is Psalm 31:5. And then Jesus breathes his last. Someone has observed that just as stars are brightest when

Cause of Jesus' Death

Those who were crucified had to push themselves up with their feet in order to breathe. Imagine the pain each breath caused as the nail wounds were aggravated and the back's lacerated skin slid over the rough wood of the cross. At some point pain and exhaustion took over or the person became unconscious and no effort was made to breathe. This meant the person died of suffocation. Another theory is that the combination of loss of blood, buildup of fluid in the lungs, and shallow breathing led to cardiac arrest. Crucified persons could live several days; at least one survived for nine days. The fact that Jesus died so soon indicates that the tortures he endured prior to the crucifixion must have been extremely brutal. It could also mean that his cross had no seat or foot rest that would enable him to push himself up for breath. A classic book about the death of Christ is *A Doctor At Calvary: The Passion of Our Lord Jesus Christ as Described by a Surgeon* by Pierre Barbet.

Holy Land site...

In 1842, Otto Thenius proposed that a particular hill in Jerusalem that resembled a skull was Calvary. The British General Charles Gordon promoted this idea in 1883 and believed that an ancient tomb nearby is where Jesus was buried. Many Protestants accept this "Garden Tomb" as Jesus' tomb. Archaeologists, though, date the tomb to Old Testament times, so it wasn't a "new" tomb as the Gospel specifies.

for your spiritual health...

Pray the Stations of the Cross. They are displayed in virtually every Catholic church in the world.

trivial tidbit...

The pelican is a symbol of both the passion of Christ and the Eucharist because people thought that this bird fed its young with blood by piercing its own breast. St. Gertrude once had a vision of Christ as a pelican piercing its heart with its beak.

it is darkest, in death Jesus shines most brilliantly as the light of the world. Through him the most heinous crime imaginable, the cruel execution of God, becomes a life-saving act of love.

Aftermath of the Crucifixion

The Gospels portray the impact of Jesus' death in different ways (see Matthew 27:45–54; Mark 15:33–39; Luke 23:44–47; John 19:31–37). There is darkness and the tearing of the Temple curtain. Matthew adds that there is an earthquake and rocks are split, tombs are opened, and dead saints walk the streets. He also includes an earthquake in his resurrection story. These symbols convey that the end time is happening now; the new age is here, ushered in by Jesus' death and resurrection. Matthew's Gospel reports that because of these marvels, the centurion and others proclaim, "Truly this man was God's Son." Mark has only the centurion say this, and he says it is because of the way Jesus died. Luke reports that the centurion praises God and declares, "Certainly this man was innocent." The crowd disperses, but Jesus' acquaintances stay.

John shares a special memory of the crucifixion, which he says he has witnessed. The next day was the Sabbath and, according to John, also the Passover. Of course the Jews didn't want the bodies on the cross that day, so they ask Pilate to have the legs of the men broken and the bodies removed. (The crucified couldn't push themselves up to breathe if their legs were broken.) The soldiers strike the legs of the two criminals with a heavy mallet, but when they come to Jesus, he is already dead. They don't break his legs, which strengthens the comparison of Jesus to the sacrificed Passover lamb, which was to have no broken bones. However one soldier pierces Jesus' side with a spear. Blood and water stream out. This action fulfills two prophecies: "None of his bones shall be broken" (Psalm 34:20) and "they will look on the one whom they have pierced" (Zechariah 12:10). It also has threefold symbolism. To some, the water symbolizes the sacrament of Baptism, while the blood stands for the Eucharist. Another perspective is that the flow of blood and water is the birth of the Church that Jesus brought forth in pain, almost like a woman giving birth. The outpouring also stands for the gift of the Holy Spirit.

The Cross: A Sign of Victory

St. Paul summarizes the effect of Jesus' death: "Through him God was pleased to reconcile to himself all things, whether on earth or in heaven, by making peace through the blood of the cross" (Colossians 1:20). For this reason we call the day of Jesus' death *Good* Friday.

Yet the cross was a shameful death. Scripture claims, "Anyone hung on a tree is under God's curse" (Deuteronomy 21:23). Naturally then, the first Christians were uncomfortable and quiet about the manner in which Christ died. But as time went on, they understood that Jesus reigned from the cross. By the second century crosses were a symbol of Christianity and our salvation. We make the Sign of the Cross over ourselves before and after prayer and on entering a church. Churches are built in the shape of cross. Blessings are imparted and exorcisms are performed with this sign. The cross, originally a sign of horror, has become the sign of ultimate love, a sign of love's

The Feast of the Exaltation of the Cross is celebrated on September 14. Its focus is on the cross as a sign of Christ's victory. Reflecting this positive theme, some Christian crosses are encrusted with jewels, and Christ is sometimes depicted on the cross clothed in majestic and priestly robes.

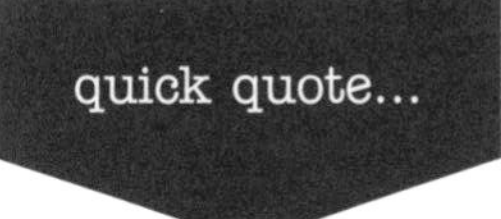

Jesus became God's unilateral disarmament.

Dorothy Sölle

victory. The fact that its beams extend in all four directions—north, south, east, and west—reminds us that on the wood of the cross Jesus has achieved salvation for the whole universe. After Jesus met evil head on and dealt it a crushing blow, he was able to pour out the abundant life he came to give. Perhaps it is not a coincidence that the word *evil* reversed spells *live*.

A few people have experienced the *stigmata*, a mystical phenomenon in which the bleeding wounds of Christ appear or are felt in their body. St. Paul claimed, "I carry the marks of Jesus branded on my body" (Galatians 6:17). St. Francis of Assisi (1182–1226) was the first one officially known to have the stigmata. St. Pio of Pietrelcina (Padre Pio), who died in 1968, bore the wounds in his hands, feet, and side for fifty years. St. Rita of Cascia (1386–1456) suffered only the wound of one thorn in her forehead.

The Burial of Jesus

After Jesus dies, he is buried almost immediately in someone else's grave (see Matthew 27:57–66; Mark 15:42–47; Luke 23:50–56; John 19:38–42). It's thought that ordinarily crucified criminals were either left on the cross or thrown into common pits, where they became prey for wild animals. Jesus is an exception. Because it was Friday and that evening was considered the beginning of the Sabbath when the "work" of burials was forbidden, Jesus had to be buried in haste. Joseph of Arimathea, who was a member of the Sanhedrin and a secret disciple of Jesus, asks Pilate if he could take the body of Jesus away. Mark notes that Pilate wonders if Jesus was already dead, so he summons the centurion and learns that Jesus has been dead some time. Pilate gives Joseph permission to take the body. John alone informs us that Nicodemus (the Pharisee who came to Jesus secretly at night) brings about a hundred pounds of myrrh and aloes and helps Joseph. They pull out the nails, lower the body of Jesus, and wrap it in linen cloth.

Although the Gospels don't mention that the body of Jesus was laid in Mary's arms, it is possible. Michelangelo's famous statue Pietà in St. Peter's Basilica in Rome renders this poignant scene. Strangely and sadly it is two members of the Sanhedrin and not the apostles who bury Jesus. By doing so, by the way, Joseph and Nicodemus would have incurred ritual impurity for seven days.

Nearby is a new tomb hewn in the limestone rock. Matthew notes that it was Joseph's tomb. Matthew and Mark state that Joseph rolls a stone against the door of the tomb. The disk-shaped stones, which kept animals out of the tombs, averaged about six feet in diameter, were one or two feet thick, and could weigh a ton. The Synoptics say that the women observe where the body was laid. Matthew specifically states that after Joseph departs, Mary Magdalene and the other Mary sit opposite the tomb.

Matthew's Gospel includes an episode that occurs the following day. The chief priests and Pharisees go to Pilate and tell him, "Sir, we remember what that imposter said while he was still alive, 'After three days I will rise again.'" (Apparently they remember Jesus' words better than his apostles do!) They ask Pilate to secure the tomb in case the disciples intend to steal the body and tell the people that Jesus was raised. Pilate authorizes a guard of soldiers to seal the tomb. This probably means that they stretch a cord across the stone, set the ends in wax, and imprint the wax with the official seal. To break a Roman seal without being authorized was punishable by death. It's unclear, however, whether the guards were Roman or Jewish.

trivial tidbit...

In apocryphal writings, the centurion and one of the soldiers at the foot of the cross merged into one person named Longinus. Tradition holds that he converted to the Way and became St. Longinus. In St. Peter's in Rome there is a colossal statue of him holding a lance.

trivial tidbit...

The hours for the death of Jesus in the Synoptics and in John do not correspond. This could be because the Synoptics used the Jewish way of counting hours, while John used the Roman system, which is like ours.

trivial tidbit...

The national flag of a number of countries incorporates a cross. Among them are England, Scotland, Australia, George, Switzerland, Spain, Denmark, Finland, Iceland, Norway, Sweden, Greece, Tonga, Martinique, and the Dominican Republic.

short prayer...

Hail, O Cross, our only hope!

quick quote...

Ultimately, God removes evil from the universe by absorbing it into himself.

Ray C. Stedman

Descent to the Dead

Jesus' body didn't undergo corruption. In the Creed we pray that Jesus descended "into hell" or "to the dead." This means that after Jesus was buried, he visited the abode of the dead where Adam and Eve, Abraham and Sarah, and all the other faithful Old Testament forebears were waiting, along with the good thief. There Jesus announced to them that they were freed. He had vanquished death and opened the gates of heaven.

There is no liturgy on Holy Saturday. This day is the hiatus between the old age and the new age. We observe it as the silent, still time when "the King is sleeping," resting in his tomb. Holy Saturday is called the Second Sabbath, for it is the second time after creation when God rests. Like Mary, the mother of Jesus, on this day we await in faith and hope for Jesus to awaken.

Crucifixion Symbols in Nature

Here are three symbols of the crucifixion:

✦ The *Passion flower* is named for the crucifixion because Spanish Christian missionaries saw in it the symbols of crucifixion. The central column is the pillar of the scourging, and the tendrils are the whips. The radial filaments, which can number more than a hundred, represent the crown of thorns. In Spain therefore, the Passion flower is known as *Espina de Cristo* (Christ's Thorn). The top three stigmata represent the nails, and the lower five anthers stand for the wounds in the hands, feet, and side. The ovary is the hammer. The leaf shape is a spear. The rays within the flower form a halo for Jesus' divinity. The ten petals and sepals represent ten apostles (omitting Judas the betrayer and John the faithful). The flower is said to stay open three days, signifying the time between Jesus death and the resurrection as well as his three-year ministry.

✦ A *sand dollar* also bears Christian symbols. On the top side there is an Easter lily that has the five-pointed Star of Bethlehem in the center. Five narrow openings symbolize the four nail holes and the spear wound of the crucified Christ. On the other side are the Christmas poinsettia and a bell. Inside the shell are five "doves of peace." Some say that these are the angels that sang to shepherds on the first Christmas.

✦ There is a legend that at one time the *dogwood tree* was tall and mighty. Because of its strong wood, it was used for Jesus' cross. The dogwood was ashamed of this and begged Jesus for forgiveness. Jesus took pity on the dogwood and made the tree slender and twisted so that it would never again be used for a cross. As a reminder of its role in history, however, the dogwood tree's blossoms are in the shape of a cross. In the center of each blossom is a crown of thorns, and the outer edge of each of the four petals has a red nail print.

24 Lord: The Resurrection

A class was preparing an Easter play, and children were volunteering for the parts. One little boy hadn't raised his hand for any part. When the teacher asked what role he would like, he declared, "I want to be the stone that is rolled away and lets Jesus out!"

That boy had the right idea. The most important happening in history is that Jesus is freed from death. In all the immensity of the universe, our little blue planet spinning around one of a trillion suns was graced by God being born as a human being, suffering and dying as we all must, and then leaving behind an empty tomb. Ever since then we have pondered and celebrated the mystery of God's unfathomable love for us. St. Paul states that if Jesus hadn't risen from the dead, our faith would be in vain (see 1 Corinthians 15:14). If there had been no resurrection, Jesus would have disappeared in the sands of time with the other would-be Jewish "messiahs." His stupendous rising from the dead was the climax of his life on earth and his vindication for his faith in his Father. It gave credibility to his teachings, restored his followers' courage, and ignited a new religion that spread through the world like wildfire. Jesus, the Incorrupt One, is "the pioneer and perfecter of our faith" (Hebrews 12:2).

trivial tidbit...

The phoenix is a symbol of Jesus, for this mythological bird dies in flames every 500 years and then rises again from its ashes. The peacock too figures in Christian art as a symbol of immortality because of a legend that its flesh is incorruptible. Also, the eyes of the peacock's tail feathers stand for the all-seeing God.

The resurrection of Jesus was unique. The day of resurrection is known as the eighth day because it heralds the new creation. The paschal mystery, which encompasses the suffering, death, resurrection, and ascension of Jesus, reveals his divine sovereignty. After the resurrection, the followers of Jesus called him *Kyrios* ("Lord"). Before the resurrection they had addressed Jesus with the Aramaic for *Lord*, which is *Mar*, a title of respect comparable to "Sir." They realized that Jesus now was fully *Kyrios*, the Greek word for *Lord* that was used in place of the name of God. The main message of the disciples as they went about proclaiming the good news was "Jesus is Lord," that is, "Jesus is God."

The Miracle of Miracles

The resurrection of Jesus was not a reincarnation, which means that a living being dies and comes back to life as a different being. In fact, Catholics do not believe in reincarnation. Certainly the risen Jesus was the same person as Jesus of Nazareth and had the same body. Yet Jesus' rising was also more than the resuscitations experienced by Lazarus, the son of the widow of Naim, and Jairus's daughter. They would all die a second time; Jesus wouldn't. Jesus came forth from the tomb no longer bound by space or time. He had an entirely new mode of existence—we call it a "glorified" body. At first, his own disciples didn't even recognize him, for example, Mary Magdalene, the Emmaus disciples, and the seven apostles who were fishing when he appeared on the shore.

We say that Jesus is the new or second Adam. Where Adam's disobedience brought about death for us, Jesus' obedience yields eternal life. Jesus is the firstborn of the new creation. Because Jesus rose, we know that we can trust in his promises, in particular the promise that we too will rise someday. Jesus has vanquished our greatest enemy, death, and with it all fear. The story of his life has a happy ending, and so will ours.

The Gospel accounts of the resurrection differ significantly. This is understandable because of the nature of the event and the time that elapsed before anyone wrote down the accounts. This much is certain: On Good Friday and Holy Saturday, the followers of Jesus were shrouded in sorrow as they grieved for him. They were in shock from his violent execution. Furthermore, except for John, the apostles, especially Peter, are laden with guilt. Imagine then their exhilaration, confusion, and delirious joy on discovering that Jesus had somehow been raised from the dead. No wonder their memories and consequently their stories of the event are garbled. Although no one observed Jesus actually rising from the dead within his tomb, numerous eyewitnesses attested to the fact that he was very much alive.

trivial tidbit...

The earliest extant art that depicts Jesus rising out of the tomb instead of already risen dates to about 1020 A.D., almost a millennium after the original event.

quick quote...

The wages of sin is death, but the free gift of God is eternal life in Christ Jesus our Lord.

Romans 6:23

Matthew's and Mark's Accounts of the Resurrection

In the Gospels of Matthew and Mark (see Matthew 28:1–10; Mark 16:1–13), at dawn on the first day of the week, that is, Sunday, Mary Magdalene, Mary the mother of James (and Mark adds Salome) go to the tomb. Mark says that they bring spices to anoint Jesus' body, since they were forbidden by law to do this work on the Jewish Sabbath, the day before. In a

a cool website...

Go to www.shroud.com for an overview of the latest research on the Shroud of Turin.

trivial tidbit...

The shroud, with patches covering fire damage removed, was scheduled for a rare public viewing in spring of 2010. It was previously displayed in 2000. The Vatican has owned the shroud since 1983.

The Shroud of Turin

In Turin, Italy, there is a shroud that is a hotly contested enigma. The linen cloth, 14.5 feet by and 3.5 feet, bears the imprint of a scourged and crucified man believed by some to be Jesus. Recently a similar face was discovered on the reverse side. The shroud is kept in a climate-controlled urn in the chapel of the cathedral. The shroud came to Turin in 1578, but documents show that it was known in France in the 1300s. In 1898, the negative of a photo of the shroud revealed a positive image of the man. In 1988, radiocarbon-14 testing was carried out to date the shroud. Three tests indicated that the cloth was no older than 1260. But people have since argued that the piece of cloth that was tested was part of a patch. The shroud has a weave characteristic of first-century Palestine, and pollen in the fibers are from plants that grow only there. Scientists cannot explain how the imprint on the shroud was made. One theory is that somehow a flash of light from Jesus' resurrection marked the cloth. The Shroud of Turin, like Veronica's Veil and other items of popular piety, is not an article of Catholic faith. Rather, it demonstrates the hunger of people to be in touch with the historical person of Jesus. Even better, for Catholics at least, is the Eucharist, where we actually become one with him!

very touching detail, the women discuss who will roll away the large stone from the entrance of the tomb. Little do they know that this tomb was the womb of new, glorified life.

Matthew's report is fantastic. There is an earthquake and a dazzling angel rolls away the stone and sits on it, a sign of triumph over death. These events frighten the guards, who tremble and faint dead away. Mark simply relates that the women enter the tomb and see a young man in a white robe seated on it. The women do not faint, but they have to be dumbfounded. The angel reassures them, "Do not be afraid. I know that you are looking for Jesus who was crucified. He is not here; for he has been raised as he said. Come, see the place where he lay." The angel tells the women to go quickly and report this to the disciples, along with the news that Jesus is going to Galilee, where they'll see him. Jesus could have appeared to these disciples in person, but he chose to use messengers to deliver the news of his resurrection.

Mark reports that the women, amazed and frightened out of their wits, flee and say nothing to anyone. In some of the oldest manuscripts, Mark's Gospel abruptly stops here. An added ending explains that the women relay the news to the disciples, who then begin to proclaim eternal salvation to the world. In a second and longer ending in Mark, Mary Magdalene first sees Jesus and then tells the disciples, who don't believe her. Jesus then appears to two disciples on the road to a town called Emmaus, who report back and also are not believed.

Matthew's Gospel elaborates that the women depart from the tomb with great fear and great joy to

trivial tidbit...

Although we may calculate that Jesus was in the tomb only one day and two nights, in the Jewish (and biblical) way of speaking of time, it was three days before his resurrection.

You ascended from before our eyes, and we turned away grieving, only to find you in our hearts.

St. Augustine

tell the apostles. On the way suddenly the risen Jesus meets the women disciples and says, "Greetings!" They take hold of his feet and worship him. Then Jesus says, "Do not be afraid," and repeats the angel's instructions, adding, "Go and tell my brothers to go to Galilee." He calls the apostles "brothers," for he has already forgiven them.

Matthew also reports that some of the guards let the chief priests know about the crisis at the tomb. After consulting the elders, the priests bribe the soldiers with a large sum of money to say that the disciples came and took the body while they were asleep. This is a risky agreement for the soldiers because the punishment for sleeping on duty was death. However, the priests promise to defend the guards if the governor hears the tale. This story of the stolen corpse then circulates (see Matthew 28:11–15), although robbers certainly wouldn't have stripped the corpse and left the linens behind…neatly folded at that!

In Matthew's Gospel, the eleven disciples (as he calls the apostles) then go to a mountain in Galilee as directed. There Jesus appears to them and they worship him, though some still doubt. (It is hard to understand how they could doubt with Jesus standing right in front of them, but then it must have been hard for them to believe their own eyes.) Their faith is not strong yet; the Holy Spirit won't come upon them for another nine days. Jesus gives the eleven what has come to be known as the great commission. He says, "All authority in heaven and on earth has been given to me. Go therefore and make disciples of all nations, baptizing them in the name of the Father and of the Son and of the Holy Spirit, and teaching them to obey everything that I have commanded you. And remember I am with you always to the end of the age" (Matthew 28:16–20). And with that the Gospel of Matthew ends.

Mark's longer ending is similar to Matthew's, but he includes the ascension of Jesus. He says that Jesus appears to the eleven while they are eating and first scolds them for not believing those who had already seen him. He then commissions them: "Go out to all the world and proclaim the good news to all creation." He promises that those who believe and are baptized will do marvelous things: cast out demons in his name, speak in tongues, pick up snakes, drink poison without being harmed, and heal the sick by laying hands on them. Then Jesus is taken up into heaven and is seated at the right hand of God. The disciples proclaim the good news with the Lord working with them, and their message is confirmed by signs. They carry on the mission of Jesus and share his power.

Holy Land site...

Within the Church of the Holy Sepulcher in Jerusalem there is a tomb traditionally honored as Jesus' tomb. An outer "Chapel of the Angel" leads to a chamber that contains a marble-covered slab thought to be where Jesus was laid to rest. Where the church stands there was once a Roman temple to the goddess Aphrodite.

Luke's Account of the Resurrection

Luke has a significantly different account than Matthew and Mark (see Luke 24:1–12). He says that the women bringing the spices to anoint Jesus go inside the open tomb and find it empty. Suddenly two men in dazzling clothes stand before them at the tomb. Terrified, the women bow their faces to the ground. The men inquire, "Why do you look for the living among the dead?" They remind the women that Jesus said he would be handed over, crucified, and rise on the third day. The women, among them Mary Magdalene, Joanne, and Mary, the mother of James, go and break the news to the apostles and others. Although

trivial tidbit...

Mary Magdalene is the only one standing by the cross whom all four Gospels name.

women were not legal witnesses in the Jewish culture, Jesus chooses women to be the first witnesses of his resurrection. The apostles, however, do not believe the women. (When has this ever happened before or since?) Nevertheless, Peter, and only impetuous Peter, speeds to the tomb, stops and peers in, and sees the linen burial clothes by themselves. He goes home "amazed."

John's Account of the Resurrection

It's John who gives us one of our favorite Easter stories (see John 20:1–18). Mary Magdalene bravely makes her way to the tomb while it's still dark and sees that the stone was removed. She concludes that the body of Jesus has been stolen. Frantic, she runs to Peter and the disciple Jesus loved (presumably John) and breathlessly says, "They have taken the Lord out of the tomb and we do not know where they have laid him." Peter and John race to the tomb. John arrives first, bends downs to look in the tomb, and sees the linen wrappings lying there. He doesn't enter, deferring to Peter. The older apostle arrives (you can almost hear him gasping for breath) and enters the tomb. He sees the linen wrappings and, separate from them, the head cloth neatly rolled up. John then walks into the tomb too. John says that this disciple "saw and believed" even though "as yet they did not understand the scripture" that Jesus must rise from the dead. Then, kind of anticlimactically, the two apostles return home.

Not Mary Magdalene. She continues to stand weeping outside of the tomb. She bends to look into it and sees two angels in white sitting where Jesus' body had been, one at the head, the other at the foot.

They ask, "Woman, why are you weeping?" She says, "They have taken away my Lord, and I do not know where they have laid him." Then Mary turns around and sees Jesus standing there, but she doesn't recognize him. Either his new life significantly transforms his appearance, or Mary's tears blur her vision. Jesus too asks, "Woman, why are you weeping? Whom are you looking for?" Assuming that he is the gardener, Mary begs, "Sir, if you have carried him away, tell me where you have laid him and I will take him away." She's in such distress that she speaks nonsense, proposing to carry the body of an adult man herself. Jesus says only: "Mary." When she hears him pronounce her name with the same tenderness as he must have said it many times before, she realizes that it is Jesus who stands before her, alive. She turns and says, *"Rabbouni,"* which means "my master." Overjoyed, Mary apparently flings her arms around Jesus, for he cautions her, "Do not hold on to me because I have not yet ascended to the Father." Then Jesus directs her, "Go to my brothers and say to them, 'I am ascended to my Father and your Father, to my God and your God.' " Mary goes to the disciples and announces the good news. She declares, "I have seen the Lord," and delivers Jesus' message to the rest of the disciples.

The Lord has changed all our sunsets to sunrise.

St. Clement of Alexandria

On the Way to Emmaus

Luke alone tells of an encounter with the risen Lord on the road to Emmaus that shows his playfulness, among other things (see Luke 24:13–35). On Easter Sunday two disappointed disciples leave Jerusalem for Emmaus, which is some seven miles away. One is Cleopas and the other, who is unnamed, could have been

trivial tidbit...

According to one legend, Cleopas was the brother of St. Joseph, and therefore, the uncle of Jesus.

for your spiritual health...

Reflect on one way the risen Lord might be present to you now in a way that you don't recognize him.

his wife. As they walk along, talking about the bizarre events of the day, Jesus joins them, but they don't recognize him and he doesn't introduce himself. He asks what they were discussing, and they stand still, their faces sad. Cleopas answers, "Are you the only stranger in Jerusalem who doesn't know that things that have taken place?" Jesus plays dumb and asks, "What things?" The two travelers reply, "About Jesus of Nazareth, who was a prophet mighty in deed and word." They proceed to recount how Jesus was crucified but women had seen his empty tomb and an angel who said he was alive. Moreover, some disciples had also seen the empty tomb but hadn't seen Jesus. Despite this news, the two are dejected because they had hoped Jesus was the one to redeem Israel. What the astounding women's stories and the empty tomb signify does not occur to them. Then their mysterious companion, the very one they have been discussing, exclaims, "Oh, how foolish you are and how slow of heart to believe all that the prophets have declared!" Jesus asks, "Was it not necessary that the Messiah should suffer these things and then enter into his glory?" Then he tutors them, interpreting all that Scripture said about him. His words dispel their dark mood.

As they near Emmaus, Jesus walks ahead as if to go on. But his two companions, obviously fascinated by Jesus, urge him to stay with them because night is coming. So Jesus goes into the inn with them. While he is eating with them, he takes bread, blesses and breaks it, and gives it to them. With this they realize his identity and he vanishes. The disciples, reflecting back on their conversation, ask, "Weren't our hearts burning within us while he was talking to us on the road?" They return to Jerusalem to find the eleven apostles and others excitedly talking about how the risen Lord had appeared to Peter. (It could be that shame for denying our Lord compelled Peter to isolate himself from the other apostles. So Jesus was able to appear to him alone for a private reconciliation, giving Peter a chance to say, "I'm sorry for betraying you.") Then the Emmaus travelers share their story of how Jesus walked with them incognito and was revealed to them in the breaking of the bread.

The "breaking of the bread" was the early Christians' expression for the Eucharist. The Emmaus story is a mirror image of the Mass. First Jesus explains Scripture (the Liturgy of the Word), and then he shares a meal of bread (the Liturgy of the Eucharist).

quick quote...

In one guise or another Christ always meets us on the road, burns holes in our hearts, explains the latest crucifixion to us and sends us back—to Galilee and our abandoned discipleship.

Ronald Rolheiser, O.M.I.

Appearance to the Disciples

Luke and John offer different stories of Jesus' appearances to his disciples (see Luke 24:36–42; John 20:19–23). In Luke while the Emmaus travelers are speaking to the apostles, Jesus suddenly stands in their midst. Jesus' new level of existence gives him powers for which locked doors mean nothing. He greets his friends with the usual Jewish greeting, "Shalom," or "Peace be with you." On this occasion the words are powerful. The last time the apostles were with Jesus they were running for their lives while he was being taken prisoner. And Peter had denied him. With shame and guilt lying heavy on them, the apostles are sorely in need of peace. In addition, hearing the details of Jesus' death must have been devastating for them. They were in shock and wondered why God hadn't rescued Jesus.

big book search...

Look up 1 Peter 1:8–9 and read what is said about those of us who do not see Jesus Christ. It should make you feel good about your faith.

At the sight of Jesus, the apostles at first are terrified, thinking they are seeing a ghost. Jesus asks why they're frightened and doubtful, and he says, "Look at my hands and my feet and see that it is I myself." Jesus is recognized not by his face but by his holy wounds. He invites, "Touch me and see; for a ghost does not have flesh and bones as you see that I have." When the disciples are joyful but still disbelieve, Jesus asks for something to eat. They give him a piece of broiled fish and he eats it, thereby proving he's not a ghost, but also showing that he again shares table fellowship with them as a close friend. Jesus proceeds to explain that in Scripture the Messiah is to suffer and rise on the third day and that redemption and forgiveness is to be proclaimed in his name to all nations. He says, "You are witnesses of these things." Then Jesus promises the Holy Spirit.

John too reports that on Easter evening the disciples are behind locked doors for fear of the Jews. The disciples knew that because their leader was killed, their lives too were in jeopardy. All of a sudden to their great joy Jesus is standing with them. He greets them with "Peace be with you." He, the "Prince of Peace" (Isaiah 9:6), calms their turbulent hearts with the peace that is the hallmark of God's rule. Then Jesus shows them his hands and sides where his wounds are obvious. In case there is any doubt that he has forgiven them their weakness and understands their fear, Jesus reiterates, "Peace be with you." Then he missions them. He declares, "As the Father sent me, so I send you." He breathes on the disciples, an act that calls to mind God breathing on Adam to bring him to life. Jesus says, "Receive the Holy Spirit. If you forgive the sins of any, they are forgiven them; if you retain the sins of any, they are retained." The Church understands that by these words Jesus bestowed on the apostles the power to forgive sins and instituted the Sacraments of Reconciliation and Holy Orders.

Appearance for Thomas's Sake

Thomas was missing when Jesus came (see John 20:24–29). Maybe he was the one daring enough to venture out to get provisions for the rest and so should have come down in history as "courageous Thomas" rather than "doubting Thomas." This positive nickname agrees with the image of Thomas who, when Jesus declares he is going where his life is in danger, boldly says to the other apostles, "Let us also go that we may die with him" (John 11:16).

When Thomas returns, the apostles jubilantly announce, "We have seen the Lord!" Naturally Thomas must be somewhat hurt that Jesus chose to appear when he wasn't there. Rather than expressing disappointment at missing Jesus' visit, Thomas boldly asserts, "Unless I see the marks of the nails in his hands, and put my finger in the mark of the nail and my hand in his side, I will not believe." The next week must have been a long, hard one for Thomas. Then on the following Sunday, although the doors were shut, Jesus visits again and says, "Peace be with you." He invites Thomas, "Put your finger here and see my hands. Reach out your hand and put it in my side. Do not doubt but believe." This is more than enough proof for Thomas. He exclaims, "My Lord and my God!" (We don't know whether or not Thomas actually accepted Jesus' invitation to touch his wounds.)

Because the first resurrection appearances occurred on Sunday, the first day of the week, this day became known as the *eighth day*, the day of the new creation and of new life. The first Christians gathered to celebrate on this day, the Lord's Day, in addition to observing the Jewish Saturday Sabbath. In 321 Emperor Constantine officially made Sunday the Christian Sabbath and day of rest.

quick quote...

Let him Easter in us,
be a dayspring to the
dimness of us.

Gerard Manley Hopkins, S.J.

trivial tidbit...

George Frederic Handel's oratorio "Messiah" composed in 1741 encompasses the life of Jesus. Its highlight is the well-loved "Hallelujah" chorus, whose words are taken from the Book of Revelation.

Jesus then makes the statement that consoles us who are not gifted with a personal visit from him: "Blessed are those who have not seen and yet have come to believe."

There is no record that Jesus appeared to Caiaphas, Herod, or Pilate to say, "I told you so." Instead he came to those who were his friends and supporters in life, and they came to believe in him. What's more, although his body was glorified, it bore the scars of the crucifixion, as lasting testimony to his love for us.

Easter Symbols

✦ *Easter eggs* represent the tomb from which new life emerges.

✦ *Rabbits* are prolific and so are symbols of fertility.

✦ *Spring flowers* bloom after the dead of winter and are signs of new life.

✦ *The rising sun* is like Christ who rose from darkness and brought light to the world.

✦ *New clothes* for Easter symbolize new life.

✦ *Easter lilies* with their simple trumpet-shaped form and bright white color are associated with the pure new life of resurrection.

✦ *Butterflies* that emerge from cocoons transformed from caterpillars signify new, glorified life.

✦ *The paschal candle* stands for Jesus as the light of the world.

Breakfast on the Beach

Another post resurrection story found only in John (see John 21:1–14) occurs at the Sea of Galilee. Peter, Thomas, Nathanael, James, John and two other apostles are together. They are doing nothing after Jesus' appearances to them and are probably wondering what will happen next. Peter announces, "I'm going fishing," and they all decide to join him. All night the seven men fish but catch nothing. At dawn Jesus stands on the bank and calls, "Children, you have no fish, have you?" When they shout back, "No," he tells them to cast their net on the right side where they will find fish. They do as he says and catch so many fish that they can't haul the heavy net onto the boat. The beloved disciple, assumed to be John, exclaims to Peter, "It is the Lord!" Peter, true to style, dives into the sea and eagerly swims to Jesus. The other six apostles follow in the boat, dragging the net the hundred yards or so to shore.

On the beach the apostles see fish frying over a charcoal fire and some bread. Jesus tells them to bring some of their fish too. He considerately involves them in providing the meal. Peter goes back to the boat and hauls the net ashore. We're told that there were one hundred and fifty-three large fish, but the net doesn't tear. (The exact number suggests that the proud fishermen must have counted the fish.) Jesus invites the disciples to breakfast and again assumes the role of servant and serves them. They don't ask who he is because they know.

After breakfast Jesus graciously initiates a dialogue that gives Peter the opportunity to make up for his three denials at another charcoal fire (the one

short prayer...

My God and my all!

quick quote...

If you confess with your lips that Jesus is Lord and believe in your heart that God raised him from the dead, you will be saved.

Romans 10:9

quick quote...

Where Peter is, there is the Church. Where the Church is, there is Jesus Christ. Where Jesus Christ is, there is eternal salvation.

St. Ambrose

in the courtyard of the High Priest on the night before he died) by three declarations of love (see John 21:15–19). Jesus asks Peter, "Simon son of John, do you love me more than these?" Peter says, "Yes, Lord; you know that I love you." Jesus commands, "Feed my lambs." Again Jesus asks, "Simon son of John, do you love me?" And Peter responds, "Yes, Lord; you know that I love you." This time Jesus says, "Tend my sheep." A third time Jesus asks, and Peter is hurt (and probably a bit exasperated). He replies, "Lord, you know everything, you know that I love you." And Jesus says, "Tend my sheep." In this dialogue Jesus is turning over the care of his people, the Church, to Peter. Notice that Jesus isn't embarrassed at asking for an expression of love from this burly fisherman.

Then Jesus says that when Peter grows old he will stretch out his hands and someone will fasten a belt around him and take him where he does not want to go. This probably refers to Peter's martyrdom. Jesus says, to Peter, "Follow me." Peter will follow Jesus so closely that eventually he too will die on the cross.

Then Peter asks what will happen to John, and Jesus answers, "If it's my will that he remain until I come, what is that to you? Follow me!" It is interesting to note that in John's Gospel, Jesus' last words are these: "Follow me." In Mark's Gospel they are his first words.

The Ascension

The risen Jesus must have appeared more times than the Gospels record. This is confirmed by St. Paul: "He appeared to more than five hundred brothers and sisters at one time" (1 Corinthians 15:6). Also, although the Gospels do not tell of the risen Jesus appearing to his mother Mary, certainly he came to her in a personal and intimate reunion.

Sometime after the resurrection, some think immediately after, Jesus returns to his Father in heaven, a mystery called the ascension (see Mark 16:19; Luke 24:50–52; Acts 1:6–11). In Mark's and Luke's Gospels, the ascension occurs on the same day as the resurrection. It is part of Jesus' one grand movement to glory. This means that humanity is already in glory, a hint of what awaits us all.

While Matthew and John do not report the ascension, Mark includes the fact that Jesus is seated at the Father's right hand. (Mark 16:19) and Luke places the story both in his Gospel and in the Acts of the Apostles. In the Gospel he simply says that Jesus leads the apostles to Bethany, lifts his hands in blessing, withdraws from them, and is carried up into heaven. They worship Jesus and then joyfully return to Jerusalem and remain in the Temple blessing God.

In Acts, Luke provides a fuller account. After rising from the dead, Jesus appears to the apostles for forty days, teaching them about the kingdom of God. He orders them to stay in Jerusalem to await the coming of the Holy Spirit. Still under the misconception that Jesus is somehow a military messiah, the apostles ask if this is the time he will restore the kingdom to Israel. Doubtless Jesus rolls his eyes and says it not for them to know the times the Father has set. Then Jesus foretells a remarkable future for them: They will receive power when the Holy Spirit comes upon them and they will be his witnesses to the ends of the earth. At that Jesus is lifted up and a cloud takes him out of

Holy Land site...

The Church of the Primacy of St. Peter graces the shore of the Sea of Galilee and commemorates Jesus commissioning Peter to be leader of the Church. Inside the church is a rock called *Mensa Christi*, (Table of Christ), where Jesus prepared breakfast for his disciples. Outside of the church there is a large, striking, bronze statue of Peter kneeling before Jesus and declaring his love.

sight. While the disciples are gazing at this phenomenon, two men in white robes stand by them. They jolt the disciples into action by asking, "Men of Galilee, why do you stand looking up toward heaven?" The strangers reveal that Jesus will return to earth the same way he left.

The ascension is the exaltation of Jesus to the seat at the right hand of God. That means that Jesus, in his humanity, shares the divinity and power of the Father. Monsignor Ronald Knox summed up what this mystery means for us: "Human nature…has penetrated behind the last barrier, has crossed the last threshold, which separates the human from the divine. And because we are one in and with him, his achievement is ours. He is just the "first fruits." St. Paul does not hesitate to describe Christian people as here and now "enthroned above the heavens, in Christ Jesus."

In heaven, Jesus, our mediator, intercedes for us. He will come back to earth in glory at some undisclosed time in order to judge all people. This second coming of Jesus, or *parousia*, will mark the end of time and the end of the world as we know it. This is why we Catholics say that we now live in the end times, awaiting his arrival.

trivial tidbit…

The ascension of Jesus is reminiscent of the prophet Elijah being whisked up to heaven in a flaming chariot and a whirlwind at the end of his life.

quick quote…

Christ has no body now on earth but yours, no hands but yours, no feet but yours; yours are the eyes through which Christ's compassion looks out on the world, yours are the feet with which he is to go about doing good, and yours are the hands with which he blesses all the world.

St. Teresa of Avila

The Coming of the Holy Spirit

The apostles stay in Jerusalem, praying and waiting with other believers, including Mary, the mother of Jesus (see Acts 2:1–42). While there, at Peter's suggestion the group (now numbering a hundred and twenty) replaces Judas with Matthias. One of the requirements for the position of apostle was being a witness of the resurrection. This is another clue that the Lord appeared to more than the original eleven apostles and some of the women disciples.

On the Jewish feast of Pentecost, at nine o'clock in the morning, the disciples are sitting together when suddenly the house is filled with wind. Flames of fire rest on each one, and the Holy Spirit, the Spirit of God, fills them. They begin to speak in tongues. Because Pentecost was one of the feasts when Jews were obliged to go to Jerusalem, the city was packed with people from all over who speak different languages. Empowered by the Spirit, the disciples come out from the house and talk with reckless boldness to the people on the street. This radical transformation of the followers of Jesus from terrified doubters to courageous believers is one of the "proofs" of his resurrection. Everyone in the crowd can understand the disciples' words. Some people are amazed, while some think that they have had too much to drink. Then Peter delivers the first of many sermons, declaring that Jesus of Nazareth—a man known for his deeds of power, wonders, and signs, who was crucified and killed—has been raised up from the dead by God. Peter urges the people in the crowd to repent and be baptized, with dramatic results. Three thousand people that day become followers of Jesus.

Holy Land site...

On top of the Mount of Olives is the octagonal Chapel of the Ascension built in 1620. It houses a rock on the spot where Jesus ostensibly ascended to heaven. In 392, a church stood there, which was destroyed and rebuilt, with its roof open to the sky. The Muslims rebuilt this church as a mosque with a dome in 1187.

Post-Pentecost Occurrences

The followers of the Way, as the first disciples were called, live in community, share their goods, and celebrate the Eucharist (see Acts 6:8–7:60). The group grows so rapidly that seven deacons are chosen to help the apostles. The apostles and deacons work great signs among the people. Peter, for example, cures a

quick quote...

The sun penetrates crystal and makes it more dazzling. In the same way, the sanctifying Spirit indwells in souls and makes them more radiant. They become like so many powerhouses beaming grace and love around them.

St. Basil

short prayer...

Come Holy Spirit, fill the hearts of your faithful and kindle in them the fire of your love. Send forth your Spirit and they shall be created. And you shall renew the face of the earth.

crippled beggar lying at the gate of the Temple. He commands, "In the name of Jesus Christ of Nazareth, stand up and walk." And the man walks into the Temple leaping and praising God (Acts 3:1–9).

One deacon named Stephen becomes the first Christian martyr at the hands of the Jewish leaders. As Stephen is being stoned to death, he exclaims, "Look, I see the heavens opened and the Son of Man standing at the right hand of God." Ironically, one of the Pharisees present and supporting the stoning is Saul, a notorious persecutor of the Christians who becomes the great apostle Paul after he too is blessed with an experience of the risen Lord (see Acts 9:1–36).

As Saul was on his way to Damascus to persecute Christians, a brilliant light flashed and he fell to the ground. He heard a voice say, "Saul, Saul, why do you persecute me?" This statement shows how Jesus identifies himself with his people. Saul asked, "Who are you, Lord?" and the answer came, "I am Jesus, whom you are persecuting." Jesus told Saul to continue on to Damascus and wait for further instructions. Struck blind by the experience, Saul had to be led to the city. There he waited and fasted three days until Ananias, one of the early followers of Jesus, came to him. Ananias too had had a vision of Jesus and was commanded to cure Saul. After regaining his sight, Saul became a zealous Christian. In writing 1 Corinthians 8:6 he professed, "There is one God, the Father from whom are all things and for whom we exist, and one Lord, Jesus Christ, through whom are all things and through whom we exist." Paul (his Roman name) visited the apostles and learned from them. He preached the Gospel especially to Gentiles, founding new churches in towns in the area of the Mediterranean Sea. His letters to these churches that are in the New Testament predate the Gospels. Eventually Paul was imprisoned in Rome and beheaded.

Earliest Christianity

The followers of Jesus multiplied exponentially. A major reason for this was the work of Paul with the Gentiles. Peter, too, came to understand that Christianity is for Gentiles as well as for Jews. The new religion was also given impetus when Christians were persecuted by the Jews and eventually banned from the synagogues. This forced many of the early Jewish disciples to relocate to other countries, taking their faith with them and spreading it. Christians also suffered persecutions from the Roman emperors, and many were martyred. The Church witnessed the truth in the saying, "The blood of martyrs is the seed of Christians." The fierce persecutions raged until one day, before a battle, the pagan Roman emperor Constantine had a vision. He reported seeing a cross in the sky and hearing the words "In this sign you will conquer." After winning the battle, Constantine issued the Edict of Milan in 313 A.D., which established religious tolerance. Eventually Christianity became the official religion of the Roman Empire. The religion that started with a poor carpenter's son from Nazareth had exploded. Today about a third of the world's population call themselves Christian. However, throughout history Christians have disagreed, and this has divided them into virtually hundreds of faith traditions, despite their founder's prayer that all may be one.

big book search...

St. Paul was consumed with love for Christ. His letters reflect this in some very beautiful passages. Read Romans 8:35–39; 2 Corinthians 5:14–17; and Philippians 1:20–21, 3:7–11.

The feast of Sts. Peter and Paul is celebrated on June 29. On January 25 the Church celebrates the feast of the Conversion of Paul.

Christ is everything for us.

St. Ambrose

Once, when the high priest and Jewish council wanted to kill the apostles for preaching about Jesus, one wise Pharisee named Gamaliel reasoned that after two other popular Jewish leaders had been killed their followers had dispersed, so why not leave the apostles alone? He argued, "If this plan or this undertaking is of human origin, it will fail; but if it is of God, you will not be able to overthrow them—in that case you may even be found fighting against God!" (Acts 5:38–39). Surely there has been ample proof over the centuries that "this undertaking" of belief in Jesus of Nazareth has been "of God."

25 The Life: Jesus Today and Tomorrow

Every so often there is a "Jesus sighting." Markings in a cloud formation, a tree trunk, a rock, a tortilla, or the like are perceived to be an image of Jesus. Some people find this experience exciting, for to them it's a sign that Jesus is making a connection with us. Actually the vision is the result of *pareidolia*, a psychological phenomenon defined as the tendency of humans to construct familiar images from vague and random patterns. How much more phenomenal than these purported visions are the authentic connections Jesus has with us today!

The Spirit of Jesus is alive and well and present in the world. For those of us who follow Jesus, he is still Emmanuel, still "God with us." How else has his Church endured for some two thousand years? As he promised, our glorified Lord is with us always, both continuously and until the end of time. He guides, teaches, heals, strengthens, and comforts us now as surely as he did these things for his first followers. The difference is that Jesus is not visible as he was to them, and therefore we must practice the faith that he so often urged his followers to have. As Scripture assures us, "Jesus Christ is the same yesterday and today and forever" (Hebrews 13:8). Throughout the ages, he is our life, for he fills our existence with meaning and promises us entrance into eternal life, immediately and after our death. Jesus is now loose in the world, living and acting with power and love, in multiple forms.

quick quote...

Do not be afraid of Christ! He takes nothing away, and he gives you everything. When we give ourselves to him, we receive a hundredfold in return. Yes, open, open wide the doors to Christ—and you will find true life.

Pope Benedict XVI

for your spiritual health...

Make a "holy hour" before the Blessed Sacrament. This practice arose from Jesus' question to the apostles who slept during his agony in the garden: "Could you not stay awake with me for one hour?" (Matthew 26:40)

Jesus Present in the Eucharist

The Mass is the wellspring and the highest peak of Christian life. More than anything else, it is at the heart of who we are and what we believe. From the beginning Christians have met for the "breaking of the bread," celebrating this memorial of Jesus' sacrifice as he had commanded. In Paul's words, we "proclaim the death of the Lord until he comes" (1 Corinthians 11:26). At this sacred meal, among his followers gathered together, Jesus is truly present. There, through the words of the priest and the power of the Holy Spirit, bread and wine become for us the body and blood of Jesus. To Catholics these elements are no mere symbol; they actually are Jesus—his body, blood, soul, and divinity—present with us in a unique and miraculous way. That is why we call this mystery the "Real Presence." In the Eucharist, Jesus again lives and acts in our time and space.

At Mass the saving acts of Jesus are made present again. Jesus offers himself in the same sacrifice he made at the Last Supper and on Calvary, but this time we collaborate with him. We join in offering him to the Father for the redemption of the world. We also offer ourselves, our lives, and all our works to God. Then, as Jesus promised his disciples, he becomes living bread and the cup of salvation. We consume the blessed bread and wine, believing that under these forms, it is truly Jesus, the glorified Lord, who is nourishing us. By partaking of his divine life, we are all united and become more fully the mystical body of Christ. We are then sent forth to continue his mission in the world.

Besides Jesus being with us in the consecrated

bread and wine, he is with us at Mass in other ways. During the Liturgy of the Word, Jesus is present in the Scripture that is proclaimed, in particular the Gospel. In a special way Jesus is present in the priest, who represents him in offering the sacrifice. Jesus is also within every baptized person in the congregation assembled around the altar. Paul tells us, "Now you are the body of Christ and individually members of it" (1 Corinthians 12:27). If we wish to deepen our relationship with Jesus, we can do so by encountering him in the Eucharist.

Jesus invites us all to his table. In Scripture he says, "Listen! I am standing at the door knocking; if you hear my voice and open the door, I will come in to you and eat with you, and you with me" (Revelation 3:20). The word *Eucharist* means "thanksgiving." By participating in this ritual meal and most perfect prayer we say "thank you" to God for everything, but especially for the gift of his Son, who died and rose so that we might live. During the seasons of the Church year, at Mass we recall and celebrate the mysteries of the incarnation (Advent, Christmas) and redemption (Lent, Easter).

When the celebration of the Eucharist is finished, some sacred hosts are kept in our tabernacles. Jesus becomes a "prisoner for love of us" in order to be available for the sick and dying at all times. A Catholic church is truly a sacred place, the house of God, because Jesus is there in the reserved Blessed Sacrament. That is why we Catholics genuflect or bow toward the tabernacle. We can visit Jesus in church or chapel to converse with him, pour out our heart to him, or simply enjoy quietly being in his presence.

for your spiritual health...

At the beginning of the Liturgy of the Eucharist the priest raises the paten to God. Make it a practice to mentally place yourself, your life, and your work on the paten and offer it all to the Father.

short prayer...

Praised and adored,
now without end
be the Most Holy
Sacrament.

trivial tidbit...

A Jesus nut or Jesus pin is a hexagonal nut that holds the rotor blades to the body of some helicopters used during the Vietnam War. It keeps the whole thing together.

trivial tidbit...

A magnificent tapestry by Graham Sutherland called "Christ in Glory" hangs in St. Michael's Cathedral in Coventry, England. When the church was dedicated in 1962, this tapestry, which weighs nearly a ton, was the largest in the world.

A Few Unique Titles for Jesus

In the New Testament there are about one hundred and thirty titles for Jesus. Here are five unusual ones.

✦ In Revelation 3:14 Jesus calls himself *"the Amen."* He is the great "yes" to God's plan of salvation. He is a witness to all that God has done and confirms it.

✦ Paul refers to Jesus as *the rock* in 1 Corinthians 10:4. This title is derived from the rock Moses smote in the desert to bring forth water for the Israelites who were dying of thirst. On the cross Jesus was pierced by the sword, which brought forth water and blood to give us life.

✦ Jesus is called *the dayspring* or *daybreak*, meaning dawn, because he brings about a new beginning.

✦ In Revelation 22:16 Jesus calls himself *"the bright morning star."* This probably refers to the planet Venus, which shines like a bright star and is visible early in the morning after the stars have faded. It could also mean that Jesus is like the sun, which radiates light and life to the whole world.

✦ Jesus once applied Psalm 118:22 to himself: "The stone the builders rejected has become *the cornerstone."* The Church is built on Jesus. He holds us all together.

Jesus Present in the Scriptures

At the end of the Scripture readings at Mass, the lector declares, "The Word of the Lord." We Catholics believe that the Bible is the word of God in the words of human beings. God speaks to us personally through the Bible, and therefore, so does Jesus. In both the Old Testament and the New Testament, God communicates in a powerful way. Scripture states, "The word of God is active and effective, sharper than any two-edged sword" (Hebrews 4:12). Picking up the Bible and reading it, or listening to it proclaimed, is like listening to Jesus, the ultimate "Word" of God. Every contact with Scripture is an opportunity for an encounter with Jesus. Spiritual writer Louis Evely recommends that we approach Scripture in the same way as the woman with the flow of blood stretched out her hand to touch Jesus' cloak: with faith, confidence, and expectancy. Through Scripture's inspired words, Jesus counsels, consoles, and guides us today. And one thing he teaches is that founding our life on the Bible is like founding our house on rock!

Jesus Present in Church Leaders and in Us

Jesus inaugurated a movement in which he had no successor. As he said, there is only one Teacher. However, his apostles, with Peter at the helm, guided the bark of his Church through its early years. And their successors, the bishops, have continued this ministry to this day. Jesus is present in a special way in our Church leaders. The Holy Father, the bishop of Rome, is the temporal head of the Church and represents Christ. Pope Benedict XVI is the 265th pope. Just

quick quote...

Where the Bishop is, there let the multitude of believers be; even as where Jesus is, there is the Catholic Church.

St. Ignatius of Antioch

a cool website...

To stay in touch with the Church, register to receive daily e-mails from www.zenit.org. The Holy Father's talks and sermons are included in these e-mails.

The Seven Sacraments

Catholics believe that Jesus is present and at work in the seven sacraments. Through them we experience and benefit from the saving actions of his death and resurrection. In us Jesus continues what he did as he walked the streets of Israel: He converts, heals, saves, feeds, and forgives. The Eastern Churches aptly call the sacraments Holy Mysteries.

✦ *Baptism* — The graces won by Jesus are applied to us. Our sins are washed away; and we become children of God, temples of the Trinity, and members of Christ's Church. These are the effects of uniting ourselves to Jesus' death and resurrection, symbolized by our going down into the water and coming out. In baptism we vow to forsake evil and follow the Gospel.

✦ *Confirmation* — The Spirit of Jesus enlivens us in an even greater way when we are anointed and sealed in this sacrament. His gifts are more activated in us, namely wisdom, knowledge, understanding, counsel, right judgment, fortitude, and fear of the Lord. We receive grace to be more Christlike and to witness to him.

✦ *Eucharist* — Jesus unites himself to us in Communion. He nourishes and strengthens us to live his life and bonds us with other members of his Church.

✦ *Penance* — Jesus forgives our sins if we are contrite. We are reconciled with God and with the rest of the Church through the saving acts of Jesus.

✦ *Anointing of the Sick* — Jesus forgives sin and sometimes gives health of mind and body to the sick, the elderly, and those facing death.

✦ *Matrimony* — Jesus unites the bride and groom as one, a symbol of his love for the Church. He strengthens them to be faithful to their vows of love and gives them the grace they need to raise children.

✦ *Holy Orders* — Jesus ordains bishops, priests, and deacons to govern, guide, and sanctify his people.

as Jesus worked at first through Peter and the other apostles to carry on his mission, today he speaks and acts through their successors.

There is a story of a woman religious who was upset by something and was scurrying to chapel. On the way she met another sister who asked, "What's wrong? Where are you going?" "To Jesus," responded the first sister in distress. "Here I am," declared the second sister. She understood the mystery of the divine indwelling.

God dwells within each of us, making us temples of the Holy Spirit. Jesus, who is no longer limited by a physical, mortal body like ours, is present in the depths of our being, symbolized by our heart. At any moment we can focus inward and speak with him. At the Last Supper, he referred to this great mystery when he said, "I will not leave you orphaned; I am coming to you" (John 14:18). Through the Eucharist, Jesus becomes more and more one with us as we share his divine life. When distributing Communion, St. Augustine would say to each person, "Become what you receive." At the Last Supper, when Jesus compared his intimate relationship with us to a vine and branches, he exhorted us, "Abide in me as I abide in you" (John 15:4). Our lives and his are codependent, intertwined. Paul uses the expression "in Christ" one hundred and sixty-four times in his letters. He is aware that we are all immersed in Jesus and do nothing apart from him.

On earth Jesus identified with the poor and the oppressed. He taught that whatever we do for one of the "least of his brethren" he considers done to himself. Mother Teresa of Calcutta called the poor Jesus' "dis-

quick quote...

It is no longer I who live,
but it is Christ who lives
in me.

Galatians 2:20

quick quote...

But God's own descent
Into flesh was meant
As a demonstration...
Spirit enters flesh and for
all its worth
Charges into earth birth
after birth
Ever fresh and fresh.

Robert Frost

quick quote...

Next to the sacrament itself your Christian neighbor is the holiest object ever presented to your sight, because in him or her the living Christ is present.

C.S. Lewis

a cool website...

There is a new interactive website specifically for Catholics, www.mycatholicvoice.com. There you can download music and CDs from most Catholic publishers, watch live streaming of some Catholic events, join like-minded groups of Catholics, and give your opinions on current events in the world and in the Church.

tressing disguise." That is why a crucial social teaching of the Church is to show a "preferential option" for the poor and vulnerable. This means that we have an obligation to help marginalized voices to be heard and to defend the defenseless. The Church challenges us to assess lifestyles, policies, and institutions as to their impact on the poor and those who are hurting in any way. Furthermore, it obliges us to work to bring about conditions where basic human rights are maintained for everyone. This is what Jesus did and what he asks us to do as his followers.

In an extraordinary way the saints are one with Jesus. Each one radiates a certain quality of his. For example, St. Francis reflected Jesus' joy and simplicity; St. Dominic, his power to preach; and Blessed Teresa of Calcutta, his care for the poor. The "ordinary" saints in our families, neighborhoods, and workplaces do the same. We can look at them and see Jesus. On the other hand, we hope that when they look at us, they see the love and care of Jesus.

Jesus Present in the Future

Catholics believe that Jesus will return to earth at the end of time. The early Christians were under the impression that this cataclysmic event was right around the corner. In fact, some members of the Thessalonian church had stopped working. They figured, "Why bother?" St. Paul had to write them a letter and goad them to return to their occupations. Even today, every so often someone (usually not a Catholic) predicts the end of the world, and their doomsday dates come and go.

In Matthew 24:27–44 Jesus speaks at length about

the coming of the Son of Man on clouds of heaven with power and great glory. He will come like lightning that flashes from east to west. Jesus encourages his listeners to be watchful and ready, for no one but the Father knows the day and hour of this coming. The Son of Man will arrive at an unexpected time. St. Augustine astutely observed, "It is by design that Jesus hid the last day from us—so that we'd be on the lookout for him every day of our lives."

Our beliefs about the second coming of Jesus are grounded in the final book of the Bible, the Book of Revelation. This is a mystifying book because it is apocalyptic writing, which is laden with symbols. Its format is a series of visions that the author, who is traditionally the apostle who wrote the Gospel of John, experiences. Today some people read into this book dreadful, foreboding messages about the catastrophes heralding the end of the world. The real purpose of Revelation, however, was to encourage Christians, who were enduring persecutions at the time it was written, to keep the faith. The author holds out hope to them by describing the end times, when the wonderful kingdom of God that Jesus proclaimed will finally prevail. That victory will come soon, and it will come on this earth, but not on any timetable known to us.

At the outset of the Book of Revelation the Lord God states, "I am the Alpha and the Omega" (Revelation 1:8). Since alpha is the first letter of the Greek alphabet, and omega is the last, this expression signifies "I am the end all and be all of everything." In the same first chapter, a man clothed with divine symbols and radiating glory says, "I am the first and the last, and the living one. I was dead, and see, I am alive

Jesus is not known to have appeared to people as frequently as his mother, Mary, has. Some of his notable appearances are to St. Catherine of Siena (1347–1380), St. Teresa of Avila (1515–1582), St. Margaret Mary Alacoque (1647–1690), and Blessed Anne Catherine Emmerich (1774–1824).

big book search...

Read Paul's description of the resurrection of the body in 1 Corinthians 15:35–55.

forever and ever" (Revelation 1:17–18). Later, seated on a throne God again says, "I am the Alpha and the Omega, the beginning and the end" (Revelation 21:6). The book concludes with Christ declaring, "I am the Alpha and the Omega, the first and the last, the beginning and the end" (Revelation 22:13). He then says, "I am coming soon" (Revelation 22:20). The title *alpha and omega* identifies Jesus with God, who existed untold eons before the billions of stars twinkling in our universe and who will continue to exist into the unending future.

In Revelation, Jesus, the Lamb of God, is worshipped: "Worthy is the Lamb that was slaughtered to receive power and wealth and wisdom and might and honor and glory and blessing" (Revelation 5:12). All creatures sing, "To the one seated on the throne and to the Lamb be blessing and honor and glory and might forever and ever!" (Revelation 5:13).

In John's Gospel, Jesus, the Word, was present at the beginning of the world, and "all things came into being through him." And what came into being in him "was life, and the life was the light of all people" (see John 1:3–4). That Word " became flesh and lived among us" (John 14) and proclaimed the reign of God and made it a reality for the human race through his life, suffering, death, and resurrection. As we profess in the Nicene Creed, Jesus "will come again in glory to judge the living and the dead, and his kingdom will have no end."

As for the judgment that would occur at the end of the world, Jesus taught that the Father gave him authority to judge. He foretold that all the dead would hear the voice of the Son of Man and come out of

quick quote...

Christ is in agony until the end of the world, and we must not sleep during all that time.

Blaise Pascal

In Revelation John sees a scroll with seven seals. No one can open it. Then an elder says, "See, the Lion of the tribe of Judah, the Root of David, has conquered, so that he can open the scroll" (Revelation 5:5). Jesus then appears as a slaughtered lamb and opens the seals.

A Cosmic Christ

St. Paul presents Jesus as the cosmic Christ: "He is the image of the invisible God, the firstborn of all creation; for in him all things in heaven and on earth were created, ... all things have been created through him and for him. He himself is before all things, and in him all things hold together" (Colossians 1:15–17).

In a similar vein, Pierre Teilhard de Chardin (1881–1955), a Jesuit priest and a paleontologist, explained existence as a progression towards Christ, who is the culmination of everything. According to Chardin's theory, creation becomes more and more complex, reaching different stages of consciousness. At each level when a critical point is reached, there is a breakthrough to another level as a result of God's action in the world. The universe is drawn on by a supreme consciousness, which Chardin called the omega point. This power is Christ, the goal into whom everything will ultimately converge. Society is moving toward unification, and love is the cosmic energy that drives this process. Chardin believed that humankind is now merely in the age of puberty, just beginning to sense our innate powers. We are undergoing a spiritual evolution into a mystical body. It is fitting that Teilhard de Chardin died on Easter Sunday.

their graves. The good will experience the resurrection of life, and the bad will have resurrection of condemnation (see John 5:21–29). Michelangelo portrayed this universal judgment in a monumental painting that covers the wall behind the altar of the Sistine Chapel in St. Peter's Basilica. A powerful Christ with upraised right hand sends souls to doom and with his left draws the good upward. The Middle Ages produced the frightening hymn *"Dies Irae"* ("Day of Wrath"), which describes judgment day "when even saints will comfort need." Although in the Roman

quick quote...

To fall in love with God is the greatest of all romances; to seek him, the greatest adventure; to find him, the greatest human achievement.

St. Augustine

Missal of 1962 this hymn was a sequence for requiem Masses, the updated Missal of 1970 omits it. The emphasis in the Church today is not on dread but on rejoicing because of the resurrection.

Like the early Christians, we Christians look forward to the end of the world, when the kingdom of God will be fully established and all things will be made new. In the new Jerusalem, we mortals will live with God. We will behold God face-to-face. We will be with Jesus, Mary, and all the other saints. Regarding the blessed ones, Scripture assures us that God "will wipe every tear from their eyes. Death will be no more; mourning and crying and pain will be no more" (Revelation 21:4). God will be "all in all" (1 Corinthians 15:28). We will be new creatures. As the Jesuit poet Gerard Manley Hopkins put it:

> I am all at once what Christ is, since he was what I am, and
> This Jack, joke, poor potsherd, patch, matchwood, immortal diamond,
> Is immortal diamond.

That is why, with longing hearts, we Catholics pray the very last words of the Bible: "Come, Lord Jesus!" (Revelation 22:20).

The whole secret and center of human existence remains the person of Jesus Christ.

Hans Küng

All shall be well, and all shall be well, and all manner of things shall be well.

Julian of Norwich

ALSO AVAILABLE

The Confirmed Catholic's Companion The sacrament of Confirmation is not the end of a Catholic's spiritual formation—in many ways it is only the beginning. This book is a kind of "how-to" manual for newly Confirmed Catholics and "seasoned veterans" alike to live their abundantly 24/7.
paperback, 224 pages, $9.95

The Catholic Companion to Mary Who is the real Mary, and what role does she play in our lives today? This book seeks to bring Mary to life as a flesh-and-blood person, using current research, theological study, and what the experiences of millions of Catholics have revealed about the Mother of Jesus.
paperback, 176 pages, $9.95

The Catholic Companion to the Psalms The psalms are woven through Catholic devotion, culture, and history, yet for many Catholics they remain an unopened gift. This book offers a treasury of methods and information for understanding and praying the psalms, bringing them to life so they can be used for ardent, heart-to-heart conversations with God.
paperback, 126 pages, $10.95

Invitation to Catholicism Everyone from inquirers and catechumens to lifelong Catholics will welcome the easy-to-understand, logical explanations found in this clear, concise overview of Catholic beliefs and teachings. Discussion questions and activities at the end of each chapter make this an ideal text for RCIA and adult study groups.
paperback, 234 pages, $9.95

Life in Christ In a style that easy to read yet completely thorough, this adult catechism presents all aspects of Catholic teachings and beliefs. Organized by topic in a question-and-answer format, this book gives straightforward answers on Catholics traditions, church structures, as well as teachings on current issues.
paperback, 328 pages, $8.95